ECHOES OF MY FOOTSTEPS

An Autobiography by Ivan Z. Gabor

as told to Jeffrey Beal

authorHOUSE®

AuthorHouse™
1663 Liberty Drive
Bloomington, IN 47403
www.authorhouse.com
Phone: 1-800-839-8640

© *2009 Ivan Z. Gabor. All rights reserved.*

No part of this book may be reproduced, stored in a retrieval system, or transmitted by any means without the written permission of the author.

First published by AuthorHouse 12/18/2009

ISBN: 978-1-4490-5321-5 (e)
ISBN: 978-1-4490-5319-2 (sc)
ISBN: 978-1-4490-5320-8 (hc)

Printed in the United States of America
Bloomington, Indiana

This book is printed on acid-free paper.

Cover: Memorial on the Banks of the Danube in Budapest, commemorating the thousands of people murdered there during the holocaust.

Table of Contents

Forward	vii
Preface	ix
Chapter I - Miami 1	1
Chapter II - Confusion and Violence	12
Chapter III - Miami 2	26
Chapter IV - War	31
Chapter V - Miami 3	55
First Picture Section	59
Chapter VI - The Red Danube	64
Chapter VII - Miami 4	87
Chapter VIII - Struggling To Survive	94
Chapter IX - Miami 5	121
Second Picture Section	126
Chapter X - All The World's A Stage	131
Chapter XI - Miami 6	147
Chapter XII - Aliyah	155
Chapter XIII - Miami 7	170
Chapter XIV - On The Streets Of Haifa	177
Chapter XV - Miami 8	225
Chapter XVI - Army Life	228
Chapter XVII - Miami 9	246
Chapter XVIII - On My Own	249
Third Picture Section	263
Chapter XIX - Miami 10	268
Chapter XX - The New World	271
Chapter XXI - Miami 11	292
Fourth Picture Section	295
Chapter XXII - The Dirty War	300
Chapter XXIII - Miami 12	308
Epilogue	329

Forward

For many years I've worked in the motion picture industry, writing and reviewing scripts and stories. In addition to that I've helped a number of holocaust survivors write their memoirs. But with all that experience, plus a lifetime of reading novels, watching films and traveling the world, I've never come across a tale as fascinating as the one told to me by Ivan Z. Gabor. In as many years as might fill one person's life he's led half a dozen, and all with different identities to match. It sounds so improbable that if a fiction writer dared to publish such a yarn nobody would believe it. Holocaust survival stories are harrowing and make for exciting tales on their own. But in Ivan's case that's just the jumping off point. Recounting the horrors of that epoch has practically become my macabre routine, but Ivan had me shift his story's focus from the cruelty of that era to the redemptive love story that was born in its wake. Telling such an emotional tale required naked honesty on the part of its subject, and Mr. Gabor dropped every pretense, peeling back the scar tissue no matter how vulnerable it made him. Only his total candor could have brought to life such an account. It was therapeutic for both him and me, and will no doubt invite the reader to come to terms with similar issues. Ivan survived torture, death threats, terror and starvation only to have to contend with the traumatic consequences of actions molded by the hell of a war most prefer to forget. Like a tragic theatrical figure he was forced to make hard choices for which he was ultimately victimized.

Presenting a cohesive story from these kaleidoscopic fragments challenged me to not only discover an appropriate literary structure, as essential to its tone as it was to the delicate mental state of its protagonist, but also to explore basic human relationships subjugated by the savagery of war. It's a life of epic proportions, but I've endeavored to make it as accessible as possible. And although it's a tale born of the holocaust I think you'll find it less off-putting than most in this genre. Finally, if for some reason your determination to fight the good fight has diminished it is my hope that Ivan's life will reinvigorate your efforts, and that by the time you turn the last page you'll come away convinced that anything is possible.

Jeffrey Beal
Miami, Florida

PREFACE

I do not wish to bear witness to atrocities already so well archived. My tale comes to your eye and your ear by way of a voice that has grown within me for over sixty years. It's an emotional aching separate from the horror of violence and death. The suffering caused by World War Two is immeasurable, and it's documentation vast. Countless survivors have described in detail the mindless carnage that permeated their pitiable existence, as painful to recount as it was to endure. So, what can I add that might make any difference? What contribution to man's moral education can I express in a slim volume such as this? Why should I put myself through the agony of traveling back to a time of barbarism? And does anyone even care? But whenever I hurl such challenges at myself I'm reminded of the unconditional love of my family, and I am obliged to admit that, at least to a few people, it does matter. And if it is of some consequence to them, then perhaps elsewhere it might matter as well.

My trauma grew in the shadow of the war at a time when the exhilaration of liberation swept the world. While a whole planet immersed itself in jubilation I found myself on a path that led to a lifetime of anguish from which there has never been any release. No righteous army has been able to deliver me from this torment. No heroic general has conquered the demons within me. Yet, this is still a narrative of World War Two. It's about a soul forever tortured as a consequence of the immense madness that swept the European continent in that era, and of all the things to which it ultimately gave rise. Maybe by sharing it I'll attain some degree of refuge. Toward that hope I shall expose my heart as a memoir to generations unborn. Perhaps then I can come to understand the turmoil that has taunted my consciousness for three score. And if another being is better for this comprehension then I'll have to admit that is does indeed *vale la pena;* it's worth the grief.

Ivan Z. Gabor
Sunny Isles, Florida

Chapter I

Miami 1

My head is constantly awhirl. I'm perpetually bouncing back and forth between the events that molded me and the actual person I am today. By this I don't mean that I daydream about the past or reminisce. No. It's impossible to feel nostalgic about the war years, and few survivors choose to relive those times. When I say that I jump around in time I really mean that my mind refuses to march to a chronological beat. Like an accidentally discharged pistol my thoughts ricochet from one decade to the next and from one country to another. Europe, the Middle East, Soviet occupation, Latin America, the wars, the United States, the theater, and the army are all part of an uncontrollable torrent of people, events and places that hijack my mind at will, and I never know when or where it will abandon me. I find the most appropriate way to define my life is to say that I am trapped in a work of surrealism. The incongruous appearance and disappearance of disparate stimuli dictates absolutely the day to day happenings that pass as my life. I might even go so far as to say that I am a surrealistic masterpiece, constantly dealing with the entrance and exit of irregular cast members and inconsistent scenery. And let me tell you, it keeps me on my toes. So, dear reader, stay with me as I jump back and forth in my life. I'll try and make it as easy as possible on you. And whenever I need life to go easy on me I relive the night I met Rebequita.

My gleaming white Cadillac glided through the dusk across the Kennedy causeway toward Miami Beach, and with the windows down I luxuriated in the tepid breeze that annually marked the close of the long humid South Florida summer, and heralded the coming of winter. Within a month the strange American custom of changing the clocks back an hour would make this moment pitch dark, but now I relished the dimly lit expanses of water on either side of the bridge. The moored boats and swaying palms, silhouetted against the evening sky, turned the panorama into a glorious picture postcard, and my soul was imbued with a robust romantic yearning. I hadn't been in Miami, or even America for that matter, all that long, but I was already swirling in social circles that excited me. I had just enjoyed a fabulous meal at a friend's apartment on Brickell Avenue, and I was finally beginning to relish life after a long period of anxiety and aggravation. I had fled my home in Argentina because of the Dirty War, an exercise in nationalistic zeal, complete with the usual paranoid madness of anti-Semitism. A generation earlier the educated world had discovered the consequences of such intolerance, but there it was again, threatening my very existence. The Argentine army was murdering the children of my friends, and everyday the peril grew worse. After witnessing what had happened to European Jews who were incredulous of their sophisticated country's capacity to hate, my wife, two young sons and I made our way to America and safety. At the time my wife and I had been going through a separation, but survival put the relatively trivial topic of domestic strife to one side so we could relocate. And once I had my family securely settled day to day survival was once again a delicious luxury to be taken for granted. Freed from the anguish of our political situation we now had the space to redefine our marital status, and mutually relieved to see our kids safe, we resumed the path of legal separation. My mind, usually overflowing with echoes of war and a million other anxieties, had become so burdened by the strain of recent events that I sought refuge in modern men of science. A battery of tests revealed that I suffered from something called general anxiety disorder, and though my English was quite limited at that time it still sounded enough like phrases in some of the other four tongues I spoke to tell me what I already knew, that I was permanently stressed out.

So here I was, another refugee in Miami, living a life that, by comparison with what I had fled, could only be described as the good life. I felt like a newly released prisoner, eager to stretch my wings. Although I left a successful life behind in Argentina I was able to bring along enough of that success to make my family and I economically stable. And now, on the evening of November the twelfth, 1977 I was floating along in the classic American proof of that firm financial foundation, a Caddy, and there was nobody keeping tabs on me. I could do as I pleased whenever it pleased me. I had no boss and no one to report to. And momentarily free of the torture of psychological war scars I was eager to see what lay around the next American corner. I was Aladdin, steering my automatic transmission flying carpet through the exotic Miami Beach night while a Beatles oldie emanated from the car's stereo system. And when I saw that red light I felt like I could float over it, but deigned to obey it out of a mood of sheer benevolence. It turned out to be a wise decision, because that traffic signal was my red light of destiny.

I brought the body by Fisher to a stop before the crosswalk at 79th Street and Harding Avenue and observed the parade of tourists and elderly retirees walking off the early bird specials upon which they had just gorged themselves. The senior citizen male fashion of matching white shoes and belt always amused me, and with an uncontrollable grin on my face I glanced to my left, anxious to share the humorous moment with whomever might be occupying the car next to me, and my eyes came to rest on a young woman. My grin stuck on my face like a thoughtless simper until the girl turned to her right and regarded me. At that moment cosmic forces came into play, and I was blissfully dragged along on a wave of sensuality that filled me to overflowing. I was so overwhelmed by this ravishing beauty that I was stripped of my free will, and my powers of cognition were diminished to the level of mere instinct. Blessedly, the traffic light continued to glow red, and with what little sensory control remained at my bidding I managed a lame opening remark, made all the more pathetic by an accent that screamed immigrant. Spinning my hand to indicate the need for her to roll down her window I lowered the level of the lads from Liverpool and opened my mouth. To my surprise actual words issued forth.

"Excuse, you know is where Collins Avenue?"

Mispronouncing six of the seven words in my bold though poorly constructed introductory inquiry exposed my pathetically obvious attempt at delivering a glib pick-up line, but the young lady took mercy on me and responded in flawless Spanish.

"*Quisiera que le diga en español?*" Would you prefer for me to tell you in Spanish?

I was thrilled that this gorgeous creature spoke a language that suited me better, and I gratefully blurted back, "*Sí!*"

She looked half my age, filling me with self contempt over my attempted cradle robbing, but she was so breathtaking I couldn't resist the compulsion to speak to her. So I surrendered to my lecherous logic and rhetorically asked myself what harm could a little innocent flirting do?

She sweetly albeit redundantly explained what I already knew, that Collins Avenue, the longest avenue in Miami Beach, and a thoroughfare that even distant Scandinavians can pinpoint on a map, lay just two blocks ahead. She was so guileless and unaware that I was just making up an excuse to chat with her that she went to the extra trouble to explain to me that I'd have to turn left once I got to the north bound, one way road, again common knowledge in Stockholm. Emboldened by a foreign tongue I spoke so much better than English I pushed forth the conversation. And she responded just as I thought she would, in the affirmative, entrancing me even more. I told her that I had arrived recently from Argentina, and that I had a company here. This delighted her, and she shared some amazingly coincidental news.

"My boyfriend works for an Argentine company here, called Gabriel Creations."

The odds of such a thing were inconceivable. I had named my company after my eldest son Gabriel, and this girl's innocent pronouncement now had the veneer of fate about it. But I hid my amazement in order to tease her. Knowing something that she didn't momentarily gave me a power over her that I relished. It was as if I had her in my control, even if just for a second. But what I really relished was having broken the ice. And it wasn't just broken; it was obliterated. We had something in common, and could chat all night about our similarities! We were practically friends already! This fateful coincidence was exhilarating, and exploiting my advantage to full potential I pressed on.

"That's interesting. What's his name?"

"Henry Berger."

Naturally, I recognized the name of one of my salesmen and I recalled how he had often mentioned his gorgeous girlfriend, Rebeca, and how much he wanted to marry her. Well, maybe Henry saw her first, but this girl was such a knockout, and we seemed to be getting along so well, I just had to pursue our conversation, and maybe soon her. Without further hesitation I divulged the fateful coincidence that bound us, confident it would impress her. After all, if she was interested in marrying my employee just how would she feel about his superior, the big boss? Why settle for a lowly peon when you can have *el numero uno*?

"He works for me!"

Her face brightened in surprise, but so did the traffic light, only this time in green. Naturally, I didn't want our chance encounter to end, so I indicated somewhere we might continue chatting.

"Why don't we pull over and talk some more. I'd like to get to know Henry Berger's girlfriend. We can't stop here in the street."

Of course, she was so good looking I would have gladly turned off my engine and blocked traffic had she suggested it. However, common sense and proper traffic etiquette prevailed, and we turned north on Collins, me behind her, in the appropriate posture of the pursuer, and came to a stop by the curb. In so doing I took a look at her vehicle for the first time since talking to her. Once I saw her at the stop light I hadn't noticed anything else. In all honestly, had she been carried on a sedan chair like Cleopatra I don't think I would've been aware of it. But now, cruising behind her, and free of the distraction of her flowing mane and full lips, I finally had a chance to take in what mode of transportation she rode. She was indeed driving an internal combustion automobile, and was not being transported on a palanquin like the Queen of the Nile, carried aloft by a cadre of muscular slaves. In fact it was a shiny new Buick, so she too appeared to be living the American Dream.

We both got out and met between our cars. Now I could see her face to face. What a beauty! Henry was right! This young lady had a perfect face and figure, and was totally enchanting. Then she caught me off guard with a flirtatious joke.

"I didn't know my boyfriend's boss was so handsome."

This completely disarmed me. Was she being coquettish? No, that wasn't possible. After all, Henry had talked about marrying her. Of course, he did say that he wanted to, but not that it was a done deal. Who could blame Henry for desiring to have this girl to himself forever, and projecting his deepest wishes out loud, as if doing so might actually make them come true? What a lucky guy this Henry is! On the other hand, who could blame me for pursuing this conversation deeper? For some time already I had been under the spell of this strange evening, and only now did it start to make sense. This romantic aura was culminated in meeting this girl! But she quickly dashed that notion by dropping the other comedic shoe saying, "But of course, you're too old for me!"

The words hit me between the eyes and woke me up. Lust had overruled my reason. What would such a lovely thing as this have to do with middle aged me? She was right; I was too old for her! I was momentarily shaken. What a fool I was, driving around in my fancy Fisher chassis like some decrepit Don Juan. But I shook off my disappointment and plunged back into the conversation, only now I changed gears to a more platonic speed.

"Henry told me your name. It's Rebeca, isn't it?"

"Yes, but he never mentioned yours."

"Ivan Gabor. *Mucho gusto.*"

We chatted innocently, and even the topic of her upcoming nuptials came up. Apparently Henry's dreams were actually going to come true, while my illusions of love were dying. But I persisted in our innocent exchange. She told me they were planning a wedding, and I hid my jealousy with some halfhearted congratulations. Then she gave me some background, how she was the only daughter of Cuban immigrants. That didn't surprise me, because every other person I had met since coming to Miami was a Cuban immigrant. Then she turned things around by getting more personal with me.

"Are you married?"

No woman asks a man about his marital status out of bored curiosity. There has to be a reason. Either she's interested for herself or someone else. In this case I hoped it was the former. And if she was checking on my warranty then I had to figure out if she was interested in a love affair or marriage. In any case, after years in South America I came to the conclusion that most Latin women are extremely possessive, and even a love affair, supposedly devoid of pensive musing on pressing matrimony, has to offer the girl some degree of exclusivity and the hope of eventual vows. As for me I must confess that, at that time in my life, getting married again was the furthest thing from my mind. A torrid love affair with a beautiful Cuban maiden was far more desirable. I pictured us frolicking on the beach, letting the warm waves break around us as we embraced on the sand, Hollywood style. Of course, even if I were spoken for, this girl was so tempting I might have lied about it anyway. As it was though, I told the truth.

"I'm single. My wife and I became separated when we were living in Argentina. We came here together to protect our kids, but now the separation is in effect again. We don't live together, and we'll be getting a divorce soon."

I was overenthusiastic in my rush to assure her of my legal and moral availability and probably sounded desperate. A woman hates that in a man. But she seemed content with the basic facts of my reply, that

I was relatively free. However, if any glimmer of hope of satisfying my lust with this girl beat within my heart she immediately smashed it.

"Would you like me to introduce you to somebody?"

This turned our conversation on its head. Upside down now, as I was, I was unable to navigate through any sensible sentence. Too tongue tied to loosen the knot all I could do was follow her lead.

"Sure. Who would you like me to meet?"

"*A mi mamá*!" My mother!

Defeat. Total, ice cold deprivation. I had no chance with this girl. The bell rang and I was flat on the mat, Caesar's thumb was turned down, and the Captain of the firing squad was offering me my last smoke. What hubris had clouded my mind? In what fantasy world did I dwell? Clearly, I was never even in the running! From the moment she laid eyes on me she had been sizing me up for her lonely mother. This girl probably drove all over town hunting for a potential second husband for the poor widow, and I was probably candidate number twenty seven for the week. Today it was Miami Beach, and tomorrow it would be Coral Gables. Half the male population of South Florida had probably gotten the once over by this innocent little lady, the bait in the fatal snare. Her shiny new Buick was a Venus fly trap, sucking in men toward her mother's bridal canopy. But as disappointed as I was not to be on her fast list for lovers, I was still under a compulsion to agree to anything she suggested. So, if she wanted me to meet her mother, I'd do it. If I was too old for this young thing maybe I was right for her mother. So I stayed. Anything, just to remain another moment in her company. Then a grim thought swept through my mind. If I actually did marry her mother I'd be forever vexed by being stepfather to a girl whom I once desired in a decidedly un-parental fashion. I'd suffer from the Lolita complex until my dying day! Be that as it may, I was so satisfied by her physical proximity our topic of conversation was immaterial, and I agreed that it would indeed be nice to meet her mother. I didn't mean it, but I submitted the classic American assent that even I couldn't mispronounce, "Okay!"

This delighted her and I took advantage of her momentarily dropped defenses to force upon her my business card. This was the first actual proof that what I had spoken was true. I was indeed who I said I was, that I ran a certain business, and had a certain employee. Up until then I could have been merely throwing pick-up lines. After all, she was the one who provided the facts, while I merely insisted that I was part of it all. She had offered her boyfriend's name and other data, and I just went along. Swept away on a hormonal tide of desire as I was, I might have exaggerated my importance, health or financial standing just to improve my chances of even a moment's ardor with such an irresistible woman. As fate would have it however, we had enough reality in common to avoid such deceit. And while a more suspicious female might have early on requested such evidence as I now offered, young Rebeca was trusting enough to have long since made the decision to take me at my word. But perhaps this confidence was not intended so much for me as for my card, and I took it that her eager acceptance of it was nothing more than documentation to assist her in keeping accurate records of her methodical search for her mother's next victim. Apparently, she would call up and make some arrangement for me to apply for the stepfather position. But still, at this last moment before parting company it was natural for me to hope that I might yet enjoy a destiny with her far less platonic than potential parent replacement. But those last fading hopes died a frozen death as we shook hands, and drove off our separate ways into the breezy Miami Beach night.

Like so many brief romantic encounters it had been a thrill, quickly followed by a melancholy disappointment. As for the girl, I doubt it had been any kind of thrill for her at all. It was a classic May/December scenario, and I was a common fool for getting caught up in it. For all my illusions of a shiny American car and sexual conquest, I was just another forty year old male, under the sway of a text book case of middle age panic. I needed a good talking to, and to make sure I understood that lecture I harangued myself in one of the four languages I spoke better than English. By this stage in my life I was fluent in Spanish, Yiddish, Hebrew, and the native tongue of my birthplace, Hungary. That language is a most effective medium for giving someone the sauce, and my parents used it to set me straight a hundred times. As I mentally shook myself, the foreign echo of those words took me back to what I had struggled so long to suppress, life during the war.

Chapter II

Confusion and Violence

The dreamlike surreal state I inhabit is not unique. Anyone can relate to it, because everyone used to be a kid, and kids always experience this planet as a verifiable surrealistic event, understanding nothing, while finding it fascinating at the same time. Even in childhood this world, our home planet, always looked insane to me. My plight is that I've never outgrown that feeling, and even as an adult I continue to occupy that same terrain. Most kids grow up and, perplexed by the world's mystery, ultimately pretend to have a handle on things. Perhaps this is man's eternal existential dilemma, seeing madness everywhere, yet impotent to impact it for the better, simply bluff their way through it. It's been that way since I was a kid, and it's never lost its grip on me. And, as I've already decided that my experiences are worth sharing, I'll try and stay within accessible mental and literary boundaries, the better to communicate, and let you appreciate, the major event of my life and our age, World War Two. My entire life is nothing but its prolonged aftermath. Ever moving, never stable, my memories are full of visions of fleeing, or being dragged from one temporary refuge to another. This is that war's persistent and haunting legacy. Invasion, resettlement, deportation, prisoners, displaced persons, refugees, immigration. If the war didn't kill us it was a very close call, barely keeping one step ahead of it. And it relentlessly persists in pursuing me. We had to be eliminated, because we were not who we should have been. The identity crisis was a plague. To the Romanians and Hungarians I was always the other, and to both a Jew. In Israel I was a European. In Argentina I was Israeli, and the Americans insist that I'm Argentinean. It seems I'm always one step behind. Who am I and where do I belong?

For hundreds of years it was hard for many Hungarians to know just who they were or where they came from. This is because she continually lost the wars in which she fought, and had to cede territory to the winners. Over the years half of Hungary became spoils of war. Yugoslavia to the south, Austria to the west, Czechoslovakia on the north, and Romania to the east had been whittling away at Hungary for centuries. Her most recent loss was the result of the Great War. In 1914 she had been obliged to go along with Austria, her partner in empire, and the rest of the Central Powers, including Germany and the Ottoman Empire. They fought the Allied powers, composed of France, England, Italy, Russia and the United States. The Allies won and the Central powers were divested of empire. Worse than that Hungary had to surrender her eastern territory of Transylvania to Romania. This place with the eerie sounding name is a beautiful province, home not just to fictional vampires but to my all too real family. And they, as well as the hundreds of thousands of other Hungarians who lived there, were forced to become Romanians, switching nationality and allegiance. While map makers found this arrangement good for business the people who inhabited these border regions were bitter, and utterly disinterested in adopting Romanian culture. They continued to speak Magyar and considered themselves Hungarian in every way. Transylvania was their ancestral homeland and they did their best to ignore Romania. Into that confusion I appeared on the twelfth of September, 1934. It was Hungary when, as babies, my parents brought a little *nachis* into the lives of my grandparents -my father in 1903 and my mother in 1910- but it was Romania by the time both of them reached voting age. Linguistically and culturally Transylvania continued to be Hungarian, and even when I entered the public school system's kindergarten I didn't learn Romanian. I was technically born and raised in a country whose language was totally unknown to me. We lived a comfortable life in the small city of Baia-Mare, about sixty miles from the Hungarian border, politically within the borders of Romania, yet tenaciously clinging to Hungarian individuality. This is the bizarre and contrary environment in which I was raised.

Jews had lived in Transylvania since the third century. They had originally arrived from the Roman province of Pannonia as domestic slaves and servants helping the Romans manage their commerce. It wasn't even Hungary yet. So, long before the Christians arrived, and five hundred years before Attila the Hun's pagan conquest of the region, our people were there, practicing the worship of a single God. But our numbers were small, and we had to deal with the whims of the many. Sadly, the many could never make up their mind, and we were kicked out and invited back continually. Finally, around 1,000AD we were given equal rights with the gentiles which was an advanced notion for Eastern Europe. Then someone from Germany named Arpad took control of Hungary and declared that marriages between Jews and non-Jews were no longer legal, making him officially the first German to persecute Hungarian Jews. In 1239 Bela the VI appealed to the Pope to let the Jews participate in life again. Around the turn of the 18th century the Jews in that region were told to live in small villages, and to keep out of the big cities. So, they settled into *shtetls*, or hamlets, and developed cooperative farms. Then, in 1848 the many decided to let Jews back into the cities, and my forefathers settled there, my paternal ancestors in Baia-Mare and the maternal side of my family in nearby Baia-Pire. My mother's father was an industrialist and he prospered in the lumber trade. Even though anti-Semitism was always just under the surface life was relatively good for the Jews in that region. But in 1882 that tranquility was shattered with a resurgence of gentile paranoia based on that old Blood Libel nonsense. Blood Libel was a centuries old bogus charge that Jews killed Christian children in order to drain their blood to make matzo. Periodically, this myth resurfaced to assuage the frustration of some embittered gentiles who needed a scapegoat on which to vent their frustrations over one thing or another. In this case it escalated to such a point that there were pogroms against us, both in the shtetls and in Baia Mare proper. Subsequently this charge of blood libel was proved false, and the Jews returned, this time with enough confidence to build a big synagogue. Freedom once again bloomed for the Jews of that region and they became major players in many areas, such as business, the arts and industry. In 1909 the well known and respected Weiszer family bought the bankrupt Phenix glass works and converted it into the biggest chemical manufacturer in the whole country. Baia Mare became a center of a culture and commerce, and the Jews were a vital part of it. Of its fifteen thousand citizens about seven percent were Jewish. The next political change however, the Treaty of Versailles, saw further changes in Jewish fortunes. When the Austro-Hungarian Empire dissolved Baia-Mare became Romanian, and brought with it a brief era of anti-Semitism, and many Jews lost their jobs. Meanwhile, across the border Hungarian Jews were advancing in agriculture, medicine, manufacturing and banking. And as the war to end all wars became buried in memory, the little city of my birth again transformed itself into one of the most cosmopolitan municipalities in the region. By the time I was born our home town was again Romanian, even if you never heard a discouraging word in that particular idiom.

Let me tell you, when you speak a foreign language within your own country it can definitely lead to a serious identity crisis. Our national identity was no more tangible than a dream, and such uncertainty taints an individual with a palpable surreal aura. To further qualify my parents as surreal citizens they were born into the Jewish faith. Of course, Judaism is no more surrealistic than any other religion, but its distinct language and customs tend to throw its practitioners into sharp contrast with the general gentile European social milieu, suggesting approximation to the broad definition of that mysterious artistic term. To deal with this clear cut incongruity a socio-religious movement arose in Europe called Reform Judaism. It preached assimilation, urging Jews to fit in with the prevailing social milieu, while still maintaining their theology and rituals. This mostly consisted of modifying their external appearance by shaving, cutting their hair like the gentiles, and dressing like them as well. Millions of Jews, fed up with constant discrimination, made all the easier by their overt countenance, eagerly subscribed to this reform, my parents included. But many of our relatives were religious, and they clung to the ways of their forefathers, avoiding any plan to emulate *goyim*.

My maternal grandpa, Samuel Mayer, was a pious man, but he was also quite successful in commerce, having been a lumber baron in his youth and later opening the first commercial gas station in the region. He earned handsomely, and both he and my grandma dressed like solid upper middle class citizens, and even had the luxury of live-in domestics. And it is mostly thanks to them that I learned something of Jewish customs. They even saw to it that I became a little familiar with the Hebrew language, and I occasionally attended *shabbos* services with my grandpa. On the way there we had to pass a Catholic Church, and there were always people milling around outside, often yelling insults at us for being Jews. To their eternal credit my grandparents were known not so much for their economic success, but for their generosity. Grandfather Samuel can be found on the pages of the Who's Who of its day, as being noted for his kindness. When he prospered he gave to all charities, and when he didn't he still invited the poor home to eat. He was famous for his heart of gold and was the richer therefore. It gives me satisfaction to know that Hitler never got his diseased claws on him.

My father, Armin Grossman and my mother, nee Ilus Mayer, were a good match. They were both believers in assimilation, and paid scant attention to their roots. They were content to behave and dress in the fashion of the day, and they looked just like any other Hungarians, proudly identifying themselves as such. Actually, as can be attested to through photographic evidence, they probably looked even better than most Hungarians. My father was an especially dapper gentleman, a real Beau Brummel. He was so impeccably attired that whenever he went out he reminded me of the mannequins in store windows, showing off the latest styles. And Ilus, or Ilushka as she was called, was one of the most beautiful women of the whole region, as well as being respected as a cultured, refined lady. In her home was the only piano in town and she delighted people with her playing. Nobody seemed to care what her religion was. Jews at that time participated in all walks of Hungarian life, and she was voted Miss Baia Mare, and even made it as far as runner up for Miss Transylvania. She was also the perfect match for my father in that she was always arrayed in the latest fashions. If she was going down to the corner for an aspirin she looked like she had stepped off the cover of Vogue. Her gloves matched her shoes, her hat was at just the right tilt, and her dress was right out of a Hollywood movie.

If the title Miss Transylvania doesn't have a surreal ring to it then I don't know what does! But the point is that when my mother was a beauty queen she wasn't put into a Jewish beauty pageant, or a special Jewish category among the contestants. Jews were not restricted from any institution, public or private, and they frequented the local swimming pool in the summer, and the ice skating rink and ski resorts in winter. Indeed, the culture that evolved along that stretch of the mighty Danube River did so along lines of relative tolerance toward one's fellow man and woman. Apparently so, at any rate.

My parents met in 1932, and with so much talk of war in Europe they reflected deeply on whether or not it was wise to bring children into the world. But they were in love and felt secure in Baia-Mare, so I made my way onto their agenda.

By 1939 our home town had grown to about twenty five thousand, with Jews accounting for about twenty percent. Whether due to assimilation or not, most of them did not feel threatened by either their community or government. They prospered, their neighbors were friendly, and war seemed a million miles away. But that huge distance was about to close dramatically, and fitting in would prove to be a poor tactic in promoting acceptance of the Hebrew People. Ultimately, assimilation offered no rescue whatsoever from the Final Solution. The clothes and haircuts did nothing once the Third Reich invaded Poland, and countries all across Europe were forced to pick sides.

To seduce Hungarian leaders Adolph Hitler cagily promised them the return of Transylvania in exchange for taking up the banner of fascism. As the avaricious Nazi dictator had already proven himself adept at grabbing up European real estate, his offer was accepted. Next thing we know we witnessed the old red, white and green flag of Hungary leading a parade of its troops down the streets of Baia-Mare, which was now called by its original Hungarian name of Nagybanya. Considering ourselves Hungarian, and pathetically clueless as to what this would lead to, we joined in the gay reunification celebration. I even decked out my bicycle with ribbons for the grand occasion. We were ignorantly applauding the arrival of the very people who would soon persecute us.

At first the Hungarian-German pact, or even the war itself, didn't affect us. It was on the radio, in the press, and movie newsreels in the theater, but for a five year old like me in 1939, the newsreels were indistinguishable from the theatrical motion pictures, and so didn't seem any more realistic. The cinemas had their established schedule. First came the cartoon which was total escapism, creating a mood of fantasy that made the next part of the program, the newsreel, seem likewise unreal. So, when I saw the triumphant blitzkrieg up on the giant silver screen it was just as surreally distracting as any other celluloid entertainment. Even for big people like my father the war was a mere topic of conversation. And as for Der Fuhrer's anti-Semitic ranting it seemed equally distant and disconnected from our reality. Hungary was too civilized and sophisticated for such hate mongering. As for me, I didn't expend any of my time or mental energy in reflecting on dire political situations. Anything beyond food and play was abstract and best left to adults. As those adults were my parents I had even less reason to fret. I don't know if being raised in a sheltered manner was due to the influence of gentile or reformed Jewish culture, but I definitely know that I, little Freddy, was a pampered child.

I was the first male born into an extended family with no other children, so I was doted upon by my parents, aunts, uncles, cousins, grandparents and even great grandparents. Part of my spoiled upbringing consisted of my father's determination to protect me from the more unpleasant manifestations of life on this planet. This practice of ignoring reality qualifies the prevailing mood of my rearing as surreal.

As protective as my father was even more so was my mother. She was not a typical *hausfrau* by any means –being a crowned beauty queen will have its affect- but she was as determined as any female to guard her pups. Of course this was the norm for Jewish mothers of that period. I don't mean to caste aspersion on modern women as being inferior matriarchs, but there was something feral and protective about women in the first half of the last century that reflected an incomparable surrender and dedication on the part of anyone wearing the mantle of motherhood. My own mother did not shrink from such obligation, and she was as consumed by the instinct to safeguard her children as much as any woman of her generation. She fed me, cleaned me, dressed me, and saw to my education and amusement. If necessary she was also prepared to kill on my behalf or give her own life that I may survive. Eventually, my awareness of that maternal instinct contributed to a lifelong guilt complex over her sacrifice.

For the first two years of the war my surreal upbringing was in full swing. Reality was kept as far from my corner of the universe as possible. But when 1941 rolled around Hungary dusted off its banner of anti-Semitism and waved it in the face of the Jewish community, making the truth impossible to ignore. My father, a licensed CPA, was employed by the prestigious Cosa Nostra Hungarian-Romanian Bank. He was a cultured gentleman, and a respected member of the community, but with the state sponsored resurgence of anti-Semitism everyone was scrutinized for any taint of the dreaded Jew virus. If you were even one fourth Hebrew, which means having just one Jewish grandparent, your membership in the Hungarian club was revoked. Armin's impeccable Hebrew pedigree assured him of that. Of course, digging into his ancestry was hardly necessary once the first step of investigation, analyzing his name, was executed. His Christian name could very well have belonged to a gentile, but with a last name like Grossman it was all too obvious that he was a son of Abraham. The new rules prohibited anyone of such ancestry from holding a responsible position, so one day he showed up for work to learn that he was fired. His haircut and suit could not overcome the detrimental stigma of his name. It was a directive all the way from Germany to start getting tough with the Jews, and depriving us of white collar jobs was first on the list.

My father, accustomed to hiding the brutality of ugly reality from me, as well as from my mother whenever possible, now saw the handwriting on the wall. So, even though he saw his dismissal, and those of countless other Jewish Hungarians, as temporary anomalies, he decided to hedge his bets and change our family name. It went from very Jewish sounding Grossman to generic Gabor, the Hungarian equivalent of Smith. Anyway, who knew for sure just how many generations of our family had used the name Grossman? As members of the tribe we should have had some Semitic sounding name like Moishe ben Asher or Benjamin Neftali. But, except for those Jews who had proudly held on to their ancient tribal surnames, like Cohen or Levy, everyone we knew had last names that sounded Russian or French or German, like Grossman. But father was convinced that a common and popular name like Gabor would allow us to blend into Hungarian homogeneity and keep us from harm's way. As an extra safeguard, my father gave me the very gentile sounding nickname of Freddy. Thus I evolved from Alfred Grossman into Freddy Gabor.

The changing of the names was just the first step. To further protect us he moved us from provincial Nagybanya, where everyone knew their neighbor and neighbor's religion, to metropolitan Budapest where blending in was a viable tactic. This was not an extension of the Reform tactic of fitting in, but rather an overt attempt to become covert by simply vanishing into the woodwork. Jews in the countryside were far too easily identified and arrested. But Budapest was big and impersonal, and offered a chance of anonymity and survival to those who were audacious enough to try. Name changing was a big help, but we had to literally disappear into the endless sea of souls that lived in the anonymous housing complexes of a major city to become completely nondescript. Thus, in 1942 we settled into a nice three bedroom apartment in the residential district on the east side of town. That side was more proletariat than the western bank of the Danube, and offered us the best chance of refuge. There, we did not stand out at all. There were so many people on every block it was conceivable to live there for years and still not meet everyone. Our neighborhood was more densely populated than our home town, and perfectly suited our purposes.

At that time my maternal grandmother also came to live with us. At the age of seventy my grandfather died of a heart attack just weeks prior to our move. He was the only member of our family to pass away from natural causes during the war. And his dying at that time actually saved my grandma's life. Had he lived even just a few months longer my grandma, who was much younger, would've stayed with him in their rural home in Baia-Mare. She'd have been at his side even as the Gestapo kicked in the door of their picturesque cottage and dragged them off to Auschwitz. That's what happened to their own parents, my great grandparents, in the nearby town of Baia-Pire, and to most of our other relatives as well. They all died in the gas chambers upon their arrival at the camp and were incinerated at once. But coming to Budapest gave my *balabusta* of a grandmother a chance for survival, just as it did my mother and me, and eventually tens of thousands of other Jews who took the risk of hiding in plain sight in the rooms, cellars and attics of our teeming capital.

The vast majority of people in European urban centers have always lived in apartment buildings. Free standing houses are almost exclusively the residence of choice in the countryside, but apartment buildings housed, and continue to house, most urban citizenry on the Great Continent. These buildings have always been sound structures, modeled after medieval fortresses. In those times the peasants lived outside the walls of the local castle, and when enemies attacked they sought refuge in its interior courtyard. Likewise, all apartment buildings had interior courtyards, and the lower economic strata, the modern equivalent of the peasant class, occupied those apartments that faced inward, where water pumps and public bathrooms were found. The units that faced the street however, were considered far more prestigious, and demanded higher rents. They cost more, because they came with a view. The serfs on the courtyard side of the building only saw the courtyard, while the nobles on the street could see, depending on what floor and direction they faced, sunrises or sunsets, sweeping panoramas of the Danube and the architectural splendor of one of the most beautiful metropolises in the world. I don't remember our specific vista, but I do remember that we had indoor plumbing and a small maid's quarters. While we weren't rich my father had always provided his family with a comfortable middle class existence. We enjoyed all the trappings of our social station, such as preferred education, plentiful food, and a domestic servant. And when we moved to Budapest that was not diminished. Although democratization had made great strides in Europe, such bourgeoisie notions as royalty and social class persisted, and where you lived was one of the determinant factors in that die-hard caste system. Basically, the location of your apartment identified you. I was unaware of the elite position of our residence, but my mother doubtless enjoyed living on the street side, and my father probably felt pride to be able to provide us with such status.

An unwanted side effect of preferred housing was exposure to the parades of the fascist Arrow-Cross Party, known as the Nyilasok. This was the Hungarian equivalent of the Nazi Party, and its ranks were populated by juvenile delinquents, bullies, thugs and other social rejects. But they were armed social rejects, venting a hundred years of built up anti-social angst in the direction of the officially sanctioned, outnumbered, unarmed scapegoat targets, the eternally foreign Jews. These ultranationalists routinely murdered people, regardless of age or sex, by either beating them to death or shooting them. Their preferred method of assassination was to march their victims to the banks of the Danube and shoot them so that their bodies fell neatly into the swiftly eastward flowing current and disappear, eliminating the need to dispose of cadavers. For sport they merely beat people with savage ferocity. It goes without saying that they were to be avoided at any cost. To heighten that danger they set up their headquarters right around the corner from our building, and they loved to strut in parades right under our window with abysmal frequency. Singing anthems of hate they carried placards denouncing Jews, communists, foreigners, homosexuals, gypsies, and any other minorities they chose to harass. Those placards, as well as their armbands and make-shift uniforms, all sported the arrow-cross symbol. Just as the German fascists had their infamous swastika emblem, the Hungarian Nyilas fascists had their own. The Nazis perverted the ancient Hindu totem of purity to represent cruelty, and the Nyilasok appropriated the symbol of supposedly peaceful Christianity, adorning its four ends with fierce pointed arrowheads. But as rampantly as this menace grew, all the harder my father strove to hide it from me. It was a daunting and ridiculous task for him to habitually regard my queries as unworthy of serious reply.

"What are those arrows, father?"

"Oh, nothing. They'll go away soon."

"Father, why are those people singing mean songs about Jews?"

"Don't worry son, it really doesn't mean anything."

"Papa, is that man Hitler going to kill everyone?"

"Oh, he's very, very far away, Freddy. Don't worry about him."

And so it went. With few alternative sources of news I blindly accepted the fantasy world foisted upon me. Like little Lord Buddha I was brought up ignorant of the maladies of the world. For some reason my parents thought it best to delude me. It was always act one in the theater of the absurd, located in the galaxy of the surreal. When we moved to Budapest I was seven years old, spoiled and blithely clueless. With food and affection still in great supply I was utterly unconcerned over our rung on the social ladder or the political atmosphere. Over the course of the next few years however, I would become as worldly as anyone. Close proximity to war will do that.

Chapter III

Miami 2

Two weeks after I met that young girl at the traffic light I was once again dedicated to my business, and not giving her a second thought. For the first few days afterwards I tried to become absorbed in my work, but the presence of Henry Berger was a constant reminder, and I could hardly forget a woman that my employee habitually praised.

"I tell you, Mr. Gabor, I must be the luckiest man in the world. I can't wait until I'm married. Just the thought of having such a gorgeous wife as her by my side for the rest of my life makes me feel blessed a thousand times over. That's what it is alright! I'm blessed! I tell you! I'm blessed!"

Finally, I had to put an end to it.

"Okay Henry, I got it! I think we all got it. And we're all very glad for you. Now give us a break. Okay? Let's get back to work. We got a line to get ready."

Then I decided to dispense with Henry for the time being.

"Anyway Henry, you should be out selling our line. Nobody here is gonna buy!"

He didn't appreciate having his boasting squashed like that, but it really was getting annoying. Of course, what annoyed me most was the fact that, having already met his betrothed, I had become overwhelmingly jealous of him. But while I reflected on that I also had to ponder as to how he didn't seem to know that we had met. My encounter with his fiancé was brief, except for what lingered in my mind, but apparently she had chosen to keep it from him. This led me to contemplate a world of possibilities. Maybe she had been drawn to me and wanted to keep a mature man in reserve in case she wearied of an immature young pup of a salesman. I've heard of such things happening, so why not with me? Or was she still planning to introduce me to her mom. Or maybe it was something else entirely. Perhaps she didn't want to suffer the ignominy of having me reject her poor mother, causing her shame and embarrassment. After all, if nobody knew about me then that potential stigma would never exist. So, it was safest for her to keep me under wraps, and only reveal my identity if a union with mother seemed imminent. Of the two choices I must admit that I greatly favored the former. Such meditation can drive one wild however, so I plunged into my work as intensely as I suggested to Henry. I wanted to clear my mind of this damsel as much as I wanted to free myself of the guilt over my desire to steal my employee's fiancé. Besides, he was so obsessed with this girl I have no doubt he'd go mad if he were left in the lurch. Anyway, I'm not the kind of person to intentionally cause anyone heartache, so I thought it best to leave Henry Berger to his bliss, and just forget about a woman I knew for a total of ten minutes. And the best way to forget personal problems is to jump into the deep end of the work pool. If I was going to conquer America, as I had Argentina, I had to focus.

    A few weeks after telling Henry Berger to put a lid on his yammering I was hard at work on the coming debut of my first line of teen clothing in America. Gabriel Creations had been growing, and I was looking forward to introducing my line to a broad market. The American Dream was holding its carrot out for me to grab, and love and family were the furthest things from my mind when my secretary interrupted.

"You have a phone call."

I broke my concentration. "From who?"

Then destiny came banging again on my door, though I didn't know it.

"Rebeca," she said.

I had done such a good job of forgetting the girl from the traffic light the name didn't grab me. I actually thought it was the name of my car insurance agent, so I took the call. A voice far sweeter than my insurance agent came on the line and spoke in Spanish.

"*Hola*, Ivan?"

It might sound like I'm trying to be cool, but the truth is I actually didn't remember her name at that moment. I realized it wasn't my insurance agent, so I was momentarily confused. But the fetching voice on the other end of the line persisted.

She said, "You don't remember?"

"No," I replied. A silence passed. Again she asked, "You really don't remember?!" My mind was so full of clothes and deadlines I was at a loss. Then it hit me.

"Ahh, you're the fiancé of Henry Berger, the girl who wanted me to meet her mamá!" Now I was a fountain of information. But I demonstrated that I was in possession of the facts without revealing any personal enthusiasm over her call. And her answer was equally free of emotion.

"Sí," she said.

She said yes, but not like anyone especially overjoyed about it. She was not a giddy bride to be, gushing over her coming nuptials. Her answer did not second my emotion. It was a flat, monosyllabic and noncommittal confirmation. But I did not make much of it. Rather, I took a guess at what motivated her call.

"So, you want me to meet your mother?"

Wasn't this, after all, the reason why she had my card, and the reason why she called? She'd already told me that I was too old for her. Yet she didn't seem to be walking on air over the notion of marrying Henry Berger either. But I didn't repeat my question preferring to let the silence grow. And grow. What was probably three seconds seemed like a hundred, yet she said nothing. One might almost assume that the line had gone dead, but it's not so difficult to tell the difference between dead air and a dead line. After a respectable span of time had elapsed it was time to test the waters.

"*Hola*," I said. *Hola*? Are you still there?"

She finally admitted, "*Sí.*"

The Spanish affirmative word was her brief contribution to our conversation, and after a few more moments it became clear that the ball was in my side of the court. I was nervous about misinterpreting her service, but I took a chance and lobed one over the net.

"Did you call for some other reason besides wanting me to meet your mother?"

Now silence spoke for her. The eighteen year old was too intimidated by the forty one year old. She was simply too timid to talk. The ball lay on the clay, and I was totally at sea. Then it occurred to me that she might want to talk with me. Of course, this could have been wishful thinking on my part, but I still felt uncomfortable about robbing the cradle or Henry Berger's dreams. Finally, with nowhere else to go I took a chance.

"Would you like to meet me somewhere?"

"*Sí.*"

Echoes Of My Footsteps

That syllable again. But this time it spoke volumes. This was clearly what she had been waiting for. Her reply was minimal but expansive. It filled the room. Many times I've relived that moment and that day in my mind. It's true that I was cool at first, not recognizing her name. But it was no act. And I used to believe that I stayed aloof, nobly considering the youth of the girl and the feelings of my employee. But time has been kind to me, and nonjudgmental regarding the true nature of my feelings. Back then I was deep in the throes of reliving my lusty adolescence, constantly seeking out the company of willing single women, and I'd be fooling myself, though very few others, if I tried to present any other image. Equally true however, was the fact that there was something more profound than the allure of mere physical attraction. While she got to me on a sensual level she also reached my mind. And when she surrendered that tiny Castilian syllable it made my day. Naturally, I didn't hesitate to confirm. "Why not! Let's meet somewhere!" The next thing I knew I was in my Caddy on my way to a sidewalk café on Biscayne Boulevard.

Chapter IV

War

If you are a decent person, opposed to hurting others, war itself is the ultimate surreal event, because nothing about it makes a lick of sense and it looks completely out of place. Observe the gentle contours of the farms and hillsides of central Europe and its undulating waterways, and you'll see that the appearance of sharply angled tanks and machines of destruction seem as unnatural and incongruous an arrangement as any demented artist could ever concoct. It's utterly nightmarish. Nature's palette of earth tones is invaded by uncomplimentary murky grays and blacks. The vast serene blue of the firmament is rent by buzzing mechanical dive bombing insects. A virtual still life is destroyed even before the first bright red salvo is fired. Ugliness clashing with beauty, the ultimate expression of surrealism, but an exhibition few had the luxury not to attend.

So, the first influence in my life, besides the subliminal affection of my upbringing, was war. I am not however just another shell shocked war refugee. My calamities are primarily postwar. Of course, had there been no war at all perhaps my mental state would still have evolved to its present state, and this haunts me too. But these confusing confessions are premature! Before you become as consumed by anxious mystery as I already am, allow me to impart a bit of what that conflict felt like first hand.

Doubtless you've already read about war, and maybe more than a little about this one in particular. If you have then you know that it was hellish and painful, and I do not wish to force upon you one extra disagreeable moment by making you go through it again. Brevity will be my guideline while still sharing with you its all consuming mood of tension, best summed up by comprehending the two overwhelming constants of fear and hunger. Your mind is always afraid that you'll be savagely beaten or violently killed, and your body is continually famished. There is no calm or satisfaction. Utter anxiety reigns where peace should prevail. What's wrong with this picture? Horrific surrealism.

When my father got fired and we moved to Budapest I dwelled in a state of blissful ignorance. Hungary was imposing its anti-Jewish laws in accordance with their treaty with Germany, but I was unaware of any of it until one day at public school I got my first lesson. There was an air raid drill and the teacher announced that all of the children should line up in preparation to go down into the cellar. Then she said something odd that I didn't understand. She announced that the Jewish kids had to go to the end of the line. That was the first inkling that I was different, and that my life valued less than the others. My consciousness was beginning to wake up, but my father continued to try and numb it and hide things from me, like the total disappearance of my family. I was accustomed to seeing my relatives all the time. I was used to constant visits from aunts and cousins. After all, I was the darling of the family and hardly a day went by when some relative didn't come to our door. Some were assimilated, like my folks, but some were ultra orthodox. I remember my second cousin Nandor and his family. He wasn't technically my uncle, but because of the age difference that's what I called him. He was Hasidic and always trying to convince my dad to commit to Judaism. But he was warm with me despite the cold ears upon which his proselytizing fell.

"Please Nandor," my dad used to say. "We're religious enough. Besides, now's not the best time to parade around with a beard and *payis*, if you know what I mean." But now there was no Uncle Nandor or anyone else, and their absence seemed so sudden to me it was as if they vanished. One day I looked around and realized relatives weren't coming around any more. So, I asked my father, "Where is everybody?" Still believing my immature brain couldn't deal with reality he continued to keep me on a need-to-know basis, simply replying, "They're gone." This existentially frank and dismally incomplete reply was not what I sought, but as always, I had to accept it.

By 1944 most of the Jews in countries conquered by the Nazis were either in ghettos or concentration camps. But with millions already liquidated, the Jews of Hungary had thus far escaped the carnage. This contributed to the feeling of people like my father that Hungary was unique. What happened in other countries, though we did not know the real extent of it, wouldn't happen here. And this also contributed to the game my father played with me. The object of this bizarre game was supposedly to protect me. Though things were getting progressively worse for Jews, he still told me that we were safe. Once, we were walking by a church, and some kids called out, "Rotten Jews! You won't be around much longer!" I had never heard such talk, but my father immediately told me not to worry about it. He insisted that it would all blow over.

This charade collapsed before my eyes one day while we were walking down the street. My father had just taken me to the Transportation Museum, a place I loved. It was filled with old planes, trains and automobiles, and was near Heroes' Square, another one of my favorite places in the old city. We were strolling down Andrassy Boulevard, a broad, beautiful thoroughfare lined with outdoor cafes and tall trees. There was a man coming our way, weaving back and forth, and when he caught up to us I could see that he was drunk. He was incoherently screaming and yelling, and my father asked him, "What's all the noise about?" The man stopped and cried out, "It's the end of Hungary! The Germans are in the street!"

The mood of the day was shattered, to say the least. This man was making a doomsday pronouncement, and I was utterly confused. I had to know what he meant.

"Father, what does he mean?"

My father persisted in keeping me in the dark.

"Oh, he's just drunk!"

I don't know what's worse, that he still tried to keep the truth from me, or that he lied to himself. The truth was that he just couldn't believe or accept it. The Jews had given so much to Hungarian culture. How was it possible that the Germans were here and that we were going to be persecuted?! But he must have considered that it might be so, because he took me by the hand and headed for home with a greater stride than was his custom. When we turned the corner on our street we ran into a parade of boys waving swastika and arrow-cross flags.

By that time we were supposed to have been wearing the yellow Star of David patch on our clothing, as well as obeying curfew and other anti-Jewish restrictions, though it had been only occasionally enforced. But now that the Germans were here the Nyilasok became even stricter and more murderous than their Nazi overseers. For example, they loved to find Jews without the Star of David. It gave them an excuse to practice the kind of violence that filled their hearts with perverse joy. It all meant that my father and I were in a race to reach the refuge of our apartment before being spotted in the street without the obligatory yellow Mogen David. Being the coddled boy that I was the yellow star patch was yet another vitally important artifact of our situation that eluded me. Everyone else seemed to get it though. Jews, under threat of the harshest penalties imaginable, were required to wear that patch on their clothing at all times when in the street. This was a matter of life and death, yet the elders of my family persisted in keeping me in the dark, mystically convinced that a ten year old Jewish lad, heir to the genes of normally intelligent people, and just a few years shy of attaining manhood himself, was somehow incapable of comprehending or accepting reality. I cannot wrap my present consciousness around this mystery without assigning such weirdness a surrealistic designation. The state of my cognition, trained to remain a perennial child, was so utterly clueless about the Yellow Star's real significance that I saw it simply for its aesthetic value. I regret to confess that when they first introduced it I was so out of touch I thought it was an attractive wardrobe accessory.

The patches themselves in every sense were totally incongruous. Objects had signs on them, not people. Only uniformed members of society, such as soldiers, policemen and public servants, displayed insignia; not private citizens. Wearing them, while not arbitrary, seemed so, rendering the heretofore unknown patches anomalies, and absolute candidates for surrealism. We had to debase ourselves by parading around with signs on our bodies. This dehumanizing tactic stripped us of our integrity, and to add insult to injury, as well as heighten the sense of incongruity, we were obliged to spend our own money to purchase them. They were actually sold like any other product! Stores carried them, and enterprising individuals went door to door selling them. In addition they came in different grades. Some were plain cotton while others fancy velvet. The first one I saw was the plush variety and I immediately voiced my approval. I actually desired it and was proud to have it sewn on my jacket, completing the chic look of my matching short pants and knee socks ensemble. A more ignorant child never walked the streets of Budapest.

In a larger cultural sense, taking into consideration the context of European culture, it really wasn't surprising that Jews ended up wearing generic name tags. We had already been geographically segregated for centuries. At different times we were either welcomed into or expelled from whole countries. Russian Czars, for example, could never definitively decide if we were welcome or not. And it was only a generation or two previous to my birth that a zone known as the *pale* had been exclusively designated as kosher for Jewish habitation. And in other countries we were periodically crowded into ghettos, only to be let out after some time, then forced back in again in a bizarre cycle.

The parade of the Nyilas punks seemed more rampant than any previous demonstration. Emboldened by the presence of their armed Nazi overlords they broadcast stern warnings through bullhorns to the people gathered on the sidewalks.

"All Jews between the ages of twenty-one and forty-five must immediately report to the authorities! Yellow Star emblems must be worn on clothes at all times! Six o'clock curfew will be strictly enforced!"

I did not have to ask my father what was going on, nor did he offer a feeble spin on the event. I could read the signs, and they weren't any too friendly toward us. Added to that the urgent tugging of my father's hand as we hurried home, and I knew we were in real danger. I might not have been immediately aware that we were in imminent peril of being murdered in cold blood, but the view from my ivory tower was now clouded.

The first command of the fascists regarding Jews was to employ them as slave labor. The Russians were bombing Hungary, creating mountains of rubble. So as not to waste badly needed combat troops on the menial task of cleaning up after air raids Jewish men were conscripted into a labor battalion and sent wherever they were needed. And my father was in that broad age range that included him among its ranks. At that time he had been trying to learn a new profession, because Jews were no longer allowed in the white collar trades. Jewish doctors, lawyers, bankers and teachers had no chance of retaining their positions, so my father hoped he might be left in peace if he became a blue collar worker. He studied metallurgy, hoping to be of some practical use to the new ruling class, buying more time as we waited for the Russians to liberate us. But a different kind of manual labor awaited him. Along with the rest of the able bodied Jews in his age group he was conscripted by the Nyilasok into the Jewish Forced Labor Brigade to clear away rubble. As he had been previously drafted into the Hungarian army as an accountant we were not panic stricken. My mother probably just assumed, or at least hoped, that this new stint would also be temporary. He was taken away, leaving me, my grandmother and my mother to carry on until his possible return. As daunting as it was to bring new life into that world, people still succumbed to human passions, and my father left my mother in the family way. Conceivably, he left without even knowing it.

Almost as soon as my father was taken away another pronouncement was made. This order made it necessary for us to move from our deluxe apartment. The government was now concentrating Jews in the cities by moving them into specially designated buildings. They did this in preparation for moving us all to the ghetto, ultimately to more efficiently facilitate mass deportations to the concentration camps. There were apartment buildings decorated with giant Stars of David on them, and we were required to move into one. To add further insult we had to move into the interior units. Of course, compared to what awaited us this was a trivial inconvenience. The worst hovel in Budapest was a deluxe suite compared to concentration camp barracks. To take advantage of the disenfranchisement of Budapest Jews some gentiles took the first step in bettering their own living arrangement. In our case a Christian woman came to our flat and made us an offer we couldn't refuse.

"Look, the building where I live has been designated a Jewish building. It's nearby. Your address is Csengery Utca, number fifty-one, and mine is number sixty-one. So, you can move into my apartment and I'll move into yours and watch it for you."

She was cheerful and pleasant and tried her best to make it sound as if she was doing us a favor. With the command of the fascists ringing in our ears we had to accept this arrangement. Oddly enough, some Gentile families elected to remain in their homes, even if their buildings were designated as Jewish. Habit can be a strange task master. They had lived there so long, and were so settled in, they just couldn't imagine moving. In those cases their apartments were usually on the outside. To have that coveted honor could not be ameliorated even by war. Such class distinction spilled over into the most absurd territories, like cellars. The Russian air raids, for which we had rehearsed in school, were going on all over the city, and everyone hid from them in the cellars of their buildings, Jew and Gentile alike. When the siren wailed we all sought refuge there. In those days every building used coal for heat and it was delivered through a chute into the basement, which was divided into separate bins for each unit. And though the same bomb would kill us all the Christians maintained a racially segregated cellar, with them cowering in one part, while we Jews were obliged to seek refuge over by the dustier coal bin section. Of course, by then the dust of the coal was all that was left. Delivery of the precious heating fuel had long since stopped. To avoid freezing to death we were burning the furniture in the apartment. Every week our décor became less and less decorative as it was fed bit by bit into the ever hungry mouth of our iron stove. Meanwhile, down in the cellar, we hunkered down in the last dusty coal residue in Budapest, riding out the air raids. Meanwhile, the gentiles did their own hunkering down, but in the classier and cleaner dirt and dust of the surreal caste system. Of course, there were some central bomb shelters in the city where any Christian was welcome. Jews verbotten. We didn't know how long we'd be in the Jewish designated building, or if we'd ever see our old apartment again.

After we were in the Jewish designated building about a week a Nyilas woman came in and did the unimaginable. She took my mother and some other women away to a nearby brick factory to work for them under penalty of death. They just came and took her away, without warning or ceremony. I ran after her, begging to let her stay with me.

"Please, don't take my mother away. Please!"

The fascist women sneered at me as if a bug was crawling on them.

"Shut up, you little Jewish rat! Now get back if you know what's good for you!"

Now, I was without either of my parents. And my mother was everything a parent should be. She was the provider, the boss, the captain of our ship. Without her I felt as if the air had been kicked out of me. But my grandmother immediately stepped up to the plate and filled that emotional chasm, making it possible for me to survive that impossible moment. She smothered me in her warm embrace and spoke soothingly.

"Don't worry, *Freddela*. I'm sure she'll come back soon. They just need her and the other woman for a day or two. You'll see. She'll be back."

Jewish work brigades brought bricks to the factory on the edge of town, collected from the rubble of Russian bombing raids, and the women were recruited to put them into categories. The women had to stack bricks until the sun went down, making it impossible to see any more. Then they stopped and the entire factory was locked shut. They were fed little and basically worked to death.

The war offered such reversal of fortune as to be unfathomable. Here was my mother, a former beauty queen, slaving away under watchful eyes and rifle barrels. What could she have been thinking? Was she outraged, offended, or just plain frightened? Knowing my mother I would say that just one thought hung in her mind. She was not offended at having to perform menial physical labor, nor was she was frightened for herself. All she could think about was protecting the child inside of her and getting back to her nine year old son and protecting him too. I'm certain it was all that permeated her consciousness that entire day of arduous toil. Furthermore, her instinctual maternal urge made her determined to escape. So, as soon as the guards locked the gates she began exploring for weaknesses in the factory's security. She crept along in the shadows, eyeing every gate, door and window. Miraculously, in less than an hour, she found an unguarded gate that led to the street. It was a combination of Nyilas incompetence and luck that let her find it. Of course, it was often a Nyilas game to trick a freedom loving prisoner with an unprotected door and then open fire as soon as she stepped out into the street. But fortune put its cloak of invisibility over my mother that night and allowed her to sneak through a gate that a negligent fascist had left ajar. She removed her shoes and walked as quietly and as stealthily as a cat, making her way out of the brick factory and, under cover of night, all the way back to us. What joyous relief! I hugged my mother like she'd been away for a year. And I cannot imagine the joy my grandmother felt at seeing her daughter return from the land of the dead. The very next day all of the prisoners at that brick factory were rounded up and put on transports to Auschwitz.

There's not too much to explain about the rest of my family. Besides, you've heard it all before. Six million times before. Most of my relatives were shipped off to Auschwitz in southern Poland and liquidated. The ever efficient Germans kept loading trains bound for the camps. The transports returned empty and were then reloaded. Back and forth they went, again and again, as the ghetto population plummeted. To keep us off those trains my mother was in full survival mode, coming up with plans for our salvation. One such plan came to us from our recent past, back when we lived in the outside apartment and could afford domestic help. We had a maid named Sonia, a friendly gentile woman from Russia who was sympathetic to our predicament. She offered us a possible avenue of escape involving a Christian woman she knew who worked at the huge locomotive factory on an island in the Danube River. That plant, the biggest in Hungary, had been owned and run by Jewish industrialists, the Weisman-Fried family. Of course, it had been expropriated by the fascist government as were all such businesses. This vast theft bears irrefutable evidence that the real motivating factor behind the absurd campaign waged against the Jews was plain old fashioned avarice. The factory, now run by Nyilasok appointed managers, continued to operate, and its employees still held their jobs, though its Jewish ranks were purged. The woman who Sonia knew was prepared to hide some Jews in her large house as long as it was financially worthwhile to her. Motivated by greed, many gentiles were prepared to feign empathy in exchange for some measure of wealth. So, my mother collected all her jewelry, right down to her wedding ring, calculating that it was worth at least our lives. She wrapped it all up in a large kerchief, thrust it into her pocket, firmly grasped my hand in hers and trudged off to barter for our safety. She took me along in case she made the deal quickly, and she'd return for grandma afterwards. Of course, I was kept in the dark about this. My mother had long subscribed to my father's plan of keeping little Freddy ignorant, so she didn't share her agenda with me. So, even though I had no idea where we were going, I trusted my mother, and that was good enough for both of us. In any case, I was always a good boy and did as I was bid. Doing otherwise was unimaginable. Such was life during the war. Actually, that was the way of life in Europe for many years before that. One minded one's parents. The war simply heightened that reality. Disobeying mom or dad could cost your life, whether Jew or gentile. It was madness to disobey your parents. In this case it was extremely sensitive. We had to accomplish a certain task, but as usual, I was on a need-to-not-to-know basis. She had to get us there, and either leave me there and return for grandma, or get back with me. In either case she'd have to do it all before the six o'clock curfew. Our gentile apartment in the Jewish building was just two rooms, and going into the other room and whispering was the sole option for privacy. Without telling me directly, the way she urgently murmured to grandma told me plenty.

We caught trolley number six, and settled into some empty seats as unobtrusively as possible. Jews were still allowed on public conveyances, just as long as they sported their yellow stars. After about a mile we were the only people momentarily left on the trolley, and I was bursting with curiosity and anxiety to ask my mother where we were off to, but I knew that I was meant to be seen and not heard, and kept mum.

After about an hour we got off the trolley. Mother consulted the scrap of paper that Sonia had given her and then did something that repulsed and terrified me. After reading it, silently moving her lips in concentration to memorize it, she looked both ways to see if we were observed, and swallowed it. It had been agreed that, in case we were caught, there would no evidence to incriminate anyone else. To heighten the anxiety even more mother pulled me into the shadow of an alcove, produced a small knife and started removing the stitches from my yellow Star of David. She stuffed our patches into her pocket, because as arranged she could not implicate this woman. If strange people were spotted in her neighborhood it would certainly only complicate things if they were Jews.

Following Sonia's instructions we found the house. We knocked lightly, so as not to attract any attention. This too was deliberate and planned. Though too soft to be heard under normal circumstances, my mother's light rapping was immediately responded to, and the door was quickly pulled open. The woman quietly commanded us to enter without hesitation. It was not a cordial invitation, but an insistent order. She was as afraid as anyone else of the consequences, because things went heavy on gentiles who hid Jews. We stepped in as quickly as she bid.

The lady did not look to me like anyone prepared to do a good deed, and she wasted no time with small talk or cordiality.

"Well, let me see it."

My mother pulled out the kerchief from her coat pocket and handed it to the woman. She immediately opened it and studied the contents. After just a few seconds a grimace fell across her meaty unattractive face, and she slowly shook her head from side to side in a display of decisive disapproval. She practically threw the package back at my mother.

"I'm not going to risk my life for such a pathetic amount of jewelry as this. Be gone!"

She grabbed mother by the sleeve, dragged her to the door, and pushed us outside, shutting the barrier in a subdued kind of slam. The whole transaction had not taken thirty seconds. My mother looked dejected and just stood there for a few moments. Of course, if you know the facts you could easily understand why she turned us away. The penalty for helping a Jew was so severe it's a wonder anyone did so at all, regardless of the economic benefit. Not far from the Plaza of Heroes were street lamps that served as gallows. From them the Nazis hanged any souls kind hearted enough to aid or hide a Jew. Sometimes they were beheaded to punctuate the lesson. Signs adorned the bodies proclaiming *Jew-lovers*. Human beings hanging from trees and lamp posts are a ghoulish and nightmarishly surreal sight, even as war time images go.

I really didn't comprehend the scene, except that it was a devastating disappointment. My mother sighed, took another deep breath, grabbed me by the hand, and we hurried off back to our apartment where my grandmother anxiously awaited our return. If my mother had been successful then she would have left me temporarily with the sourpuss gentile woman and returned to our apartment to fetch grandma along with some essential belongings. Success or failure she still would have been exposed to another trip outside. What was worse was that it had been a slow journey down to this woman's house, and it was now approaching six. My mother had been confident that her jewelry would have bought our safety and a first night's asylum in that woman's house. But it did not come to pass and we had to run the risk of being caught outside by the Nyilasok. On the way my mother reversed our operation and sewed our yellow stars back on with a needle and thread she had brought along just in case. It was bad enough to miss curfew, but even worse without the stars. Thankfully no policemen of any sort, or anti-Semitic public minded citizen, shared our trolley.

Every few seconds my mother checked her watch. At six o'clock she let out a sigh, and cursed that gentile woman. We were now past curfew. But the fact was that we really didn't fathom just how dangerous that really was.

The trolley clanked to a stop at exactly ten after six. We got off and tried our best not to attract attention by running. Panting, with mere yards separating us from the refuge of our home, we were spotted by a Nyilas hooligan.

"Halt! What are you Jews doing outside after curfew?"

This was, of course, a question that did not require a response. All such inquiries were rhetorical and anyone answering them invited worse retribution. We were told to follow him with our hands raised over our heads. They took us to a building next door to the Hotel Royale, a Budapest landmark famed for its elegance. Visitors relished the creature comforts of the Royale, but nobody looked forward to a visit to its neighbor. It was a place of torture and death. Of course, I was still too ignorant to understand it completely, but my mother was aware of what might await us within. Everyone knew that people were interrogated there, usually never to be seen or heard from again.

Once inside we were taken to an interior patio. At once a Nyilas woman took over. She might have been of the female gender, but all hints of femininity had fled this Lady Macbeth long ago. She marched us to a red bricked cellar with an earthen floor under a dome roof and stood us against the wall next to a dozen others in similar posture.

"Up against the wall and spread your arms!"

I was never more terrified in my life. Even to the dull likes of me this was clearly dangerous. I followed the example of my mother and the others already leaning against the wall with the flats of their hands against it. As my natural course of action I looked over to my mother. The guard snapped, "Eyes straight ahead!"

More guards came in and grabbed one of the men near us and dragged him away to another room. We heard screaming and a gun shot, then silence. I was petrified.

The fact that I couldn't look at my mother was one of the most horrific parts of this procedure. I was accustomed to looking to her for every cue in my life. Now, I was on my own. I starred at the wall in front of me, utterly lost.

They grabbed and dragged another man to that room. Screams, a shot, silence. They came for another. Then another. Only a few remained before they would get to us. So, with one minute left to live, and desperation as her only guide, mother launched into an act of subterfuge designed to distract our captors and would be murderers. As already explained, my mother's normally well honed survival instincts were sharpened to a razor fine edge by the onset of hostilities in Europe. Where once she was typically protective of her brood, now she was a cunning animal, unafraid to employ any tactic, no matter how dismal the odds, to buy even a moment's stay of execution. If she could slow their hand for even a second she might employ that extra time to devise a more elaborate ruse with which to save my life. Now however, there was no question of subtlety. Her baby was about to be sacrificed to some absurd notion of racial superiority, and such social surrealism could not be tolerated. Out of sheer desperation she formulated a minimalist plan in one of the two seconds remaining, and in the other she put it into motion. It was a million to one shot that it would work, but it was all we had. She jutted out her four month pregnant stomach and cried out, "I'm in pain! I'm in pain!" The Nyilasok were heartless, murderous vermin, as likely to kill a baby as anyone else, but my mother hoped she might strike a faint chord in what little remained of the maternal instinct of this Nyilas woman. And while she hoped this she continued wailing in mock agony.

"I need a doctor! Help!"

It seemed futile, but she pursued her histrionics with noble dedication. She writhed around with bulging eyes and bellowing affliction, oblivious to whether or not she was eliciting the desired response. She was transcendental to the Nyilas torture chamber and the record of torment that had transpired there every day for years. Many before in this room had cried out in anguish most sincere, all to the gleeful satisfaction of their tormentors. Why would they segregate accidental, coincidental or incidental pain from the continual agony they caused? It made no sense, but it was all mother had to work with. And she did not let up.

Convulsions and moans poured out of my mother without a break, and each second that passed without a threat, kick, punch or gunshot from the Nyilasok encouraged her performance even more. Such thoughts might have consciously flashed through her mind like a desperate pep-talk.

"It's working! Keep it up! They're buying it! You can do it!"

I can't imagine what the other prisoners were thinking through all this, except that they were relieved to have their sentences commuted even momentarily. One member of that audience who was immediately convinced was me. I actually thought she was in pain. Of course, my theatrical review was immaterial. The opinion my mother most cherished at this moment was that of the Nyilas guard. She had to make an impression on the half percent of the one shred of sympathy remaining in that hardened and callous bosom. If it was still there it might urge her to react like someone half way normal. And, after an eternally long five seconds of synthetic shooting pains her audition was

Echoes Of My Footsteps

rewarded. The guard, though skeptical, gave my mother the benefit of the doubt.

"Alright," sneered the guard. "I'll take you to the hospital. But if you're faking you're dead!"

It was actually ridiculous. They were intent on killing her, but if she was in pain they'd attend to that first. And once that was resolved they could go back to killing her. It was the very essence of surrealism.

The guard paid no attention to me whatsoever, and when they started toward the door my mother just grabbed my hand and dragged me along. Not if my hand had been made of metal and welded to my mother's own hand could I have been any more firmly attached to her. As for my part, I remained silent and invisible. But on the way out I saw that we walked over dirt that had been soaked with blood. And I saw bodies on the ground at the end of the wall. I had never seen a corpse before, and if not for hearing the shots I might have not known that they were dead. There was no doubt of it now.

The hospital was a five block walk, and my mother had to stagger all the way there, trying to make her abdomen protrude as much as possible, and keep moaning. The guard walked alongside, observing her every gesture. As mother's fear was the one authentic emotion present it was not a challenge for her to produce tears; they came on their own. By this time of course I too was overwhelmed with apprehension, convinced as I was that something was wrong with my poor mother's pregnancy. As soon as we arrived at the hospital the guard begrudgingly rang the bell while mother moaned and wailed. After a few more sobs the door opened and a shaft of light flowed out engulfing us all in its protective aura. With the brightness flooding our eyes we beheld the silhouette of a nurse adorned with a halo. She immediately admitted us into the stark white hospital interior as my mother pursued her histrionics. Observing my mother's condition, and exacerbated by her cries of pain, the angel of mercy wasted no time in enlisting a doctor in our cause. Not leaving another moment for the Arrow Guard witch to reconsider a young doctor manifested himself in our midst. The maniacal hag stood a few inches off to the side and behind us, allowing my mother a fraction of a second in which to tell the doctor the whole story with a desperate wide eyed glance, hoping he was true to his oath to do no harm. So far, my mother had managed to convince a fascistic, rabidly anti-Semitic murderess, intent on killing us, to take her to a place of safety. That in itself was incredible. The second phase of her plan consisted of convincing a medical professional, employed by that fascist government, of the veracity of her distress. If she could accomplish that then the Nyilas problem might be cancelled. Of course that rested squarely on the hope that the doctor would recognize the true nature of my mother's condition, as opposed to premature birth, and offer his voluntary aid. To reinforce the terror in her eyes she leaned forward imperceptively and whispered just as low that she was only in her fifth month. The doctor understood everything and honored his oath. He would not aid or abet the Nyilasok.

The fascist bitch declared that she would accompany her captive every step of the way, but the doctor imposed his authority and demanded she wait without, and escorted my mother into the sacred sanctuary of the examination room. All this time my mother's hand and mine were one, so I too entered the sanctity of the small clean room. Once behind closed doors the doctor studied his two pitiable Jews, and contributed to the theatricality of the evening by emitting some typical diagnosis sounds, "Hmm. Uh huh." This was for the benefit of the suspicious guard, in case she was listening at the door. The next second he opened that door and informed the Nyilas woman, "She must stay here tonight," and retreated back inside the neutral zone inside. Dejected and bitter, yet obedient to the Aryan looking doctor's diagnosis, our dejected would-be assassin turned and dragged herself away, probably determined to commit some extraordinarily viscous mayhem in order to compensate for losing two victims.

My mother wept and trembled from the utter anxiety of the situation. She was elated to be sure, but also frightened out of her wits. We were seconds away from being shot in cold blood, and she might have even been forced to watch me die first. Such things were common, usually accompanied by mocking laughter. But, thanks to my mother's daring, and the luck of finding a truly honorable member of the medical profession, we were still breathing. This young doctor sympathized with us, but he knew he would have to send us back out into the cold black night, exposed to the jackals in waiting. Our presence was a danger to him. The warm, protective hospital kept records, and he knew that mother really wasn't ill. He knew he'd have to make a full report on this patient and be forced to justify his actions. This case would have to disappear into the night. So, he took out his scalpel and removed the yellow patches from our clothes. He knew our best chance was to pass for gentile. Going out now with bright signs on our chests was suicide.

Mother thanked the doctor and we prepared to go back outside. We were terrified that the Nyilas matron might not have believed the doctor and would be waiting for us, but we stepped out into a cold and blessedly unpopulated street. Either that Nyilas bitch was not dedicated enough to wait for us, or she had plenty of other innocent women and children to bully and butcher.

We had been saved from the frying pan, but now were in the fire. If ten after six meant death what then of eight thirty? And, instead of being one block from home, as we were when arrested, we were now five long city blocks away. Our only allies at this moment were speed and darkness. We were guilty of two major crimes at that moment, breaking curfew and parading without stars. And, just because we had survived one encounter with the Nyilasok that night, we were not granted any safe passage back home. The exact same threat of death dogged us. But mother thought it better to pass as gentiles than blatantly announce our true identity with those damning scraps of yellow cloth.

Five blocks can take ten minutes under normal circumstances, but normality had long since disappeared from Budapest. We sought out the shadows on either side of the street as if they were safe zones, but the clopping that our shoes made sounded like kettle drums to our frightened ears, echoing off the brick buildings, summoning every Nyilasok, Gestapo, SS trooper and policeman within ear shot. And, while the shadows hid us, they could just as well hide an enemy. Rounding each corner brought a new menace. A common street lamp was like a searchlight. Every foot was a mile, every block a trek. Just an hour earlier I might have dumbly let myself be dragged along by my mother, without the need of any other level of awareness. But the crash course on survival I had just experienced honed my senses to a new state of alert. Their full potential had heretofore lay dormant and now they were awaken, fresh from the sleep of an overly protected youth, and finally ready for full engagement. My eyes darted from side to side, scanning the environment like the potential prey of a cagey predator, and my hearing picked up every sound. Even extra sensory perception was now within my grasp. Of course, none of these freshly attuned senses gave us any assurance of a safe journey home, but I felt that now I would at least perceive any threat coming, and be that much more prepared.

Even with all that determined preparation our five block trek home was still a crap shoot, and the consequences would be beyond the imagination of any sane person. Again, they would fall into the realm of the surreal. Tardiness usually makes the average person nervous.

Kids are afraid their parents might punish them for getting home too late by depriving them of some inconsequential frivolity. And spouses often suffer rapprochement and accusations of infidelity. But imagine if Cinderella's punishment for staying out past the stroke of twelve was death! It's necessary to imagine it, because common sense tells us it's ridiculous. But the entire war was that way. The punishment for not wearing a patch was death. The penalty for helping a Jew was death. And the penalty just for being a Jew, the son of a Jew, or the grandson of a Jew was death. Reason and sanity were on hiatus.

We walked with an unnatural gait, carefully placing our feet down so as not to make a sound. Step by feline step we closed the gulf between no man's land and home, keeping the image of grandma in my mind as a goal. And by kind fate's intervention, not a soul, friend or foe, crossed our path. Night held so many unseen dangers hardly anyone ventured out any more. By the time we made it home we were exhausted from the physical and psychic stress of the day and had wet ourselves from sheer terror. Grandma was insane with relief to see her daughter and grandson still alive, and we all wept together. I now understood our peril. Finally knowing the score I was almost sorry I did.

There was no doubt that my mother had been brave and resourceful. And I cannot deny that I owed her my life that night. But, as all survivors will tell you, blind dumb luck was our most ubiquitous accomplice. We were outnumbered by a million to one, unarmed, incapable of communicating with anyone beyond the sound of our voice, clearly identified by badges, and our whereabouts were known to both fascist authorities and the police. The odds were incalculably stacked against us. So, we were almost totally dependent on people and things beyond our feeble ability to affect them. But as reliant on the unknown as we were we also had to make some effort on our own behalf. Luck alone could not level the playing field. So mom and grandma made plans on how to stay out of the clutches of the fascists for the next few days. They figured that, after the brick factory and Hotel Royale episodes they might come looking for us. That meant that our current residence was unsafe. We had to lay even lower than usual for now, and our options were limited. Hoping for the best, we snuck into the cellar of a nearby gentile building, hunkered down on the ground and waited. Of course, anyone in the upper floors could've spotted us and turned us in, but that's where the luck part of the plan came in. As it is, we weren't there long. We couldn't be. Our meager provisions ran out quickly and we had to reemerge to continue scrounging. Until then however we just sat there as quietly as possible, enduring hunger, cold, and the deprivations of our circumstances.

Try to envision what life is like under these circumstances. Food is rationed out in small handfuls. We cannot remove or change our clothes. Our sanitary conditions, or lack thereof, consists of finding a corner, digging a small hole, and then filling it in again. And washing was impossible. We prayed for rain or snow, either of which provided us with some form of water. Without water we were as doomed as being discovered. And there's nothing to pass the time. The one thing we had to keep up morale was conversation. It was whispered, but it prevented us from going totally mad.

"Remember so and so? What was the name of that movie? The Germans can't last forever; after all, they do have enemies. Maybe the British will beat them soon? Maybe the Russians? I heard women fight alongside men in their army. I wonder how dad is."

We had seen a picture of my father when he was first conscripted into the army and it didn't look so bad. Maybe he'd be okay in the work brigade too. Perhaps the worst was behind us. We had to hope for that. Without hope we had nothing. Grandma added prayer to our hope, and after a few uneventful days we sewed our yellow stars back on and returned to our hovel of an apartment which by comparison now appeared tolerable.

As the war dragged on the roles of good and evil switched sides in a surreal context. When the conflict first broke out violent aggression starkly contrasted with the tranquility of a world at peace. But now, five years into the war, violence was the norm, and acts of kindness seemed surreal by comparison. Such considerations are, in and of themselves, surreal, because life ought to be peaceful, and decency not the exception. Such was reality in the dreary Budapest winter of 1944.

Chapter V

Miami 3

Winters in Miami are glorious. The vacation capital's notorious summer heat and humidity take their own hiatus when the year is new, and the residents, far too long cooped up in a state of air conditioned hibernation, enthusiastically take to the great outdoors. Convertible tops come down, seasonal clothing emerges from its plastic cocoon, and everyone dines al fresco. This young girl and I had chosen a well frequented sidewalk café on Biscayne Boulevard, the most popular thoroughfare in town. This was no clandestine rendezvous, so I didn't feel like some dirty old man, out to take advantage of a sweet young thing. I was just going there to find out her dilemma to see if I could help. I was her mentor, older and supposedly wiser. That's what I told myself, and would have told anyone else who might have asked. But I don't know how believable it sounded. I can't deny that I was looking forward to our meeting for reasons other than benevolently bestowing my sagacity upon the younger generation. There was something about this student that didn't come off like a typical college kid. She was uncannily adult and sophisticated. And, as a man, I couldn't resist it. I told myself to keep things cool, but had to repeat it to myself like a mantra once I saw her at the table waiting for me. She was only eighteen, but she was so well dressed and poised she had the appearance of a more mature woman. When she greeted me she was not the light hearted girl from our first encounter. And she wasted no time in getting to the point of our reunion.

"I want to talk to you, because I need to confide in someone. I need to very much!"

Immediately my heart went out to her. I could see that she was troubled, and I couldn't help but feel honored that it was at my humble doorstep that she sought refuge. That might not sound romantic or sexual, but that's how it hit me! This young damsel had perceived something deep within me that gave her confidence. Perhaps without even meaning to, her sixth sense had probed me and found me worthy of her trust. Unplanned and unexpectedly we had both found something worth pursuing. And now the floodgates opened, and she revealed her heart and mind to me.

"Would you marry someone you didn't love?"

At once I understood everything. But she didn't even give me time to respond.

"I don't love Henry Berger. My family wants me to marry him."

I don't have to tell you that this was actually good news to me. Obviously, I wasn't happy she was in a fix, but I was certainly glad to hear that yammering Henry Berger would be silenced forever, and that I might even qualify as his replacement. Of course, marriage was the furthest thing from my mind, but if I could be the new man in her life, even if only the new platonic man, I felt triumphant. First, the matter at hand. I had to find out more about her dilemma in order to be of some Earthly good to her.

"The whole family?"

Now she told me something that helped clear up a lot of loose ends for me.

"Well, not my father. He's Sephardic, and not fanatical about getting me married off."

Father? So, her mother wasn't a lonely widow lady, but a divorced one.

"Even though my folks are divorced they're still very protective of me. I'm their only daughter, and they want to be sure I'm what they called properly settled. And Henry? Well, they find him suitable. He's Jewish, decent looking, relatively my age, earns a nice living and is wild about me. And that's another problem right there!"

I finally had a chance to put in two cents and I confirmed her assessment.

"That's a fact. He never stops talking about you."

"I know! Last night I told him and he went berserk. I even asked him for some of my personal things back and he refused. So, I told him if he keeps them I'm keeping his engagement ring. But I got a bad feeling I haven't seen the last of him. And I know for sure I haven't heard the last of this from my parents."

She now fell silent and looked deeply into my eyes. It was my turn to speak, and I needed to say the right thing. She deserved good advice, and it was a distraction to have her look into my soul with those big brown limpid pools. I needed to concentrate on helping her with an open and generous heart, and not be derailed by a torrid gaze.

"First off, this isn't the middle ages. Arranged marriages are a thing of the past. You can't just marry someone because your parents tell you to. No love? No marriage!"

I believed every word I was saying, and she was delighted to hear someone around her parent's age agree with her for a change. But that didn't change the fact that she was still alone in her fight. She needed much more than someone to empathize with her. She needed an ally, and I felt as if I was being recruited, even if subliminally. Of course, troops of this kind must serve on a strictly voluntary basis, and faced with the prospect of getting involved in Rebeca's life I wasn't about to become a mercenary.

"If you need my support you got it!"

"Gracias, Ivan. I needed a friend. Thanks."

I wanted to encourage her even more, so I asked, "So, what now, Rebeca?"

"Well, I'll go home and confront my mother. Now that I have some support I know I can do it. Thanks, Ivan."

Some support she said. She didn't personalize it by saying it was specifically my support. It was just some generic support to her. I was in her corner, but I didn't feel insulted over her lack of intimate regard. I was thrilled to have been called by her in the first place. It was true that I had put her out of my mind while focusing on my coming fashion debut, but I was flattered to have been called by a beautiful young woman over her personal problems. Of course, I was old enough to be her father, and that I was originally brought into her life only as a candidate to marry her mother, but now that the light of potential step-parenthood was dimming, and the torch of personal friendship was brightening, I was content. And I was further encouraged by the fact that she called me by name. She had my business card and might have called me *Señor* Gabor. But I wasn't merely *Señor* to her. I was Ivan. A relationship was blooming.

1. The idyllic life of middle class Jews in Hungary before the war. My family enjoys a summer day by the lake.
2. My maternal Grandparents.
3. Typical intersection in the commercial district of Budapest, on the east side of the Danube, circa 1938.
4. My great grandfather, who had an audience with Emperor Franz Joseph on behalf of the Jewish community back in the days of the empire.
5. My mother as a little girl in Baia Mare, or Nagybanya as it was called in Hungary.

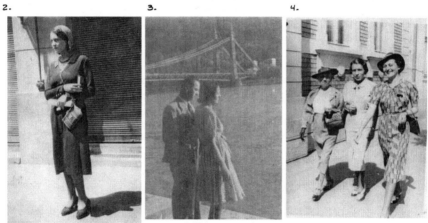

1. Grandma and mom looking out the window of my grandparents' house in Baia-Mare.
2. My mother at 18, around the time she was crowned Miss Baia-Mare.
3. My parents loved to stroll together along the banks of the Danube. You can see how much in love they were. Soon after this my mother, grandma and I were brought here to be killed by a firing squad.
4. The madness of war invaded so quickly it's frightening to consider that these photos were taken just months before. Here is my mother, every inch the fashion plate, accompanied by her cousin and aunt who were sent to the gas chambers not long afterwards.

1. Baby Alfred and papa.
2. Me and my puppy love Nora. Look at her and imagine somebody shoving her into a gas chamber, and you'll understand how inconceivable that war was. Behind here is her mother. She and my mother (to her left on the bench) were considered the two great beauties of Baia-Mare.
3. My first photo.
4. Mom, me and grandma in front of trolley #6 which almost carried us to our death.
5. Mom and I in Baia Mare.
6. My parents on their wedding day.

1.

2.

3.

4.

6.

5.

1. My mother, friends and me at a government office in Budapest.
2. No longer Alfred, I was now Freddy, in our new neighborhood in Budapest.
3. Oblivious to the coming storm my parents and I out for a stroll in Baia-Mare, shortly before the movie to Budapest. In the back is the bank where my father worked.
4. A neighbor in the Jewish Brigade foolishly grinning at his fate. He and his entire family perished in a concentration camp.
5. Mere weeks before my father was forcibly taken away to slave in the Jewish Brigade.
6. This photo was given to me by one of Baia-Mare's few Jewish survivors, the girl on the left in the back. She saved it for me for over 50 years. I am on the left and my puppy love, Nora is next to me. Besides myself and the girl who saved the photo everyone else in this picture died in a concentration camp.

1.

2.

3.

4.

5.

6.

1. Pointing at a poster on the omnipresent iron obelisks that bore ads and, during the war, anti-Semitic propaganda, and still later publicity for my play.
2. Mailing a letter to my dad in the Brigade just a month before I had to put on the Star of David patch.
3. Posing in front of a policeman who would soon be hunting us.
4. At war's beginning my father was drafted into the the Hungarian army for his accounting skills. He's smiling to keep up a stiff upper lip for us.
5. Uncle Nandor and his wife Margit. They were orthodox, but altered their appearance to evade capture. Soon after this was taken they were working with Raoul Wallenberg forging Swedish visas to save thirty thousand Jews, including us.
6. Me and mom just weeks before the horror began.

Chapter VI

The Red Danube

Use the word surreal and people usually envision funny looking melting watches on a barren dreamscape shore. But my perspective is far graver and less illusory. What's more, I see it everywhere, giving rise to an uncomfortable impression that practically the whole world is insane. Regarding this last perspective, most of the so-called civilized world is in agreement with me when it comes to World War Two. How could you think otherwise? One hysterical nut rants some utter nonsense, and fifty million people wind up dead. Certainly, there can be no more awful example of what the dictionary calls the incongruous arrangement and presentation of subject matter in a dream like setting. To say the whole war was a nightmare from start to finish is a statement in very little need of defense. And the emotions elicited by bringing it to mind constitute a morass that consumes any attempt to reason its why and wherefore. How can one reason the totally unreasonable? Of course, this conjecture comes by way of the blessings of distance. At this point in history I'm comfortably separated by time and circumstance from the numbing pain and gut wrenching fear of that awful time and place. However, any mental speculation about the existential parameters of experience find precious little room to blossom inside a head being pummeled by Nyilas bullies. To add to the incongruity it was a lovely summer day, the kind which makes one glad to be alive.

Once that well meaning doctor had removed our patches we decided to continue passing ourselves off as gentiles. Of course, we were far from the first to do so. After all, it wasn't that much of a challenge. We didn't resemble the cartoonish poster caricatures of kinky haired, hook-nosed, unshaven Jewish demons, and we talked like any other Hungarians. The weak link in our chain mail was the lack of presentable identification papers. We had none, which meant we were living on borrowed time at best. But, with our average appearance, and no patches to betray us, we might survive long enough to greet our Russian liberators.

Survival meant, not just avoiding arrest, but finding food to eat as well. After all, if we were free to venture out more often that meant we had more time to search for food, the number one pastime of war torn Europe, besides avoiding bullets. Near or far, the presence of gunfire was the background soundtrack of life in Budapest.

Desperately searching for food in a continent that was basically one big farm with a few widely scattered urban centers was yet another incredible example of the nightmarish mockery of reality called World War Two. There was food indeed, but it was earmarked for the killers. People in uniforms got ninety percent of anything edible. Women, children, and the old were rationed. And the subhuman Jews were on their own.

Confident we'd soon greet the determined Soviets or mythical Americans, and sans the yellow Star of David patch I ventured out into the daylight in search of food. Removing the patch convinced me I'd last longer out there, and with that extra time I might actually bring home the bacon. But confidence bested common sense, because I implemented the plan without taking the care to examine my disguise for defects. That imprudence led to my failure to remove the remnants of threads left around the edges of the excised patch. It was as obvious as the nose on the poster Jew's face. Nyilas gangsters spotted it at once, and wasted no time in attacking. These particular hoodlums were the worst of the breed, teenagers. It's conceivable that an adult fascist might not apply himself with the same fervent dedication in the beating of a young child as the teenaged variety of this scurrilous gang. A grownup very well might enjoy it, but he'd also be the most likely candidate among his species to exhibit a modicum of restraint, especially in public, lest he suffer some shame for it. Fourteen, fifteen and sixteen year olds, on the other hand, found exceptional joy in thrashing a kid. It was their specialty. They loved insulting, beating and shooting everyone, but ganging up on a defenseless kid was for them the piece d' resistance of mayhem. These savages delighted in spreading terror, causing pain, and killing the weakest among our population.

"Hey you, you filthy Jew! What are you doing out in public without your star?"

Immediately, several others joined him.

"Jew! He's a Jew!"

I maintained my innocence, with "Who's a Jew?" But the stitches on my clothing gave credible testimony to back up their accusations. Next they grabbed at my clothing.

"Pull his pants down! Pull 'em down!"

They wanted to confirm their catch of the day, as well as humiliate me at the same time. They never tired of it. But I held on to my pants, finally calling out, "Alright! I'm a Jew! So what?!"

It was violence incarnate. Without the formality of further accusation they lashed out and hit me so hard I fell to the ground. With the wind kicked out of me there was no thought of escaping. Of course, even if I hadn't fallen down they'd have pursued me like a pride of ravenous hyenas intent on finishing off a wounded bison calf. I never had a chance. As I desperately struggled to take a breath they fell on me like a school of piranha, pummeling me with their fists, boots and clubs. In seconds I was bleeding from wounds on my head, face, torso and limbs. I did my best to cover up, but it was futile. While they struck they cursed me, their insults serving to urge them on, and they became hysterical in their frenzy to kill another blaspheming member of Abraham's tribe.

"Stinking Jew. Rotten kike!"

I almost got to my knees, in the hope of fleeing, but they kicked me back down and continued stomping. When I tried to stand my hands momentarily left my head as I tried to push up from the unyielding stone street. In that split second their hard bony fists struck me in the nose and mouth and temples. Blood streamed down my face, mixed with my sweat, and filled my eyes, its acrid salinity burning my senses. I blinked some of it out of my eyes, only to have more of it pour back in at once. I was so defenseless I just shut my eyes to at least block out the sight of my tormentors. Countless wallops subdued me, and the bashing and pounding was a blur of pain. Clearly they were planning on going beyond the typical perfunctory punishment in preparation for arrest. Instead they were committed to meting out the harshest possible execution of sentence. They were going to beat me to death, as I myself had previously witnessed. Beyond the usual hatred they were fueled by anger motivated by the fact that could foresee their own approaching doom. Their whole nasty regime was under attack by intensified Allied air raids, bolstered by land assaults from the approaching Red army. Their days were numbered and they knew it, so they took out their frustration on anyone unlucky enough to cross paths with them. These fascists could not give a good showing of themselves in the face of armed foes, so they avenged their coming defeat upon the imagined and defenseless enemies that lived among them. They were the ultimate examples of cowards and bullies. The primary fascists, the Nazis, had an escape clause in their grand plan for Hungary; they'd simply abandon the place and beat it back to the Fatherland. The secondary Nyilas fascists were Hungarians and had no far off refuge to protect them. But this country was unique among the nations taken over by the Nazis. In the other lands occupied, and then deserted, by the Third Reich, the populace uniformly celebrated, with reprisals reserved for collaborators. Hungarian fascists however, persisted in their vain war against the Jews even after their German masters fled. By the time they attacked me the hand writing on the wall was crystal clear, yet they persisted in their lost cause, torturing and killing as many women and children as they could. They had absolutely nothing to win by beating or killing me, but they relished every blow. And with each one I felt weaker. The pain was so intense I prayed for them to just get it over with and kill me. At least the agony would end. The pain, the suffering, the hunger, the cold, the hate would all cease. But witnesses to this horrific scene, not as drunk with power, and bolstered by reports of advancing Allied troops, saw the benefit in shrinking from the task at hand and dared to step forward in my defense. A few passing gentiles spoke up in a most eloquent fashion to dissuade the brutes from their passion, and others were gutsy enough to call down from the windows of their apartments.

"He's had enough!"

"Leave him alone!"

"Don't let his blood be on your hands!"

I was already half dead so I don't know exactly what words were most effective, but somehow the bastards became convinced that I did have enough for one day, and the beating stopped.

I was all scrapes, blood, gashes, tears, gouges, mucous, cuts, saliva, rips, sweat, welts, vomit, dirt, and all consuming pain. It hurt even to breathe, and I was soaked in my own urine. But slowly I became aware that I was still conscious and alive, and that nobody was hitting me anymore. The slurs persisted, and my head was ringing, but I came to my senses enough to crawl back home where my horrified, weeping mother and grandma tended to my wounds.

As I've already explained, my rescue was due to the intercession of kind strangers. And that obvious principal is nothing more than random chance. Certainly those people who opened their mouths in my defense were noble and good, and deserved to carry the mantle of true Christendom. But, as far as it related to me, it was blind dumb luck, something over which I had no control. I got lucky, and that's all there was to it. Nobody in my circumstance could claim otherwise. Most Jews who were saved from extermination during the war were likewise the beneficiaries of *mazel,* good fortune. It's true that there were some fighters who took matters into their own hands, and bought their salvation through guts and guile. And there were cells of armed Jewish partisans in the forest, as well as occasional ghetto uprisings, and even a camp revolt. But the vast majority of Jews were emaciated and powerless prisoners, living and dying at the whim of their captors. The rest just hid. Any among those who rode out the storm will be the first to admit that they only have inexplicable *mazel* to thank. Relying on fickle and unpredictable luck as a survival plan does not sound like a prudent tactic, but in retrospect it seemed as if we had little choice. As proof I submit the two most terrible and traumatic incidents of our lives.

With mere months remaining to the conflict, not that we knew as much at that time, the round up and deportation of Jews intensified. My grandmother, pregnant mother, and I were all living together in one small apartment in a Jewish designated building, venturing out only for food. After my beating I was more scared than ever to go out. I was a mass of welts and scars. My eyes were both blackened, there were cuts along my scalp, and every bone and joint ached. In addition to all that puss was oozing out of sores on my neck. By then I had developed a condition, caused by a lack of vitamin D, and it caused running sores to develop on my neck. Many died from this and other such conditions caused from malnutrition. The war had claimed my body even if death had not yet performed its coup de grace. I almost constantly felt as I did during my beating. My whole body throbbed. Why couldn't it just end? Then, it almost did.

Had we known how deliciously close the Allies were we would've been encouraged. But we never heard any news of the outside world, and confidence eluded us as long as the fascists kept their strangle hold on the city. They controlled the radio, newspapers, and the posters on the round metal kiosks that dotted the city. All of this media boasted endless German triumph and served to keep us in fear and anxiety. And while some Russian artillery units might have been approaching our eastern outskirts the Nazis still held the population in its grip. Nothing can demonstrate that perfect power more than the mass arrests that were now a daily part of life in the capital, and we felt no surprise when we fell under their shiny cold boots. We accepted it as our inevitable, predetermined fate.

In the early winter of 1944 a mass arrest occurred, and all the inhabitants of our building were taken out and marched toward the ghetto, the next step in our destined deportation to a concentration camp. The significance of this was unmistakable. Our turn had finally come. We were doomed, along with the countless other Hungarian Jews who had gone this route before. Our entire building was cleared of Jews. We slogged along like zombies, abandoned and alone. There were no Yankee GIs coming to the rescue, and the Russians were just a mirage. All our options were closed. We were dead. But as we marched toward our black fate a most bizarre and unmistakably surreal event was coming toward us from a plateau so secret we had no idea it even existed. It came roaring up to us in the form of a shiny black limo. It caught everyone's attention equally, brutal tormentors and frightened victims alike. Its brakes squealed as it careened to a stop, and out jumped a man who then leapt up onto the magical car's running boards. As soon as he did he broke out in loud glorious speech.

"We are with the Swedish Embassy and have s*huspass* -visa- for many of you here!"

Next he started to call out Jewish sounding names. He spoke with great authority and without fear. He looked absolutely heroic. Then my mother and grandmother blurted out at the same time, "My God, it's Nandorbaci!"

It was true! My ardently religious uncle Nandor, now free of facial hair and dressed like a typical Hungarian peasant, was standing a few meters away from us, waving these papers, these *shuspasses*, and calling out names. If anyone would have told me that I had an uncle that was still alive in Budapest I would have cackled at the irony of such a ridiculous statement. And if you would have added that he was about to jump out of an ambassador's limousine right in front of me I wouldn't have even taken it seriously enough to be offended by the cavalier indifference of such callous whimsy. No such reality was possible. It was unimaginable and inconceivable, yet here he was. He had hidden underground, and survived long enough to be rescued by the very same man who was now about to rescue us. Nandor stood on the running boards, making him taller than anyone else around, imbued with authority, calling out names and saving lives. When he called out a name happy people ran forward and claimed their sanctified Swedish visas. Uncle Nandor issued shuspasses and bold announcements.

"We are with the Swedish Embassy and we have visas for many people here!"

I didn't really comprehend what all of this specifically meant, and it contributed to my usual state of confusion. Apparently, even death was incomprehensible to me. But our marching had stopped, and excitement replaced mother's and grandmother's usual terror. It must have been good. And as I grasped for these threads of understanding I heard our own names called out by Uncle Nandor.

"*Shuspass. Shuspass* for the Gabor family. Ilus, Freddy, Zelma."

My mother and grandma looked at each other with dismay, and Nandor continued.

"Please come forward for your *Shuspass.*"

Gabriel has sounded his trumpet and Saint Peter opened the gateway to Heaven. We rushed to the car and grabbed our papers, affording one incredulous look deep into the eyes of my uncle who returned the glance with a brief but equally intense stare. During this exchange we stood next to the shiny limo, which looked like a vision from a dream to me. I peered within it and beheld the man who was our true savior. I didn't know it at the time, but the dignified, aristocratic looking and well dressed young man sitting in the back seat was one of the most famous saviors of the Jews of World War Two. Raoul Wallenberg was the ultimate Righteous Gentile, but he looked as if he could have been one of the Aryan occupiers. His saintly actions did indeed contradict his physical countenance, for he was determined to save as many Jews from the Nazis as possible. I stood there transfixed by the beatific image of this true Aryan as my uncle continued.

"You have all been issued Swedish visas and are now under the protection of the neutral Swedish government. Take your papers to one of our Swedish Protective Houses at once. You will be safe there. Hurry!"

Not if God Himself had descended from the clouds would we have been more awestruck. Here was a Germanic looking man interfering with others of his type on our behalf. Blessed surrealism.

At once, several angry and uniformed SS officers approached the car. They ordered him to get out, but he blithely rolled down his window and produced some papers and made his own demands which included respecting his authority. The famed Swedish diplomat did not falter, and he persuaded the bewildered Nazis to stay their bloody hands. As bloodthirsty as the Third Reich was it always sought to exude the aura of propriety. They claimed the mantle of civilization, and as such always gave the impression it obeyed the established laws of civilized men. They didn't even persecute the Jews until they changed the laws to make it legal to do so. Thus, they were duty bound to honor the official state of neutrality that existed between their two countries. There were a handful of European nations that enjoyed such political indifference, and Germany begrudgingly honored those treaties, keeping a simulated smile of toleration on their frustrated faces through all their dealings. For example, a bearded Rabbi bearing a passport from a country such as Spain or Sweden could theoretically approach Adolph Eichmann and wish him a good shabbos, and escape retribution. And Wallenberg exploited that loophole to the max. He even bent those rules. In this case the Swedish Embassy had issued three thousand visas to Jews, and he printed up ten times that many. As a matter of fact, Nandor's wife was part of the crew that produced the counterfeit papers. The Shuspass was an impressive looking document, and all its recipients felt secure and protected. And, as the Nazi officials had no proof to the contrary, they had to honor them all, even if ninety percent of them were forgeries. They would do so, at least for the time being. As my uncle was handing them out he repeated his instructions of salvation to the chosen few of the chosen people who were to make their way to a Swedish Protective House. These were buildings that housed members of the Swedish Diplomatic mission to Hungary, and all such places granted diplomatic immunity to anyone seeking asylum within its walls. Without hearing another syllable we ran off in search of one.

This incident, a mere footnote in the history of the war, saved our lives, at least for them time being. As luck had it we were marching along the very spot where the limo pulled up. Not everyone heard him, and most of the sad parade marched on as Nandor made his speech. But we heard him, as did those around us, and received the blessed fake documents. However, had that car stopped fifty yards behind us we'd have been goners. That day he only managed to save the last two hundred people on that line, and we were part of that group. Ultimately he saved a hundred and fifty times that many.

In our desperate rush to get to the Swedish Embassy we first passed the Vatican protected house and tried to gain entrance there with our Swedish documents. The Vatican was also neutral and had a presence in Budapest. They did what they could to help, but had to follow the same rules. They expressed regret that they could not let us, and pointed out that our documents were specifically for a Swedish protected house. They urged us to get there as soon as possible, and even pointed the way. The Vatican, Spain and Switzerland all had protective houses in Budapest, but nobody had nearly so many as did the angelic Swedes.

We flew to a Swedish house and, waving our documents in the faces of the guards, rushed inside. So many documents had been printed and issued, the interior of the building looked like rush hour on the subway. Our home for the next two days was one stair between the second and third floors of the building, and we felt fortunate to have it. Below us were the pathetic remnants of another family, and on the stair above another. Maneuvering those staircases was a real challenge, but nobody complained. Our hosts even provided us with a little food. God bless Sweden forever and ever.

Kids will be kids, and although certain death waited for us just outside the door, we gravitated to each other and found spirit to play. We took off some our buttons and played tiddlywinks, placing great importance in our innocent pastime. Hours earlier we were on a death march, and now here we were, squeezing buttons between our fingers, imagining great goals and triumphs, oblivious to our imminent execution. I continued to distract myself from the dark reality outside with this quaint game for the few weeks we stayed there. After the first two days there on the stairs we were resettled into a small room, following their redistribution model of three families to a room, all sleeping on the floor. Now we felt not just lucky, but honored. The Swedes were our saviors, and we couldn't stop talking about the aristocratic diplomat in the limo. But, even as we discussed our great fortune Gestapo officials were expressing doubt as to the veracity of our papers, and were plotting with determination to get us into their clutches. Thankfully, they were too preoccupied with the advancing Red forces to dedicate as much time to us as they would have liked. But ultimately their compulsion to kill eroded their grudging adherence to protocol, and they grew weary of the diplomatic protection afforded the reviled Jews. Finally, they reverted to their usual posture of might-is-right and resumed their program of mass murder by placing the dilemma in the hands of their subordinate fascists, the Nyilasok. No veneer of Geneva Conventions or bureaucracy had ever hindered the Hungarian bullies, so they wasted no time in attacking the Swedish Protected houses. They came banging on the doors of our sanctuary with their rifle butts, shouting as they did. We were on the fourth floor when I heard the noise, but we stayed where we were, hopeful that our Swedish white knight would appear and calm the situation. But he did not appear, and we were all dragged out, screaming and begging for mercy. Some confronted the Nyilasok, waving their schuss-passes.

"You have no rights here! We are under the protection of the Swedish government!"

"Those papers don't mean a thing to us, you scum! Get outside! Now!"

I looked down and saw that they were lining people up. Everyone had their hands raised in the air as if they were criminals or prisoners of war. The bullies were shouting worse than ever and kicking their victims into line. Then some cars came roaring up and our spirits lifted. The Swedes were here in force! But our hopes were dashed as we observed barbaric Nyilasok, instead of civilized Swedes, jumping out of the vehicles, waving their weapons and adding to the raucous mayhem. They brandished pistols, submachine guns and shotguns. Upon seeing this several people in line dropped their hands and ran. And just as quickly they were mowed down. We were aghast. Unarmed civilians, women and children, were shot down at point blank range in cold blood. They were innocent, just trying to save themselves. Shot from behind they were flung to the cold wet cobblestones, their blood spilling out around their lifeless bodies. One of them, a playmate of mine, was blasted with a shotgun and thrown several yards by the impact. Mangled, nearly cut in half, he lay splayed out across the blood spattered street. Moments earlier he had been just like me. We played on the stairs together, and now his little body was ripped apart. That vision was the most terrifying moment of my life. And now I was next.

More fascist shouting and everyone who was left stood with their hands thrust even higher into the air. There was more yelling downstairs, and now we all had to go outside. It was chaos. As each of us was marched outside we had to raise our hands. Women and children wept. Men begged for mercy. Nyilasok screamed for us to shut up and march.

It was clear that the vast Russian army from the East, and the American forces from the west, would soon batter Hungary and punish its leaders, yet the fascists persisted in their diabolical design to murder as many Jews as possible in the time allotted them. Had we known how close rescue was we would have felt even more persecuted and frustrated. But our only thought now was where were they taking us? Was it to the ghetto? Was it the train station? But the longer we marched the longer we lived. And we were grateful for every precious second left to us.

We were marched through the streets, and we passed by hundreds of gentiles, our fellow citizens. Some showed sympathy in their faces, and some even cried for us. But some cackled at our misfortune, gleefully calling out, "Now you'll get it, stinking Jewish scum! You won't be taking advantage of us any more!"

These people also threw things at us, and rushed forward to kick and hit us. They especially brutalized the more traditional looking, like bearded old men. The fear I had felt at my beating and for breaking curfew paled before this terror. Now, there would be no mercy for pregnant women, old folks or kids. We were marched through the heartless gray ruins of Budapest, and step by step fear clutched tighter and tighter at our throats. All the while the armed hoodlums taunted us with insults, and ordered us to keep marching with hands raised.

"March you kikes! Turn here! Don't slow down you swine! Keep those hands up! March you filthy rats. March!"

People in line were talking among themselves.

"Where are they taking us? To the Ghetto? No! To the train station. They're going to take us somewhere and we won't return."

Hearing this I started to cry, "Mama, I want to live! Grandma, help me!"

But mama was crying, and grandma was praying, both with lifeless eyes.

As we marched along more Nyilasok arrived, swelling their ranks to over a hundred. Usually it only took a few armed men to handle a crowd of civilians. But now they came out in droves to enjoy the slaughter. They would make short work of us.

After twenty minutes we came to the Danube, to a point about two blocks from one of its bridges. It was so cold ice was already floating in the rigid waters. They lined us up along the banks of the river, screaming and yelling the whole time. They were hysterical with blood lust.

I looked down at the river and recalled how when we first moved here I enjoyed coming here with my papa. It was lovely, and I remembered playing there and watching boats cruise by. All my memories of it were beautiful, but now shattered by the shrieking Nyilasok.

"Turn around! Shut up. Don't talk! You, take off that coat! You too! You, you Jew bitch, take off those shoes. And you, and you! Kick them over here! All of you, keep your hands up!"

Were they just going to rob us of our clothes? Was that what this was all about?

"Turn around. Face the river you Jew scum!"

Sobs and prayers. Frozen panic among the hundreds of us lined up along the icy banks of the Danube on that cold, drizzling, miserable, November afternoon. And then, for a moment, there was absolute quiet. An entire city froze in its tracks. Time stood still, and the wind held its breath. One large thumping heartbeat for all of the humanity of Budapest resounded. Then the shooting began.

The noise of the guns and the screaming cannot be imagined, and the fear is impossible to relate. People were being blasted to bits, the force of the bullets propelling their bodies into the water a few feet below the cement banks. The shooting started at the extreme end of the line, nearest to the bridge to our left, and we were about a hundred yards away.

"Mama, I don't want to die. Mama!"

My cries were mixed with a terrible discordant choir of desperate plaintiff screams. People choked on their vomit, paralyzed with terror. Women pulled their children's faces into their bodies just before it came. Most closed their eyes. Some turned and called out, "God curse you evil bastards! You and your children will die like this! Your death is coming soon!"

Some of the killers fired their weapons wildly at their victims, while some took special aim at necks and heads. Blood and chunks of flesh and skin and brain flew through the air. Deafening gunfire. Shrieking agony. Closer and closer, the spray of hot, jagged death inched toward us. Just yards away the bullets were closing in, and now, mixed with the wailing, I could hear the buzzing projectiles parting the air and the flesh of victims just a foot or two away. And suddenly fear gave way to surreal thought. I reached into my pocket to fetch out a little piece of bread I had saved. Dying was certain for me, and I thought that afterwards my grandmother and mother could perhaps share this morsel. I even held it out to them. In the middle of this death and savage mayhem it was an insane gesture, and I probably seized the thought just to escape the reality of what was about to overwhelm me. And just as that incongruous image dashed through my mind the shooting stopped. There was weeping. There was moaning. But the noise of the guns, and the men who used them, was gone.

My eyes were shut tight, awaiting my death, and for several more seconds after the silence fell upon us I was still afraid to open my eyes. As long as I couldn't see my killers maybe I could elude them. I was a Jewish ostrich on the banks of the Danube. My heart raced. My senses functioned. I heard and felt the wind. Was this how death felt? Then I heard voices. Human voices. Someone said, "They're gone!" So I dared to peek through my squinted eyes. I turned back around and saw that our tormentors had fled. It was true! They were gone. We were alive!

Apparently, some other Nyilasok had brought emergency orders to our killers to stop for some reason, and they all ran off. Miraculously, just like that. We looked from side to side. We touched ourselves to see if we had been shot. For a few more moments everything went quiet. Nobody moved or spoke. No cars drove by. It even seemed as if the river stopped flowing. Then someone came to their senses and yelled, "Run!"

We all took off, my mother's hand grasping mine. She gave her other to grandma, and we moved as one toward some unknown refuge. We were not even aware of the cold any more. We were still among the living, and that was enough. We ran wildly for blocks, and then grandma called out, "We have to make it to a Swedish house."

Almost at once we saw one and we dashed towards it like desperate Olympic sprinters. It was amazing that my mother could run at all, because she was about seven months pregnant. And of course, grandma was older. And we were all weak from hunger. But we had somehow been spared, and we couldn't waste a second. Our would be murderers had vanished, but they might return any moment, so we had to make it to a building and hide. Some mysterious great fortune had intervened in our lives yet again. It didn't seem fit to show its face to others in that line, but rather wait for some inexplicable reason to make its appearance only now.

This scene had been staged hundreds of times before. Innocent civilians were marched to the river, forced to take off their shoes and coats, and then blasted into the icy waters below. No less than twenty thousand of us were murdered in this fashion. But on that day, the very last of the mass executions, the Nyilasok had no time to retrieve the shoes and coats. Fearing for their own lives the assassins ran away without stopping to collect their usual booty. As eerie evidence of the slaughter, the shoes remained standing there, some tipped over on their sides. They were all that remained to offered testimony to the existence of so many mothers and sisters and sons and daughters and cousins and neighbors.

We were part of the Nyilasok's last Danube firing squad, but why it was halted we never knew. There has passed over half a century of speculation since that day, but still nobody knows for certain. Perhaps the long awaited Russians had finally entered the city, and every fascist gun was immediately needed to repel them. All of the swaggering, gun toting bullies who had for years waged war against the defenseless were suddenly recruited to confront a new and different kind of enemy. If that was the case, then this enemy was not one imagined within the dank mental catacombs of paranoia, but a real one, inspired by righteous wrath. And this new foe was unlike the previous army of unarmed civilian women, children, and the elderly. This one was uniformed, trained and, most significantly, it was armed. History tells us that the Nyilasok's Nazi masters abandoned them to their struggle with the allies, and subsequent official reports do not claim that they distinguished themselves on the field of battle. Every single hometown fascist died a miserable and violent death at the hands of the Reds, either in short lived combat or swinging from a rope, executed as war criminals. But we really don't know if that was the case on the icy banks of the Danube that day. All we know is the shooting stopped, the killers vanished, and we survived.

This incident proves to me that destiny has us all in its grip, and there is nothing we can do to influence any of it. Back at the river we were overcome with a mixture of sorrow for the victims and elation at not joining them. Hundreds were shot and fell into the icy waters. Some were killed instantly by the bullets, while others drowned. All of the bodies plunged into the river, and bits of clothing floated on its surface. After some time more articles of clothing, loosened from the current, slipped off and rose through the blood tinged water. Eerie lily pads of hats and scarves and sweaters and vests along with bizarre floating islands of corpses formed a frightful vision that haunts the memory of mankind. To this day, whenever I hear Strauss' Blue Danube, I am struck by the clash of moods; the lilting waltz providing a macabre soundtrack for the floating bodies on a blue river turned blood red. For me it's the ultimate surrealistic war image. Poets have commemorated it in verse, conveying a testament far more touching than my own miserable words. With nearly a thousand miles of Danube left, in its meandering course to the Black Sea, how many people would see the bloated, chalk white corpses float by, and what would they think? The countless half naked women and children must have conveyed some terrible message to everyone along the river's edge. This is the result of hatred and intolerance. Hitler has turned our lovely Danube into a graveyard. What has happened to our world?

Without stopping to mourn those already dead in the water, one pragmatic Scandinavian labored to lessen the slaughter. Down river from the butchery, around the first bend that hid their valiant efforts, Raoul Wallenberg and his comrades were fishing out those who had survived the carnage. Badly wounded, bleeding, half frozen and half drowned they were given one more chance at life by a few angelic Norsemen. Their sympathy was in marked contrast to others of their stock who claimed the same birthright as a license to kill.

The safe house had lost half of its roof from bombing, but it still stood. I bolted past its open gate and ran inside. It seemed empty and was as eerily quiet as the riverside had become. I ran from room to room, instinctively looking for food, but there was nothing.

During the war hunger was our constant companion. Practically all of our waking hours were dedicated to two things, avoiding capture and finding something to eat. It was never a matter of shopping. That was out of the question. Stores had little to offer as everything of value was used to supply the troops. Soldiers risked their lives, but at least they got food. I have no doubt that any of us, including the women, would have gladly taken up arms and joined the fight for two or three squares day. We probably would've done it for just one. Even if we civilians found an open shop with something edible for sale we had virtually no money. This ubiquitous situation caused commerce and capitalism to revisit their ancient ancestor, the barter system. People traded anything of value for food. After all, you can't eat jewelry or art or furniture. If you had such possessions you negotiated them for any crust of bread you were lucky enough to find. And that was for gentiles. Jews had already been disenfranchised, forced to move into dank hovels with whatever meager minimum possessions they could carry, and had practically nothing worthwhile to trade. Added to that, going out on the street could cost you your life, limiting potential hours for food searches. It's no wonder so many people died of starvation.

I went from room to room and eventually ended up standing in front of the most unimaginable of discoveries. This is not a boast that I unearthed the greatest amount of food, but I dare say it was certainly the most unexpected.

I entered the kitchen of this abandoned apartment on the ground floor and beheld a great monolithic iron stove. Back before refrigerators it was the custom to guard leftovers inside them. Rats couldn't get inside, so it was the best place to leave a plate of food. Plus, you could keep it warm for some member of your family who got home late. So,

I had high hopes that I might find some rye bread or pumpernickel, or maybe even the end of a sausage or piece of cheese. Anything was possible with such a large stove.

There was nothing on its surface, on the burners, or the shelves overhead. So, all that was left was to inspect the interior of the oven for any remnant of a glorious past feast enjoyed by the totalitarian elite.

I reached down and pulled open the massive black metal door and peered within. I had to squint for a moment to allow the retinas of my eyes adjust to its dark interior, and as the blackness gave way to detail, I could make out a deep round pan. I reached in to grab it, and as soon as I did I felt that it had some heft to it. It wasn't actually heavy, but it certainly weighed a lot more than an empty pan. No doubt, there was something in it!

Gingerly I slid the precious cargo toward me and peered down into it. I couldn't recognize what it was, but it definitely had the appearance of food. What's more it didn't smell rotten. It looked like soup, so I stuck my finger in to see if it was still edible. If it was soup it was certainly very thick soup. It didn't run down my finger like broth. It was more like porridge. Fearful of a poisonous trap left for the Reds I suspiciously sniffed my soggy digit, but sensed nothing toxic. Convinced of its innocence I gently licked my finger and was happy to find that it was sweet. As I continued to lick my finger, relishing each drop, I was reminded of a pastime I used to enjoy with both my mother and our maid, Sonia. I felt it, but I couldn't mentally make a clear image of what it was. Then it struck me. This was cake batter. As a kid I used to always lick the spoon clean when we made cakes, and this was exactly what it was. Ages before, when I had been a child, the prospect of licking the spoon clean on baking day would have satisfied my juvenile gluttony. But now I was so excited at a similar prospect that I could barely contain myself. This cake, once a luxury, would now serve to sustain us.

We had gone from being prime examples of suffering humanity to the owner of an actual cake in just minutes. It was unfathomable. Six hundred seconds earlier we were about to be shot and drown. Now we were standing before fresh cake batter. We were starving and now had something to eat. But baking a cake meant time, if there was even any fuel. So, we briefly discussed if we could wait for it to bake. The idea of having a bona fide cake to feast upon was a strong argument. And when we discovered that the stove had fuel, and that grandma had a match, all other considerations evaporated. By unanimous proclamation we committed ourselves to enduring the baking process. And, as we had no bread, we would follow Marie Antoinette's advice and eat cake.

Watched pots never boil, and watched ovens never bake, so we distracted ourselves with conversation, speculating on how this had come to pass. The former inhabitants of this apartment must have been about to bake this cake when they had to flee. Everything was all set. They had prepared the mixture, put wood in the oven, and were probably about to strike the match and light the oven when fate came to their door and dragged them away. And all this happened no more than an hour before. Who were they? They might have been Swedes, but the building might have been taken over by their enemies. Maybe they were Nazis, Nazi sympathizers, or Nyilasok. After all, they could afford the ingredients of a cake, which was not something the average nonpolitical individual could. Whoever they were they must have been in a great hurry to leave, electing to forgo the cake, a rare delicacy even for the ruling class.

Separated from our cake by heat and time I went back to rifling through the drawers and closets and shelves with the high hopes of finding something else valuable. If I could come across a little bit of tobacco, for example, I could trade it for almost anything. People went mad for tobacco. At that time it was probably more valuable than money. There was practically nothing to buy with cash and you couldn't smoke money either. But tobacco was always in demand, and if the former inhabitants of this apartment were in a hurry they might have left some behind. There was none to be found however, or anything else of worth for that matter. But I continued to search, investigating every tiny nook and cranny. Finally my nose alerted me that the cake was ready and I raced back to the kitchen. My grandmother slowly opened the oven door, and using her coat as oven mitts she extracted the golden brown treat it from the oven. The rest of the details are lost in the blur of the celebration we enjoyed. It was delicious and glorious! What a way to celebrate our freedom! The three of us consumed it bit by bit, and we felt full for the first time in months. We had finally come across some incongruity that didn't threaten our existence. It was the first enjoyable surrealism we'd known in what seemed like an eternity. It was the best meal in memory.

In the space of an hour we had gone from the security of the Swedish house to witnessing my friend's murder, to anticipating our own death, to the refuge of this building and a delicious surprise! It was inconceivable. We escaped death by mere inches, and then, our escape was rewarded with a mystery cake. It's something I will taste forever. I just have to think of it to savor its surreal sweetness.

Chapter VII

Miami 4

Just as that sweet young girl had utterly vanished after our initial meeting she was once again off my radar screen. This time however I was not so engrossed in my work that I could put her out of my mind. And I didn't even have the presence of Henry Berger to remind me. Shortly after the debut of my new line he had moved on and was no longer my employee. As it turned out though it would not be the last of him that Rebeca or I would ever see. It would take a long, long time before his little blips disappeared off our screen for good. After all, persistence is the hallmark of the good salesman. But I wasn't thinking about him or anyone else, just the image of the elegant young lady at the café. She was barely voting age, it's true, but a man doesn't so easily forget a woman who has begged his help and shared her confidence. But, as before, it was totally up to her to seek me out. I still did not have her phone number and couldn't even speculate on how to get hold of her. But I certainly did speculate on the possibilities. She could tell her mother that she wouldn't marry Henry, her mother would be convinced, and young Rebeca would continue with her education, with no further need of liaisons with older and wiser men. A second scenario had her running away from home, starting life anew, free of all traces of her previous life, including me. Then again, she might buckle under the pressure of her family and marry Henry. Large, extended, Latin families can be quite persuasive and, just to shut them up and get out of the house, she might have relented. Or maybe she just lost my business card. Anything was possible, and Ivan Gabor was just another cipher on that list, or so I thought for a few days.

A week later my secretary appeared in the door of my office to announce a repeat call from a Rebeca. This time though I knew exactly who it was that was calling me.

"*Hola*, Ivan. *Como estás?*"

I cannot lie to you, dear reader, after going so far to gain your confidence and sympathy, so I will confess to you that her call filled me with delight. I know not the man whose ego would not swell upon being sought out by a gorgeous eighteen year old. But I was still faced with the dilemma of our age difference, and I wanted to be sure to maintain a perspective, that I was her platonic confidante, not a potential replacement for my ex-salesman.

"Hola, Rebequita. I'm okay. What's new?"

I now called her by the very personal Spanish form of her name, denoting in the diminutive suffix of that idiom that she was dear little Rebeca. I had thought of her in that way, but this was the first time that I actually used it. She could have interpreted this as the typical address for a child by an adult, and that I was firmly entrenched in the role of guardian, thinking only of her safety and well being, with no taint of lust or self interest. Of course, if she were my sweetheart, that particular romance language would have me employ the very same nickname. Thus, I dove into uncertain linguistic territory which the objective use of her full, unadulterated first name would not have implied. And with the confidence she had invested in me it seemed overly formal and unwieldy to call her Señorita. Perhaps, in early times and social climates, that would have been the case, but America had a relaxing effect on all foreign customs that not even the strictest Hispanic codes could overcome, even those stretching back to Iberian antiquity. The melting pot had a tendency to put everyone on equal footing, tradition be damned, and that leniency afforded me a freedom to communicate with her in a manner that indicated concern, without utterly eliminating intimacy. My use of her nickname, and the fact that she did not correct me, reflected the honest state of our relationship up to that point. Anything was possible. But the urgency of her call left no time to speculate on etiquette. She had made a decision, and was ready to take action. What's more, I was to be an intrinsic part of her plan.

"Ivan, I want to leave home. Pick me up at my house!"

What a shock! I had considered many roads for this young lady to travel, but no speculation on my part would have ever come up with such a scenario. She was ready to make a quantum leap in her life, and I was somehow involved. Did she just want a lift, and didn't know anyone else with wheels? Or was it the presence of an authoritative male that she required in order to intimidate her mother and make her back down? Again, the urgency obviated intellectual digressions, and her silence again indicated that I draw her out.

"Rebequita. What are you saying?"

Her answer was swift, certain and insistent.

"I want to leave my home! I cannot marry without love!"

Although my official post seemed to be that of a counselor, and I should have advised her to clam down, something grabbed hold of me. The next thing I knew I jumped in my car and headed over there without bothering to fasten my seat belt. She gave me her address which turned out to be in Miami Beach. As I lived there too, and it's a city whose twenty square miles are not challenging to master, I was able to get over there before two Beatle oldies finished playing. The short trip afforded precious little time to imagine the scene at her home. Clearly she had protested her upcoming nuptials to Henry Berger, and just as clearly, her family stood firm. But was Rebequita just being a spoiled teenager exploiting the generation gap, or was there real injustice afoot that deserved interference? I sincerely agreed with her that arranged marriages were medieval, but who was I to stick my nose into the affairs of this family? I was not a relative, neighbor or old family friend. The truth was that I barely knew this girl. For all I knew she had been driving her parents crazy for years. Only in my newly adopted country for six months, I had already come to embrace the old country point of view that American adolescents had too much freedom and were a bunch of spoiled brats, presaging the fall of their entire culture. Had this little JAP used her guile to recruit me as an unwitting pawn in her frivolous design? It was a clear possibility. After all, everything I knew about her family and situation came from her. The only evidence that I could verify for myself was that Berger was unbearable. But even that perspective was tainted by jealousy. Maybe I was being completely duped, and was rash to react so obediently. She bade me rush to her side and I was burning rubber in the same heartbeat. For all I knew I was walking into a full blown soap opera. Maybe this marriage had been arranged for years to fulfill the wish of a beloved relative on their deathbed, and she was pregnant by Berger and absolutely had to wed, having already aborted several times, all to the undying shame of her family, and Berger was threatening suicide even now. Was I about to embroil myself in a huge scandal? All these alternative realities bounced around inside a cranium already confused and plagued by betrayal. Despite such doubts as my brain could invent I had to respond viscerally. My heart said this girl was innocently in trouble and without an ally in the world. I was on a noble mission to rescue her, and that was the end of that.

Her address was affixed to the prefrontal lobes of my cerebral cortex, but I needn't have been so methodical, as it was the only house in the neighborhood with a raven tressed teenager with luggage in front of it. She stood resolutely before a pretty Miami Beach bungalow, a combination of 1930's art deco and 1950's kitsch, that could exist nowhere else but in this city. The whole neighborhood was full of similar houses that all boldly combined divergent eras, unifying them with lurid hues, meant more to compliment the flora than the architecture. Beside her were the essentials of her existence: a small valise, a little portable TV, and her school books. I took account of everything, but didn't clearly identify the texts as scholastic. If I had then maybe guilt would have prevented me from any further involvement in a school girl's flight from hearth and home. As it was, all I saw was a friend in need. Of course, a more prudent person might have observed the situation and credited me with little more than being criminally insane. Having never actually confirmed that her eighteenth birthday had come and gone I might well have been guilty of violating half a dozen American laws having to do with a minor, what to speak of the classic case of a man letting his small head think in lieu of his big one.

Feeling relieved that she was alone, and not pursued by a familial posse just one vaulting leap behind her, I tossed all her worldly possessions into the back seat of the Caddy and peeled away from the scene of the crime.

"Gracias Ivan," was all she said. She was stiff, but then broke down in tears. After all, she had just left home. Why shouldn't she cry? I allowed her this private sorrow as long as I could, but finally decided to inquire as to whether or not there was any more method to her madness.

"Have you some place to go?"

"I hadn't thought that far ahead."

While I appreciated her candor, confessing her panic, I knew we couldn't drive around aimlessly. She fell silent, pondering her alternatives, and I leapt into the tacit breach.

"I'll take you to the Sheraton. It's quiet there."

She merely nodded, and repeated her Spanish word of gratitude. Otherwise she was glumly morose and silent. She probably felt that she had crossed the Rubicon with her family, and that there was no going back. This was a frightening prospect for her, and another attack of sobs overcame her. To try and calm her I blabbed on about the hotel.

"The Sheraton's in Bal Harbor. You know how quiet that neighborhood is."

Bal Harbor is one of several small municipalities that border the fabled stretch of sand known for honeymooners and retirees. They each have their own government, complete with police cars and garbage collection, but usually get dumped into the generic melting pot called Miami Beach. Even Swedes probably think the Sheraton's in Miami Beach. And back then, before every South Floridian edifice over twelve feet high got turned into a condo, it was home to many fine hotels. The Sheraton, the last anti-condo holdout, stood on the southern extreme of the village, not twenty feet from its southern municipal neighbor, the city of Surfside. That tiny town is Miami Beach's official northern neighbor, and actually separates it from Bal Harbor. To the chagrin of the mayors of both burgs, as well as the citizenry of nearby Bay Harbor Isles and Sunny Isles as well, tourists who visit there all assert that they have made the trek to world famous Miami Beach. Nobody in Oslo is impressed if you say you've been to Bal Harbor. Fact is, nobody's aware of the subtle difference when they're there, and will die without ever knowing. But for our purposes the quiet Sheraton was ideal.

I could have taken her to my apartment five minutes away on South Beach. Of course, back then, before Miami Vice, it wasn't the glamour capital it is now, with the odds being higher at that time of seeing a shuffleboard champion than a sexy celebrity. Paris Hilton wasn't even born yet. Be that it as it may, my apartment made for a perfect swinging bachelor pad. I also was lucky enough to own the nearby Essex House, an art deco palace. In other words, I knew where to take a girl for an assignation. However, I was now in white knight mode, and protecting damsels in distress was my one and only mission. So, we found neutral territory in Bal Harbor, and I was duty bound to keep things within the parameters of decency. Even hinting that she go back to my place would have been a breach of confidence so drastic that it would have destroyed forever any chance of establishing a real relationship with her. All that aside, I was too old for her. She had said it herself, and I agreed. I was just a friend. Perhaps, due to my age, Rebequita considered me a bit of a raconteur, someone experienced in the ways of the world. I could be her friend, mentor, benefactor, counselor, or any other father figure that she lacked since her own moved out over that sticky divorce. I could fill any of those shoes, but I could not so much as entertain assuming the role of lover or husband. A May-December affair was not in the offing. This was innocent friendship, and by putting her in a hotel five miles away from my apartment, basically the entire span of the city, its platonic boundaries were firmly established. Keeping myself from taking advantage of a lovely creature at her weakest was an exercise in restraint that filled me with pride. I just hoped my gallantry could continue to prevail.

Chapter VIII

Struggling To Survive

After feasting on our cake we inspected the building a little more, and discovered that other Jews had also sought refuge there. And though nobody had seen any fascist pigs for hours we all quaked with fear. In addition to that there was bombing and shelling going on which forced many of us down to the cellar. During lulls in the raids I went around the basement and empty apartments, collecting the stubs of burned candles. I busied myself molding them into whole candles which were the only light we had known for months or would continue to know for many more. While scrounging for remnants of wax I came upon another treasure, a large can of tomato paste. My mother and grandmother were able to use it to turn whatever scraps of food we found into gourmet delights for days.

We stayed in that building for about as long as the tomato paste lasted, but felt it ultimately to be a poor place to hide. It had been a Swedish safe house at one time, so it would be the first place the Nyilasok might come looking for us. We had to find another intact building.

The sound of the gunfire had been constant, but lately it caught our attention in a new way. The Nazis used rifles and submachine guns and supplemented the Arrow Cross Guard's odd assortment of weaponry with German military issue, so both of their guns sounded similar. Now the guns sounded only half familiar. They seemed to be having a conversation with new and different voices. My astute grandmother was first to notice it.

"Listen. Do you hear the guns?"

"Of course," responded my mother, "they're murdering more of our *landtsmen*."

"I don't know," continued my grandma. "Maybe. But those guns don't sound like they always do. I think someone else is here."

Wide eyed, my mother said, "You mean the Russians? Maybe that's why they ran away from the river. Or maybe it's the Americans."

"From your lips to God's ears."

I was quiet throughout all of this, but I got excited at the prospect of invading Americans. They were just a myth to us. I didn't even know anyone who had ever seen one up close. But we knew they were responsible for much of the bombing that was destroying Budapest. They were mighty, and we knew they'd smash our enemies. But to have the cowboys personally deliver us from harm would be like a miracle. But my practical grandma's logic prevailed.

"I don't know, but I think the Americans are still far away. It's probably Russian guns we've been hearing. After all, they're coming from the East. Anyway, we can't be caught in any cross fire. They may not be aiming at us, but their bullets will kill us just as surely as if we were standing by the river. We must get indoors and stay there."

We looked in a few buildings until we found one that wasn't hit by any bombing. We walked in and discovered a stairway leading to the safety of a cellar. Once we were underground we felt safer. The stairway leveled off into a corridor, and there were small rooms off of it, all packed with huddling, trembling families. No one bothered to inquire as to our faith, as orthodox survival was now the most wide spread religion. The last tiny room was empty and we moved in. We stayed there for over a week, praying for Allied victory. We couldn't really see anyone fighting, but we were certain that a battle was raging above ground between the two proponents of totalitarianism, the fascists and the communists. Every hour the sound of gunfire drew closer until finally it was just down the street. Louder and louder. Then it was directly across the street. An explosive din, it sounded like it was right in front of our building. And a mere cacophonous moment later it was right in the building. Finally, its terrifying, crackling thunder was right in the corridor, outside our tiny cubicle. Was it fascist gunfire or Allied? If it was fascist we were dead. There would be no more arrests or marches or formality of any kind. But if it was the Allies then our deliverance was at hand. This is what had fueled our hopes and filled our prayers. But the long awaited and beloved Allies were shooting everything that moved or made a sound. Once lead slugs leave their muzzles they are not selective. The bullets were about to shred the rickety old collection of wooden slats that passed as our fortress and rip us to pieces. Mother was trembling, and I was cringing by her side. We had to call out and identify ourselves, lest we be mistaken for hiding enemies. Then grandma, ever pragmatic and knowing she had nothing to lose, yelled out in Romanian and Yiddish.

"Don't shoot! We're just some poor Jews! We're civilians. Don't shoot!"

She screamed as loud as her old lungs would let her, competing with point blank blasting gun powder. Then her raspy voice fell quiet. Miraculously, so did the gunfire. Were they reloading? Taking aim? No time to hesitate. Grandma called out again in a strained mixture of syllables of Eastern European languages, a desperate hodgepodge of begging broken phrases, perhaps her last words on Earth.

"No guns! Poor Jews! Friends! No guns! Women. Children. No shoot!"

No shoot indeed! An entire moment's worth of wonderful silence. Every heartbeat was now a negotiated cease fire. A second's reprieve. More quiet. Two seconds. Please God, let it end! Three seconds. Mercy! Four seconds. A soldier called back. And thank God, Heaven and all the angels, he didn't do it in German or Hungarian. It was Russian. Beautiful, poetic Russian. The language of Tolstoy and Dostoyevsky. What lovely Cyrillic music. Now gun barrels pushed our pathetic excuse of a door open, and gorgeous, noble Red soldiers stuck their heads in. These bedraggled veterans in their worn out uniforms looked around, and satisfied we were nothing more than what we claimed, harmless Yid women and kids, smiled. A soldier, smiling at us? Incredible! And now, beyond the limits of our imagination, one of them spoke to us in a language that was the last one we would ever have dreamt would emanate from the mouth of a uniformed soul. He spoke Yiddish.

"Don't worry, little mother. We're here to free you from those Nazi pigs once and for all. You're safe now."

We were dumbfounded. Our savior, just like another famous savior, was Jewish! Grandma and mother fell down, crying in joyous rapture. Even though I didn't literally comprehend a single syllable I understood everything. We were saved. No more hiding. No more fear. Like our savior said, we were safe. All we could do to express our relief was cry. Our savior, with much to do and many more to save, addressed us again, each word falling on our ears like blessed rain on long parched earth.

"Just stay down a little longer. It's still dangerous out there. But we'll get 'em all."

He turned to go, then stopped and opened up his knapsack. He took out a large almost whole loaf of indescribably beautiful bread and tossed it to us.

"Here, you must be starving."

We smiled back and bowed. Grandma thanked him in Yiddish, and then, unable to control her unbounded joy, crawled over to him and grabbed his hand. She kissed it and held it against her cheek tenderly. After a moment he gingerly pulled it back, perhaps a little embarrassed. He said goodbye in both Yiddish and Russian and left. A minute ago we had been hugging the ground to dodge stray bullets. Now we were hugging each other and crying for joy.

Liberation is everything the word implies. Imagine being in jail, on death row, without food. Besides that, every time you leave your cell it could be for the last time. On top of that the guards may beat you to death if they feel like it, and bombs are falling on the prison constantly. You're tormented and threatened day and night, and then it just stops. No jail cell, no guards, no more beatings or bombs. That's liberation. Utter relief. Salvation. Deliverance. I was out of touch for most of the war, constrained by a consciousness that my parents had ironically molded for me. But I absolutely understood liberation. By the time the war ended, anyone who was a child when it started, and I was certainly the most juvenile of those, had been transformed into a streetwise middle aged adult. The tug of war for my intellect, fought between well meaning parents and the harsh realities of the holocaust, was bitterly contested by the former, but definitely won over by the latter.

Freedom is sweet, and among its unlimited blessings is the luxury to just sit and think. We had lived like rabbits in the wild, hounded and hunted by all things bigger than us. Moment to moment was an ever transforming world of intimidation and violence. But now that the mayhem was directed elsewhere we embraced the freedom to become human again and think about people and things besides the moment and ourselves. Afforded that liberty what most occupied our thoughts now was father. Since his absence we had dedicated our bodies and minds full time to alertness and vigilance. It would have been whimsical and dangerous to take time out to think about anything else. We had to be pragmatic to survive, and not dull our senses with sentiment. But now, father monopolized our thoughts and conversations. Where is he? When is he coming back? Is he alive? How will he find us? We decided that, if he is alive, he'll look for us where he left us, and the woman who occupied our apartment knew where we were and would tell him. Thus mother decided to return to the apartment in the Jewish designated building.

The Russians were on a murderous rampage, killing as many Germans as possible. If it looked, felt, smelt or sounded Kraut they shot, stabbed or lynched it. They were aware of German sympathizers and collaborators, and treated them as harshly as any uniformed wermachte regular. In their rage, based in no small part on revenge for the ten million Reds killed by the Third Reich, many innocent Hungarians died in a hail of friendly fire. The Soviets focused on killing Nazis with a distinct shoot now-ask later policy. This led to many innocents being killed. They were mistakenly killed, but dead just the same. In other words, the threat from violent death had not completely vanished, so we sat still for another week on that cold dirt cellar floor, as our heroic Russian Jewish savior had recommended, and rationed our delicious black bread.

Separated now by time and circumstance it's not such an extravagance to reflect on our circumstances in the ruins of Budapest. With all things taken into account, they're really quite extraordinary. Let's consider the participants. The Axis powers had millions and millions of armed and trained men in uniform, as well as a navy, an air force, armored divisions, arms manufacturing, espionage networks, propaganda, and charismatic leadership. We had a woman in her fifties, a pregnant one in her twenties, and a boy of single digit age, all unarmed and untrained. Now, let's consider the outcome. By war's end the Axis was in ruins with incalculable casualties, while our side boasted a one hundred percent survival rate without so much as a flesh wound. All things taken in account, that's a pretty surrealistic military balance sheet.

The only mode of transportation at that time was foot power. With no electricity the trolleys lay dormant, and the lack of gasoline had taxis and private autos in the same quiet state. Everybody walked everywhere, regardless of distance or danger. And we must have been like anyone else, a pathetic sight. A ragamuffin kid, an old lady in a tattered coat, and a hugely pregnant woman, all shuffling along. Like ancient Ulysses making his way home we stopped at several island apartments. It was just impossible to stay exposed to all the gun fire and bombing without seeking some shelter, even if only for a few hours. Also, we were continually on the lookout for food or anything we could trade for it. Once, while we were searching for food some kill-crazy Russian soldiers came around the corner after having just blasted some perceived enemy and came upon us, their gun barrels smoking. My mother was terrified and yelled out in Romanian, "We're Jews!" Whenever we encountered Soviet soldiers this was our tactic. The usually anti-Semitic Reds had been the first Allies to find and liberate the concentration camps, softening their hearts toward us, so even they were now sympathetic. Mainly, we used a few words of Romanian because Hungarian was hard for the Russians to learn, and Yiddish sounded too much like German. So, at least for the time being, it seemed the safest bet. Once the Red soldiers determined we were just Jews they relaxed, and sent some food our way, instead of hot lead. The Reds didn't carry the same rich treats the liberating Americans did, such as chocolate, but a crust of bread seems just as tasty to starving war refugees. We always thanked them profusely. *Spaceba* was a Russian word we all learned quickly.

Most of the places we stayed in had their windows shot out, so finding a room somewhere without the howling wind pouring in was a real amenity. No buildings had electricity or water, and many were on the verge of falling down. For drinking and washing we used melted snow, the one plentiful benefit from the harsh winter. But many buildings were too dangerous to enter. Once a building sustained a hit from a bomb it was unstable, and often collapsed in the middle of the night without warning, killing its inhabitants. As one place looked as dangerous to me as another I asked mother why we were exposing ourselves to so much danger just to get back to our less than desirable apartment in the Jewish designated building. We had already burned up nearly all the furniture of that two room flea trap, so its allure was a mystery to me. Mother explained.

"Freddy, it's the only place your father will know to look for us. He'll return to our old apartment and the gentile woman there will direct him to our Jewish apartment. Then we'll be reunited. Otherwise, we might not ever see each other again."

It made sense, but I also wondered if she had hidden something valuable there. Whatever her reason, she was determined to get to Csengery Utca, number sixty-one.

Our nomadic wandering between all these buildings was a continual obstacle course, forcing us to maneuver through a no man's land of death and destruction. Dead people, dead horses, and dead dogs littered the streets, and I'll leave it up to you to imagine the smell. And it was impossible to walk three paces in a straight line. Burnt military vehicles of every size and shape blocked our path. Chunks of smoldering armaments and charred machinery lay about everywhere. We were approaching our old neighborhood, but it was literally unrecognizable.

With death always an inch or a second away we approached the Ferdinand Bridge on our odyssey back to our apartment. This bridge, along with numerous schools, statues and bridges, was named for the victim whose assassination had caused this whole mess in the first place. A whole war was fought over some vague notion of honor, but its legacy produced nothing but this second even worse one. The bridge spanned the railroad tracks near the Nyugaty train station, on the north end of town. The station itself, as well as most of the north end of town, was engulfed in flames. We were used to seeing burning buildings, but this was a real conflagration, remarkable even for that time. It lit up the sky for days, and you could feel the heat even at a great distance. I can't imagine that anyone near it could have survived.

It's amazing what you can get used to, like those fires. More incredible is that we even got used to gunfire and bombs. To someone who has never been around explosions, great or small, that might sound incredible. But it's true. It's like people who buy houses next to railroad tracks. After a few months they don't even hear the trains roar by. Warfare simply became the soundtrack of our lives and we took it all in our stride. Of course, the constant din was made bearable by the fact that it meant that somebody was out there fighting with and killing our oppressors. In that respect, it was actually a welcome and lovely noise. So, we accustomed our ears to the rat-a-tat of Tommy guns and pistols, and the crack of rifle fire. Of course, it's one thing to hear it from within the relative safety of a brick building, and another to hear it as you maneuver your way through a war zone. Bullets whiz by constantly, and you're seriously in harm's way. Budapest was a big city and there was a lot of house to house fighting going on. The Reds were intent on a mission to seek and destroy every last fascist resistor and sympathizer.

And though the fighting might have been many blocks away the bullets could easily travel that distance with fatal results. Many died that way, and there was gory evidence of it at every step. We had to step over corpses constantly. I should add that, as pragmatism was the watchword of the day, you rarely passed a corpse without checking its pockets for food. Like I said, it's amazing what you can get used to. But, don't think for a moment that fear had fled us for good. Perhaps that is the most amazing thing of all, that we had become inured to it. For too long we had lived wrapped up in terror. It was there when we woke up, and when we passed out from exhaustion. You can't really take it in your stride, but you somehow must cope with it. If you value life it's a pragmatic reflex that allows you to carry on. If you don't then you die from the anxiety. And certainly, many people succumbed to just that, or even committed suicide over it. Of course it's not impossible to comprehend. Who wants to live like that? It is a cliché, to be sure, but a fact just the same. War is hell. And we all lived through it. There were flames and it really felt eternal.

As we approached the bridge some Russian soldiers spotted us and waved his arms.

"Are you crazy? What are you doing out here? Don't you know there's a war going on? Get inside at once!"

He motioned in one direction, as if one was safer than another, and we obediently ran there. It was a nice change to have uniformed soldiers yell at us for our benefit. And to our greater benefit he tossed us something edible in the bargain.

When we finally made it to Csengery Utca the building was an unrecognizable wasteland. The battle for Budapest had been fought on streets like this, and the aftermath was smoldering ruins that all looked the same. I think it was just my mother's feral intuition that brought us here. Part of the building had suffered from artillery shelling, and it was hard for me to push open the hulking, and now badly rusted, iron gate. We walked up to our second story unit. There never had been an elevator in the building anyway. It certainly wouldn't have suited the Nazis to give such a modern amenity to vermin like us. Of course, with no electricity, it wouldn't have worked anyway. It amazed me that my mother still had her key, or the presence of mind to hold on to it. She was the epitome of practicality, no doubt inherited from her own resourceful mother. I was incredibly fortunate to have two determined mother hens to protect me. They were really quite a handful for the fascists. And when we got to that quaint second floor apartment the key turned with a reassuring click and we were inside. Incredibly, it was unoccupied. Though our old apartment was nearby we were still afraid to go there. The Germans could counter attack, as they often successfully did, and we'd be in worse trouble for being there. So, until we knew for sure that victory was ours, we stayed in this hovel, glad to be out of the cold, and with one last chair to burn for heat and fuel.

We had been through so much. We risked arrest to go across town to bribe someone to hide us, all in vain, and suffered tremendous consequences for it. We barely escaped that when we were thrust into a maelstrom of threats, arrests, beatings, starvation, relentless cold, filth, and the bitter anguish of imminent death. We had practically been reduced to animals, hiding in burrows, scavenging for any crumb of sustenance, trembling within our own hides. To see my mother endure such travail was unimaginable to me. All my life I had observed this beauty queen, this fashion plate, this epitome of class and refinement, as if she were a porcelain doll. Who knew she possessed such reserves of strength and cunning? She had never had to prevail over anyone more daunting than a rude salesgirl at a millenary shop, and now she was dealing with armed fascists and getting the better of them. The worst prewar scarcity she knew was finding her favorite shade of lipstick sold out, and now she endured gnawing, maddening hunger, terrified of the effect the malnourishment would have on her unborn baby. What would the effect of all this be on her? Every blow leaves a scar. You cannot survive such incessant bleak circumstance and just forget about it. Not overnight. Maybe never. She didn't complain to me or her mother about any of this, because she knew there was no point. What would we do? Could I run out and buy an ice cream cone to cheer her up? Could I invite her to the movies to get her mind off of it? No. Nobody could offer any escape from this barren, dire existence. So, she did what everyone else did, bluff that it was endurable, that we were lucky to be alive, and glad to still be drawing breathe. We convinced ourselves, and then convinced everyone else. But what went through her head at night when she lay her head down on that filthy, squalid, sweat soaked bed? Thoughts of my father, her husband, her lover. Was he alive? Would she ever see him again? Thoughts of her mother. Could she hold out another month, another week, another day? Thoughts of me, her little Freddy who she reared with pride. She took such delight in dressing me in fresh, crisp outfits everyday, and now I had gone so long in the same set of clothes we couldn't even remember. What went on behind closed eyes? Was she off somewhere trying to forget? Maybe she was in Baia-Mare, playing her piano. She was in the mood for some Mozart. Now, maybe some Liszt. She played her father's favorites just to see his warm, loving smile. Keep your eyes shut tight and go far away. But such thoughts can drive you mad, and who knew what toll was taken by these months of deprivation and misery? And who knew how long before it would end, if it would end at all, and whether or not we'd make it?

Hunger does not make for a very discerning diet, so you eat whatever there is. Once mother found some starch and tried to bake it into bread. But it was just like paste that stuck to your teeth. It was filling but awful, but it was all we had to eat for two whole days. As hungry as we were though a third day of paste seemed unendurable, and we continued searching for something better to eat. Whether it infuriated our liberators or not we absolutely had to go outside to look for food. Thanks to a leg of that last chair I was warmed enough to brave going back outside in the crossfire to scavenge again. Considering that the entire population was on this same search for food it's truly amazing that we ever managed to find anything at all.

It was January 26 of 1945, and my mother, weakened by perpetual cold and hunger, feared for the life of her unborn child and for herself as well. And now, after so many children had died in the war, she was about to bring a new one into the world. Our little apartment in the old Jewish designated building had two bedrooms. Grandma slept in one, and I shared a tiny bed with my mother in the other, which kept the both of us warmer than sleeping alone. Of course, my mother wasn't thinking of her own comfort at all. She slept on the outside to make sure I was protected between the wall and her body. Even with that maternal warmth I slept with my clothes on for extra protection. My only surrender to decorum was to remove my shoes before retiring for the evening.

About a week after we got back to this apartment, in the middle of a particularly cold night, I was suddenly and violently shook by my mother.

"Freddy, the baby's coming!"

This was immediately followed by a wail that I hadn't heard since the night we were arrested by the Nyilasok and mother's impeccable method performance. This time however, the wail sounded much more authentic. It was definitely the real thing.

Even before I could react grandma burst into the room. The urgent voices of both women wove a tapestry I could barely untangle. 'Baby!

Echoes Of My Footsteps

Help! Now! Water! Dark! Help!" Finally grandma brought order to my consciousness.

"Freddy, we need help! Run, get help! Anybody! Run!"

Another wail punctuated this plea, and I leapt from bed without even bothering to put my shoes on. A half second later I was out the door, flying down the single flight of stairs that separated us from the ground level war zone. I pushed open the heavy iron gate, and dashed into the street. It was pitch black, and it bore no resemblance to the thoroughfare of a European metropolis. Six months of bombing, shelling and street fighting had transformed it into a macabre moonscape of charred corpses and the smoldering remains of military hardware. With the electrical grids long since bombed out of service only the glint of moonlight reflecting off their battered helmets could distinguish their identity. This terrain was dangerous to negotiate in the day and impossible at night. But there wasn't anyone alive out there anyway. Few dared to challenge this deadly maze. Only rats dared to roam such a macabre landscape, and they were everywhere.

A sharp cry of maternal labor rang in my ears, and I spun around toward the neighboring building. Picking my way around smoldering obstacles I dashed to the cellar entrance and yelled in.

"Somebody help my mother! She's having a baby! Help!"

Emergencies were nothing new in 1945 Budapest, and hardly anyone paid any attention to me. So, I maneuvered my way over to the next building and cried out the same anguished plea. Again, no reply. I felt desperate and powerless. Nobody would pay any attention to a little kid in the middle of this hell. At that moment I missed my father more keenly than ever. This situation required the presence of a capable adult and to me that meant my dad. I was just a kid. What could I do? It was a dilemma far beyond my meager capabilities. The birth of a baby, and especially under such circumstances, seemed inconceivable to me, and I was at a total loss.

I had to try and get to yet another building and I was actually starting to lose my way in the confusion and bleak darkness. Most of the buildings looked similar enough in peace time in broad daylight. Now, they were truly indistinguishable. As I was getting my bearings a woman's voice stopped me.

"Young man! Come back. I'm a nurse. I'll help you. Take me to your mother."

An angel of mercy emerged from the second cellar, and her voice was a calming balm. More than anything I remember that she was fat, which was odd for that time. But she was a vision of salvation to me. She recognized my childish panic and took charge.

"Take me to her. There's no time to waste!"

As I led her back she quizzed me.

"Have you ever seen a birth, young man?"

"You mean a baby?"

"I'm a nurse, and I've seen this a thousand times. Usually, Mother Nature takes over, and everything comes out alright. So don't worry."

I felt a lot better now, knowing that an honest to goodness adult, and a nurse to boot, was going to be present. Greatly relieved I was able to focus on finding our building and leading the woman up the stairs to our apartment. Of course, all she really had to do was follow her ears. Mother's wailing was probably audible for two city blocks.

We rushed in together, but while she went to my mother's side I stopped cold. What confronted me was a sight I had never imagined in my life. It was not even anything I had seen in books. My mother was splayed out across the bed with bloody sheets under her. Her legs were wide open and a wet human head was sticking out of her. I stood transfixed. My mom gave one more shriek and a baby popped out of her.

The nurse scooped it up and gave it a swat on its bottom. Right away it started to cry, which seemed to make everyone there happy. But I was too stunned to share their joy. I had never seen a female's private parts, much less in such close-up detail, and much much less my own mother's. This was so startling to me I was paralyzed. Was I supposed to be happy, like they were, or was I supposed to feel ashamed that I peeked at my mother's nakedness? And if it weren't for the nearly daily butchery I'd already witnessed I might have felt sickened by the gore. My mouth was agape, and I stared blankly. The women meanwhile were all purpose. The chubby nurse pulled some serious looking scissors out of her pocket and cut this cord of flesh that tied the baby to my mother which caused my eyes to open even wider. Then grandma came in with warm water she had prepared by melting snow with the second to the last leg from that chair. She washed the infant and swaddled it in some rags she had. Hefting the baby the nurse inspected it to see if it had all of its toes and parts in the right place. Satisfied that it did she said, "Congratulations, madam. You have a daughter. What is her name going to be?"

Zsuzsi," chimed in grandma.

Now, all the panic and chaos of the last hour evaporated into a domestic calmness that none of us had felt for a long time. Mother was calm, and grandma was content to hold her granddaughter in her arms. In spite of the dark and cold and miserable circumstances of our lives, one might have confused the atmosphere to be charged with some degree of rarely seen joy. There was a roomful of smiles, the warm glow of sunlight now making its overture, and the war seemed distant. All in all, it was a miracle. After all the tumult and anxiety the joy of new motherhood overtook my mother and she was actually happy to be with her two children, alive despite the best efforts of the war mongers. She gently told me to sit down next to her, and I eagerly joined her to behold my new sibling. But as soon as I sat down the blissful spell was broken by my realization that I couldn't feel my feet. My panic had caused me to run out bare foot at the height of a bitter Hungarian January and my feet were nearly frostbitten. Shock overtook me.

"I can't feel my legs! I can't feel my feet! Help me, grandma. Help me!"

Without hesitation my grandmother switched gears from one emergency to another. She put my feet on her warm lap and started rubbing. Despite the fact that she had just been stirred from the little bit of sleep she ever got, and had seen to all the details of delivering her granddaughter, she was now back on the front line, ministering to her grandson. She rubbed my feet with a tireless and loving dedication that was maniacal. Anyone else would have given up. My feet were as numb as a corpse's. But she rubbed and rubbed until sweat stood out on her brow. Malnourished and over fatigued she would not abate in her efforts to restore the flow of blood to my frozen toes. Her hands ached from the effort, but she would not slacken her pace. And finally, after what seemed like an even longer interval than Zsuzsi's birth, feeling returned to my feet.

"Wiggle your toes, Freddela."

I weakly willed my filthy digits to move, and we were all relieved. We were nearly hysterical at first, because it took such a long time for the numbness to subside, but my grandmother was just as maternally tenacious as her daughter, and wouldn't give up for anything. She was absolutely indefatigable.

My grandmother, Zelma Mayer, was the ultimate example of the resourceful, strong Jewish matron. She stoically endured the war, and ran every risk we did. Her husband had died a just a few weeks before the Nazi invasion, and she never had the luxury of mourning, but she tolerated every hardship like someone half her age. I don't really think we would have made it without her. She was always encouraging and positive, and when things seemed unendurable she was always there to plug the leaks. I owe my survival to her as much as to my mother. Actually, she is a rare case of an older person surviving the holocaust. Most people over fifty were rounded up by the Gestapo and shipped to extermination camps like Auschwitz. And when anyone that age was taken to such a place they were the first to be put to death, going straight from the train to the gas chambers. Doubtless, mother and Zsuzsi would have fallen into that category too. After the war, my grandma suffered from illnesses that constantly threatened her life, and at one point she almost succumbed to one of them. My sister almost died as well. Due to the malnutrition that my mother suffered through her pregnancy poor little Zsuzsi was born with a physical defect that would cause her a life of emotional and mental stress. Wars end, but the aftermath knows no truce. Its repercussions weave their way through our lives without mercy. No surrender or treaty can put them to rest. Zsuzsi was an addition to the family for which we had waited through nine months of terror and anxiety. All that time we prayed that she would actually be born, and not perish within the womb of another victim of the Third Reich. My mother had cheated death so many times, each time saving her own life and that of her unborn baby's as well. And now this miracle of life occurred in the middle of so much death. First the cake, and now my sister, dual instances of happiness made surreal by the context of an absurd normality, all imposed by miserable war.

I don't know how much time had elapsed since my mother had awaken me, but the sun was just starting to bring its welcome heat and light to a war weary planet. Grandma was exhausted by the morning's extraordinary activities, and she went back to her tiny room and collapsed on her narrow bed. Mother bade me lay down next to her. Previously, I always lay down between my mother and the wall, the dual barriers affording me a modicum of protection from the penetrating cold. But now we had to generate heat for our delicate new addition to the family. As our clan now had a baby, I got a raise to a new post, man of the house. Part of that meant giving more than I took, and that included giving my body heat to Zsuzsi. So, I lay down close to her. Our combined warmth gave us a sense of reassurance we hadn't known for too long. Maybe the worst was behind us. Maybe father would come home. Such thoughts in themselves reflected the peace that seemed to be peeking out at us from between the remnants of this conflict. There were still pockets of resistance to the Soviet juggernaut, but we felt confidant that our Russian friends would prevail. Surely, it would end soon.

Our perpetual scavenger hunt for anything edible intensified, because my mother needed to eat in order for her body to produce milk to feed her baby. Our neighbors knew about the newborn, and they were routinely reminded of the blessed event by the usual infantile wailing. Now they reflected the returning mood of peace by generously sharing what little food they had with mother. But even with this we needed more. So, I was back to my errands of trying to bring back the bacon, or in this case, horse flesh.

When it came to scavenging for food the weather did help out in one respect. It made the whole country one giant refrigerator. So, if an animal died it stayed fresh for a long time. As gas was so hard to find horses routinely replaced vehicles, and many died in the same crossfire that cut down so many humans. The giant equine corpses lay on the blood smattered snow without putrefying, a waiting meal for anyone willing to strip off a piece. Though I hadn't eaten such a thing prior to this I knew many had. For that matter, there was always the grim rumor circulating that desperate people had even eaten human flesh. I never had to confront that eerie choice, but I was certainly glad to find a horse that nobody else already had hacked apart. So, I took out my utensil, an old kitchen knife, and started chopping. The horse's open eyes scared me, so I went to the other end of the animal to escape its gaze. But I kept feeling its cold orbs following me. Finally, I covered its head in snow and returned to the task at hand. As I sawed away I noticed next to the horse's rump the charred corpse of a German soldier, and I spat on it. Before long I had a nice slab of frozen horse meat to bring back to our apartment for my resourceful grandma to cook. She had a little salt from a generous neighbor, and she turned that poor beast of burden into our gourmet brunch. We ate it, sitting around my mother and Zsuzsi, generating all the heat we could. We were Budapest sophisticates again, enjoying breakfast in bed.

Kids will find a way to play under any circumstances. Children played in the ghettos, and we played tiddlywinks on the stairs of the Swedish safe house. It's what kids do. And with the war winding down youngsters went back to playing soccer wherever and whenever possible, and I was making friends again. Besides playing we also got involved in little black market activities, like scrounging for tobacco to sell. Then, one day, there circulated among our little crew a rumor that the Russians were bringing in an entire trainload of potatoes. Potatoes?! A whole train load? This was a rumor worth verifying, and after asking around, it seemed quite reliable. At that time, the idea of such plenty seemed inconceivable. And train cars jammed to brim with the humble tuber was more attractive to us than a train load of diamonds. You can't eat diamonds. And even if we did have precious gems to sell, who had the money to buy them? Food, not shiny stones, was what we needed, and now it was all we could talk about. And though we felt certain that some of them would be distributed among the poor, finding their way to our needy bellies, my friends and I decided to avail ourselves of some extra portion as soon as that train arrived. Our patience was put to the test waiting for the spud express, and we made big plans. And once it pulled into the station in Budapest it was our sole topic of conversation. Where were they unloaded? When would they be distributed? What would be each family's ration? But my friends and I couldn't await the decision of the Soviet Party. As soon as the first Hungarian night fell on that mountain of potatoes we went down to the train yard, and scaled the perimeter wall. Before we knew it we were knee deep in lovely potatoes. We each had little sacks, and we filled them to capacity. But no sooner had we dropped the last potato into our bags than the Russian guards spotted us. Soviet authority was to be respected, and at that time our experience with armed men in uniform told us that retreat was always the wisest course of action. We had seen German soldiers and Nyilas punks shoot kids over far less, and we truly feared for our lives. The Russians fired a few shots into the air just to give us a good scare, and them a good laugh as well, but we hadn't yet earned the luxury of trying to divine the intentions of gun wielding guards. Survival during the war divided people into two categories, the quick and the dead, so we ran as fast as we could in order to stay counted among the former. But we were a lot heavier now than when we came over the wall, and the potato laden sacks made running impossible. And heaving them over the wall was out of the question for young arms malnourished by years of war. Our lust to get as many free potatoes as possible weighted our sacks and ourselves down, rendering a clean escape impossible. Like monkeys caught with a closed fist in a coconut, we were trapped by our own avarice. So, we dropped our lovely taters and made it over the wall. As soon as we were over I realized that my compatriots were far cleverer than me, because they had the quickness of thought to stuff a few into their pockets. Alas, I was not so wise, and the entire trip for me was a debacle.

The gamut of emotions that we experienced in the last few weeks was exhausting, and we couldn't help but marvel at it all. Mostly though, we felt thankful. For in spite of the hunger and cold and danger and filth we knew we were among the lucky survivors. And soon enough a day dawned when confirmation of that survival blessed us in full. The shooting stopped. No announcement. No declaration. It just stopped.

We woke up one morning to stillness, though we didn't notice anything different. Grandma looked around, had a quizzical look on he face. We looked at her, curious.

She said, "I think I just heard a bird."

We listened intently, and we heard it too. That's when we became aware that the tweet tweet had no competition. There were no sharp nine millimeter German pistol reports. There were no dull hand grenade thuds. No bursts of machine gun fire or rifle cracks. No shooting at all. We looked at each other, and slowly began to smile. It was true. All we could hear was that bird. Then we heard another. It was like a concerto. One lovely soprano bird twittered, and then the other trilled in counterpoint. And then, as if right on cue, the sun beamed down its radiant warmth. I walked outside, fearless for the first time memory. We could actually go out without the threat of getting shot. I looked out across the city and observed others like us, venturing out into peaceful sunshine. Perhaps they were looking for those birds. Or perhaps they just wanted to stand in the direct rays of the warming sun, eyes shut, smiling. For five long miserable years that simple quaint activity had not been possible. Hatred had made such a simple thing fatal. To just stand outside was now a celebration. We were no longer targets of anything more threatening than sunbeams. Our world was finally at peace.

As soon as the last vestiges of hostile forces were wiped out our liberators set up soup kitchens. Happy Hungarians lined up to get hot, nutritious soup, though it was meted out in classic communist fashion, with everyone getting soup according to their needs. I was deputed to fetch our daily ration, and I always included Zsuzsi in our head count, even though she got her soup indirectly through mother.

The war came to an end, but not the killing. Our Russian saviors were executing the Nyilasok and their collaborators as war criminals, publicly hanging them. I went to see them punished, and the site of their execution, a major intersection called the Octagon, made me think about my father, because we had often passed it on our way to visit the Transportation Museum. Like most Hungarian Jews he had survived most of the war only to be taken away in its final months by the marauding Nyilasok. And, as the news of those taken away was mostly grim, my mother and I harbored little hope he'd be back. So, it was an ecstatic surprise when we heard that horn blowing out in the street.

For many unobserved Passovers and Yom Kippurs we had listened to sirens. There was the wail of the air raid siren, warning everyone, regardless of religion or politics, to get underground. And we also heard the police siren, that unnerving, shrill two note announcement that doom was pulling up. We were accustomed to sirens but not plain horns all that much. Gasoline was exclusively for the army, so the few civilian vehicles that still operated on black market fuel were loathe to attract attention to themselves by honking. But hostilities in Hungary had ceased and here was an honest to goodness, old fashioned truck horn beeping away incessantly. By now we were no longer afraid of looking out the window, so my mother, Zsuzsi in her arms, strolled towards it to see what the racket was down on the street. But even before she got there she heard the cries of the neighbors.

"Ilushka, Ilushka! Your husband's home!"

She froze for a second, not knowing where to run to first, the window or the door. She chose the former and looked out to discover her beloved Armin standing on the running boards of a large truck, beeping that horn, waving and smiling. I ran to join mother and beheld the glorious site. In an instant we were all together on the stairs, embracing and laughing. After the emotional reunion, which included meeting his new child, my father got practical. He held aloft a large salami and announced, "We'll never be hungry again!" It was a miracle that he had returned at all, and here he was again, the provider.

My father had been forced to work as a slave for the Nazis, cleaning up rubble from Russian bombing raids. Whenever any of the laborers became too weak to continue working they were shipped off to Auschwitz. By then they all knew that this was a death sentence, and that it was only a matter of time before they went the same route. As there was nothing to lose my father plotted his escape. With his strength ebbing he waited for a moonless night and crawled under the guard fence of the encampment where the workers were kept, and kept crawling until he was a mile away. Then he saw the distant flashes of Red artillery and made his way to it. A Red Army patrol found him unconscious in the dirt and left him some bread and water. When he came to he found the mysterious care package. The food, as well as the good will that put it there, gave him the strength to carry on. Reinvigorated, he flanked the advancing Soviet forces until it brought him to the outskirts of Budapest. There he hooked up with a Red army unit. Recognizing his intelligence they gave him a role in the Soviet occupation of Hungary, administrating the delivery of food and supplies. Now that he had the authority he made his first stop his own family. He went to our old apartment to look for us and was told by its temporary tenant where to find us. Covering the single city block in record time he brought us a plethora of things we hadn't seen in years. There were grains and vegetables, soap and tooth powder, and even toilet paper. Not only did I have my father back, but he returned like a triumphant Santa Claus. We had plenty, and he made certain all our neighbors did too. Still not used to such abundance my mother and grandmother were afraid he'd give it all away, and leave us with nothing. This made him laugh, and he pulled out some papers that identified him as an important government official with all the protection of the occupying Soviet forces.

It was another installment of surrealistic dreamscape to observe my father administering a system of government that preached equality for all. But dad was one of the outside apartment crowd and, as Orwell wrote, more equal. To reinforce his point he thrust the end of the salami toward my mouth and I took a big bite. I knew the war was really over.

Like many others war survivors my poor father suffered from physical ailments brought about by the brutality of his captors and the general lack of nourishment. Worst of all he had contracted a chronic stomach infection which continued to plague him regardless of the bounty of food at his disposal. But nothing could spoil our reunion. We ate our fill, and asked him a million questions. We talked for a good long time, snacking as we relished the sound of his much missed voice. He held Zsuzsi for a long time, and then mother finally revealed that their new daughter seemed to be suffering from some malady. Without hesitating he stood and told us to follow him down to the truck. We drove to the hospital and took little Zsuzsi inside. After a preliminary examination the doctors said that she should stay there overnight for observation. We returned to the apartment, and my father spent his first night ever in the Jewish designated building that had been his family's refuge for so long. The next day we checked on Zsuzsi at the hospital, and they assured my parents that she would survive. Yes, baby Zsuzsi would continue to breath. She would see and hear and use all her senses. And she was lucky to have made it when so many babies did not. Certainly we were all grateful for the miracle of her coming through it. But, if her mother starved during the war what deadening anguish was this baby

Echoes Of My Footsteps

heir to? Putting aside the great fortune of her survival, Zsuzsi's day to day existence was not going to be easy. War leaves lasting scars on the weak. We bundled up the poor little dear, brought her home, and that night my father spent his second and last night at that apartment. It was the last night for all of us. The war was really over now, and it was time to go home. The next day father drove us all back to our old place in style. The lady who had lived there throughout the fascist regime seemed happy to receive us into our own place. Naturally, we were glad for that, but almost a little sorry for her, knowing that she was moving back to an unfurnished hovel.

The Nazis were gone, but we were still an occupied nation. Hungary was of course a spoil of war. Of course, after Nazis and Nyilasok, the Soviets were like benevolent despots. And they were not averse to employing the capable and intelligent Jews that survived to administrator their new hunk of real estate. Having a formal education and prewar job experience, my father landed a good government job. By then my father had regained some weight and my mother was elated to have her family back together again. We were one family in a million. Practically nobody could boast to have their nuclear family unit in one piece, but we did. We even had a representative from a third generation alive, my grandmother. The terrible reality was that ninety five percent of our relatives were turned to ashes. We were practically the sole survivors. Back in the town of my birth only a handful of Jews survived. After nearly a thousand summers of a continual Jewish presence in Baia Mare it was coming to an end. And all for nothing. Some duke gets shot by a disgruntled student, a frustrated artist can't make ends meet, and the whole world gets thrown into a cauldron. And for what? Afterwards people still knew hunger, broken hearts, sickness, old age, and death. Nothing changed. Beware the leader who bangs the drums of war.

As part of my father's position he was sent to the city of Debrecen for a two week orientation period. Having already been separated for too long from his beloved family he invited me to accompany him. I hadn't seen my father in nearly a year, and it was a bona fide adventure to travel with him and spend so much time at his side. We were practically inseparable while we were there. He showed me his office and what he was doing, which was to head up a new department to deal with war orphans and children disabled in the war. He was thrilled to be in a position to help young people, and poured himself into his work. He was even part of the effort to reclaim Jewish property stolen by the fascists. It was very fulfilling, and I was immensely proud of him. Wherever my father went he was respected. Some men are feared, because they wield power, and can affect lives in terrible ways. My father, on the other hand, was treated with deference because he exuded an aura of benevolence. He was kind and used his power for good.

Debrecen is a much smaller city than the grand capital of Hungary, and we enjoyed the more tranquil environment. Not being one of the major cities of Europe it hadn't been bombed to rubble by the allies, so the Reds made it their provisional administrative capitol. It was still intact, and it was my first real vacation from the war yet. There were hardly any reminders of the conflict, and it was like a rebirth to walk around the street and parks. We ate in restaurants and went to a movie or two. And by the time we returned to Budapest I felt much closer to him, and probably even begrudged the fact that he now shared himself with the rest of the family. Triply blessed with the arrivals of peace, Zsuzsi and father, we were all in absolute bliss. But what waited around the corner was so bizarrely unimaginable it almost seems like an illusion to me now. But its synergy was right in rhythm with the surrealistic nature of my life.

Chapter IX

Miami 5

Rebequita and I strode into the lobby of the Sheraton Hotel, and not an eyebrow was raised in shock or protest. The public had long since grown accustomed to seeing a mature man marrying a mere wisp of a girl. If Pablo Picasso and Charlie Chaplain could do it, why not Ivan Gabor? While I denied myself such fantasies I certainly was not ashamed to chaperon a sophisticated young woman. In any case I hardly thought of us as a couple. We were individuals of different categories sharing the same space, and that was all. As her protector I had brought her to this haven and would see to her needs. Having no idea of her financial condition I paid for her room. She thanked me demurely, with her eyes cast downward, perhaps from the shame of this imposition. I looked her in the eyes and said, "You rest now and think clearly. You should probably call your mother to let her know you're okay. She'll be out of her mind with worry."

"Yes, you're right. Thanks for everything, Ivan. Let's talk tomorrow."

She did not hug me or give me the typical Latin kiss goodbye, reminiscent of the infamous and insincere Hollywood buss. Rather, she reached out for my hand. We shook as innocents, my large male grip enveloping her soft, delicate fingers. It was the first time we touched, and it was frighteningly full of promise.

That night I lay alone thinking of nothing but her, and wondered if I was guilty of the same kind of temporary infatuation I mentally suspected of her. My life had been so full of fateful events it was impossible to brush this aside as just another pretty face. She was so much more than that. Even though she was protesting her mother's old fashioned attitude it couldn't be denied that she had brought up her daughter to be a real lady.

She called me daily and we chatted about a lot of things. The telephone seemed the safest medium for us, because physical proximity to her beauty would have influenced me too much. The distance afforded us by technology was perfect protection from the kind of light headed impulses men and woman so often fall prey to, but then later regret. Furthermore, when there is nothing possible but conversation you get an opportunity to really know someone. And of course, learning more about her allowed me to offer a more complete counsel. For example, I found out that we both loved the Beatles, which gave me the chance to offer advice by quoting a Fab Four lyric. We Can Work It Out was the first one cited. And the longer we talked the more profoundly I got to know her. Sometimes she told me things directly, and at other times I had to read between the lines. For example, though she didn't say it plainly it was clear to me that she was innocent with regards to carnal relations. As the older partner in this relationship, and more experienced in the ways of the world, it was incumbent upon me to maintain our mutual trust inviolate. But after several lengthy chats Rebequita was obviously growing fond of me. I had told her a little of my life during the war, of Israel and Argentina. Compared to the boys she knew in school I had an impressive dossier. But she was no stranger to older men. After all, hadn't all this come about over her being betrothed to the more mature Henry Berger? I was not the first non-teen on her horizon. In any case, my romance radar was not working properly, and I did not clearly perceive that Rebequita was growing more attached to me than I suspected. If I would have thought about it all I might have speculated that she was becoming infatuated with an older man, perhaps even comfortable with another father figure. In any case, it was neither projected nor encouraged from my corner. Deep down inside I probably desired her as well, but I dared not admit it. I refused to suggest that a forty two year old man steal a virginal teen away from the bosom of her family. And I would not fall into the seductive trap of a femme fatal, no matter how sincere she felt. She was just a confused kid, and it was up to me to keep things pure. I'd give her my trust, my money, my counsel, but not my heart. That was my position, solid and unassailable. It's what I wanted to believe, but it was a position that was put to the test the day she called me and permanently redesigned our relationship with seven words.

"Ivan, I want to live with you."

If any man tells you that his ego does not blast off into outer space when a beautiful woman says something like that, he's a bare faced, forked tongued, dyed in the wool liar. My own was just starting to go into orbit when I grabbed hold of myself and called for mission to abort. "Miami Beach, we have a problem!" As soon as I landed back on earth, and regained use of my vocal chords, I swallowed hard and went into my act. I told her that it was out of the question, offering every reasonable argument a shaken mentality could concoct. All civilized moral, legal and religious codes were evoked, but her debating tactic was more to the point, simply telling me that she loved me. She did not merely say that she was in love with me, but that she loved me.

Being in love was a position that too closely mirrored a temporary state of ardor. What she claimed to possess however was an abiding affection for me. She hadn't fallen for me. It was bigger. This girl loved me!

A man can only argue with a woman so long, especially if he thinks he loves her. So, I went over the potential affair in my mind. There was no longer any doubt that she was eighteen. And there was no doubt that she was the object of my own affection. With no logic to stand in the way of our mutual passion I happily allowed her to abandon distant Bal Harbor and share an apartment with me. But Rebequita was so special I didn't want her to be another conquest on my turf. She deserved so much more than my swinging bachelor pad. Wherever we'd go was a decision that would have to be hers as much as mine. This was going to be our affair. Not even the city should be the same. So, we left Miami Beach and crossed Biscayne Bay, heading west over the causeway to Miami proper. We ended up at Bay Park Tower, a locale as new to me as it was to her. It was to be our place by mutual consent. Everything must be by our mutual consent.

You can call me a sentimentalist if you like, but I've often relived our first night together. Out of respect for her we'll leave physical minutia to a minimum, but allow me to suggest that we threw the gauntlet of doubt into the faces of scientific researchers who claim that optimum passion is achieved by forty year old women and eighteen year old boys. We turned that theory on its head. I was indeed her first man, and being with her was consistent with the rest of my surrealistic life, only now it was happiness invading a terrain of desperation, instead of the usual territory occupied by frustration and doubt. Moreover, it was a rebirth to me. We both had found true love.

Rebequita wanted more than consummation. Marriage was her one and only goal. She wanted to be with me properly, with rings on our fingers. I resisted, convinced that our ardor would ultimately prove unfair to her. She was a kid, and ought to be dating California surfers with names like Biff and Todd, and eating pizza in front of the TV while watching Mork and Mindy. What was she doing with a middle aged Hungarian?

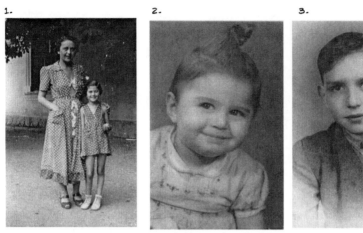

1. Like mother, like daughter. Mom and sister Zsuzsi in Budapest circa 1953. Mother took this picture and sent it to me in Haifa with the sole purpose of making me feel guilty for abandoning them. She sent many such photos as part of her not unsuccessful campaign.
2. Zsuzsi at about a year.
3. Around the time of my acting career.
4. A scene from the Young Guard.
5. Zsuzsi, accomplished on the piano at around eleven.

1-2. Shomer Hatzair camp in Hungary.
3. More camp. I'm between the two girls in the middle.
4. The same gang of kids on Aliyah stopping off in Vienna where I called my mother on the phone. I'm the boy in the second row on the left. Ernie Weisz is over my left shoulder.
5. The young Aliyah pioneers approaching the northern border of Hungary with Czechoslovakia where we crossed the river at night. This shot is taken from a book that was written about this particular Aliyah which later caused a minor scandal.

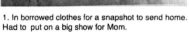

1. In borrowed clothes for a snapshot to send home. Had to put on a big show for Mom.
2. In the same borrowed togs, but revealing my true depressed mentality.
3. With best friend Natan in front of the cinema where my commie "uncle" abandoned me.
4. Wadi Salim, the worst place I ever lived.
5. Historical evidence of a rare snowfall in Haifa. Ernie Weisz and me in a snowball fight.
6. During my first week in Haifa I cavorted on the beach, allowing myself an escape from depression. The lady is unknown, but it was her relative that took the picture.

Sgt. Major Ze'ev Gabor reporting for duty. My stint in the Israeli Defense Forces was my turning point.
1. All non-coms on maneuvers. I'm second row, right.
2. Just a couple of years after my lowest point I was a different person, confident and fulfilled.
3. Guarding the frontier. I'm on top.
4. Special training session for sergeants. Capt. Massa is in the middle and I'm on his left.
5. Capt. Massa addresses the company. His back is to us, hands on his hips, and I'm on his right.
6. This is my first photo in the Israeli Defense Forces. I'm holding an Israeli made Sten sub-machine gun.

1. Top right, training my platoon in the fine art of camoflage.
2. Leading them back from an exercise.
3. Giving a lift to our company chaplain, a Rabbi of course.
4. Capt, Massa and me planning our company's exercises.
5. Early in the history of the IDF when we wore the old British helmets. I'm far right in Beret.

Chapter X

All The World's A Stage

After the fascist totalitarians got kicked out of Hungary they were replaced by the communist totalitarians. Of course, the Reds were absolute sweethearts compared to the Third Reich, and we no longer feared for our lives. But the Soviet way of doing things was daily becoming more and more restrictive. An example of Soviet intolerance was its attitude toward any organization that styled itself on western society, such as the Boy Scouts. That wholesome organization had been in Hungary since long before the war, and their resurgence afterwards was hailed as a return to the good old days. My troop was named after Forencz Toldi, our most famous writer, and it was a fantastic social outlet. The field trips, as well as the full variety of scouting activities, provided me with endless diversion, a commodity sorely absent for too long. Regrettably, the communist party branded it petty bourgeoisie and a glaring remnant of western decadence. Even though the west had saved their Red asses they now found their former allies to be oddly decadent. Just as odd, the fascists had employed exactly the same rhetoric to describe their own imagined enemies. Anyway, it all added up to shutting down the Boy Scouts.

My father foresaw the disappearance of scouting, but he also foresaw something far graver, his own demise. He must have known he didn't have long to go, because he made preparations to insure our support in his absence. His selfless love was such that he thought only of us. Practically his entire family was dead, and he knew that there was nothing he could do about it. What he could do was to protect the little of it that remained. Both he and Mom agreed that it was useless to look back, so they dedicated themselves to starting life anew. Most people were thinking about the basic necessities of life, scrambling up one hill at a time. But my dad saw the whole mountain range at a single glance, and forged ahead. He was so well educated and forward looking that he anticipated social and financial trends that might support bold new kinds of businesses. Thinking he might not have long to go he wanted to establish something stable for mom. They discussed various business strategies for post war Europe and decided to try marketing. He opened a marketing and advertising firm for mother in the Vatsi Ut district which was a rich neighborhood, ideal for the kind of clients they sought. He found a nice little office in a courtyard and called it Rapid Advertising. Mom was an eager student, and was enthusiastic to be an ad exec. And while Mom worked grandma took care of Zsuzsi.

Grandma was practically the only other surviving member of our family, and she gladly took up her role as manager of household affairs once again. She was brave, resourceful, and one hundred percent made of love. If my mother was a rock, than grandma was the mountain it came from. And though she was old she was always ready to learn new things, and kept an open ear to what went on at the ad agency.

In spite of the fact that my father held some position of authority with the proletariat loving soviets my mother did her best to resume her bourgeoisie existence. She was once again her old stylish self, smartly coordinating her ensembles with her shoes and finding just the right brooch to accent the blouse and match her earrings. Yes, on the outside she was closing in on that Miss Transylvania title, but on the inside who knew what the terrain looked like? Did she relive that day by the river as I constantly did? Sometimes I woke up in the middle of the night in our fancy outside apartment terrified the Nyilasok would pull up outside and start the yelling and shooting all over again. I visualized my pal from the Swedish house, blasted apart, lying dead and twisted in a pool of his own blood. And every day I walked past the spot where the fascist punks beat me. And how could we avoid the Danube? Every street, plaza and trolley reminded us of our torment. We had to practically hypnotize ourselves into living in the present when the past was all around us.

I was pressed into service at the ad agency, bringing ad copy to the newspaper office. My main occupation though was student. Most European kids hadn't seen the inside of a classroom in many, many semesters, and we all went into grades that better reflected our age than our academic progress. I was eleven and was enrolled in our local gimnazium, the equivalent of America's middle and senior high schools combined. Mine was called Kolscey Gimnazium, and it was one of the best in Budapest. It had suffered some war damage, so we all rolled up our sleeves, kids and adults alike, and carted off the rubble. It was tough physical labor, but I enjoyed it because my Dad worked alongside me. It made me feel proud to contribute to this community effort, and especially ecstatic to work with my dad on anything. Within a few weeks we had the venerated institution in good enough shape to shape our minds, so school was back in session. Only six classrooms were opened, but we had great professors, and I received an excellent education, ranging from the classics to science. I learned French and how to meet any mathematical challenge. And in a spirit of healing the board of education even permitted a Rabbi to come to school and lecture us.

My poor father continued to suffer from the same stomach infection he contracted while enslaved by the fascists, and no doctor seemed able to deal with it. Despite food, rest, medicine, and the dedicated loving attention of us all, his condition deteriorated. Day by day we watched him weaken, powerless to help. Finally, my beloved father succumbed to World War Two. He survived the wartime years but not its ravages. Violence couldn't do him in, but he was overwhelmed by a surreal totalitarian trauma. We always hear about the six million, but Armin Grossman was one of the millions victimized by that insanity's aftermath. I've never gotten over it, and I know mother never did either. It was bizarre to apparently survive the war only to fall victim to it afterwards. It was calculated that fifty million perished during World War Two. How may more afterwards as a result?

Thanks to the efforts of my father, and people like him, Jewish culture regained a foothold in Hungary, and he ended up spending his last days in a Jewish hospital. Such initiatives were part of the various Jewish organizations sponsored by American Jews to deal with every aspect of the post-war experience. One of the most widespread and effective was the Joint Distribution Committee which sent food, medicine and clothing. They also organized housing and reunited families. For us it was a vital link to our survival. If all else failed we could always rely on them for a square meal. They established dining halls all over Europe, and though it was mainly for Jewish survivors of the holocaust, they turned away no one. For me it was like a second home, and I often went there with my best pal, Janos Nyiri. We met at school and hit it off at once. His father was Tibor Nyiri, a noted avante writer, and it rubbed off on Janos who was destined to follow in his father's political and literary footsteps. Of course, a ready mind doesn't fill a waiting stomach, so we frequented the dining halls of the Joint Distribution Committee together. In addition to plentiful food they had social activities and entertainment and we both enjoyed many fulfilling afternoons there. Those centers also served as recruiting grounds for other Jewish organizations with varying agendas. Some were religious, teaching young people about Jewish life, while others appeared more social in nature. One group was called Shomer Hatzair. They approached me one day, as I was enjoying my free soup, and chatted with me. I told them about my Boy Scout days and they seemed sympathetic.

"Yeah, what a shame they got shut down. But you know what? We do all those things at our meetings. We go on field trips and have sing-alongs too. And by the way, it's not just for boys."

They talked to me while I ate, and convinced me to pay them a visit. At my first meeting everyone was friendly, and called each other *chaver*, which means friend in Hebrew. They used a lot of Hebrew words, and even called the meeting place a *ken*, or nest. We sang Hungarian and Israeli folk songs and I learned to dance the *hora* which I especially liked, because I got to hold hands with girls. We also went on camping trips in the forest. Sometimes it was just for an afternoon, like a picnic, and at other times we went for a whole week, pitching tents and cooking over campfires. We took a short train ride north and then hiked into the woods to a campsite. The towering trees, the heavenly aroma of pine, the chirping birds, the forest in all its glory, made those trips precious communes with nature. To city kids like us it was paradise. On one such trip my mother came out in the middle of the week to visit me to see how I was doing. She had lunch with us and chatted with the kids and counselors. I was proud that the other girls commented about how beautiful she was, and she was happy to see me involved in such a wholesome activity. I enjoyed the brief escapes from urban life and the camaraderie of the other kids. Nights were especially magical. We roasted potatoes over a crackling fire and the counselors, illuminated by the leaping orange flames, talked about Israel. They said it was beautiful and an exciting adventure. They spoke glories about the Holy Land, occasionally passing around a photo or two of a *kibbutz*. Sometimes they mentioned this thing called *Aliyah*, or return to our homeland. If Israel was going to succeed, they said, it needed people. And occasionally one of our group would be absent from a meeting or a field trip, and they'd proudly announce that he or she was *Aliyah,* returned. I became particularly friendly with one counselor named Judah Winter. He was about eighteen, which really wasn't that much older than me, but he seemed like an adult to us. He spoke to me like an adult as well, and I especially appreciated that. He was a dedicated Zionist, presenting Israel as Heaven on Earth. For my part, I was only participating for its social aspects. Anyway, there was a much more popular image of Heaven being discussed by everyone. It was called America. As long as Lady Liberty put out the welcome mat it was the destination of choice. Jewish agencies assisted in the immigration process, but the Reds, our one time saviors, were now jealously antagonistic toward anyone wishing to leave the cozy warmth of their Marxist embrace. They set up a veritable obstacle course of bureaucracy to impede any such process and turned any attempt to make one's way to America into a trying ordeal. Between the west's red tape and the east's Reds, Aliyah did offer an alternative worth considering. But all thoughts of immigration faded in the wake of the next unexpected event.

One afternoon my friend Janos Nyiri invited me to attend a theatrical performance at the National Theater. I had never seen theater on such a grand scale. Mere school pageants were all I had previously known. I immensely enjoyed it, and when we were getting up to leave someone approached me.

"Excuse me. I'm terribly sorry to bother you. I hope you enjoyed the show."

It took me by surprise, but it was a great compliment to have someone ask my opinion.

"Yes, I did."

"I'm Tamas Major, and I'm going to be directing our next play here, and I think you have just the look for one of the characters. Why don't you come tomorrow and audition?"

What an odd person! And what an odd thing to talk about. I wasn't an actor, and I never even considered such an extravagant thing. Of course, I was terribly flattered, but I really had no notion of acting, and felt compelled to refuse.

"Look, I'm no actor. Talk to my friend. He's real artistic. Not like me!"

But this fellow was determined.

"Please. Just learn some poem or something dramatic. Come tomorrow and recite it. If you have half the personality I think you do you'll get that part. And hey, acting is fun. You'll love it! It's right here at ten in the morning. Tell them Tamas the director recommends you. See you tomorrow, I hope!" And he was gone.

Janos found the whole thing wonderfully amusing.

"Freddy, he's right. This could be fun. And I think the National Theater pays their actors pretty well. What do you have to lose? I could loan you a book of French poetry that might have something perfect for you to recite. What do you say?"

"It pays?"

"Pretty good, I'd imagine."

"Okay, lend me that book. Like you say, what can I lose?"

This was in 1948, and I was only fourteen. The whole thing sounded insane to me, but Janos said I should give it a try. He was like a brother to me, and his sense of aesthetics was above question. I respected his artistic opinion even then, and if he thought I should go to the audition that was good enough for me. So I borrowed his book and memorized a poem about a violinist which was full of sensual imagery that was so far over my head it was absurd for a kid like me to recite it. Regardless, I committed the nouns and verbs and prepositions to memory and went down to the National Theater to make a fool of myself. Tamas Major was excited to see me, and giddily presented me to Hilda Gobi, the play's female lead, and one of the most highly regarded actresses in the country. She seemed to agree that I had just the right look and gave me a big kiss on the cheek. Clearly, the life of an actor was good!

There were dozens of kids trying out for that part, and I was trembling with nerves when I recited my erotic French poem. It was full of odd descriptions, like someone playing the violin between the open legs of a woman, and everyone laughed to hear the clueless kid recite the verses whose meaning was clearly lost on him. Their mocking laughter convinced me that my audition was a monumental fiasco, and I just wanted to slink away and vanish. To my amazement though, I won the role, and soon I'd be treading the boards with the most acclaimed actors in Budapest. I, little Freddy Grossman from Baia Mare, was going to star in a major play in the National Theater. To convince myself that it was true I had to repeat that information to myself fifty more times as I ran home to share the good news. Mom and grandma were amazed, and we had a glorious celebration.

"You're the star?"

"Well, it's a big role!"

"And they're paying you?"

Even though I was ignorant about this I remembered what Janos said.

"I'm not sure, but my friend Janos says it pays quite a lot!"

Ma and grandma hugged and kissed me repeatedly and said how proud they were of me. And they got even prouder when my first pay day rolled around and I received even more than my mother earned in her best week. I was now the major bread winner of the family, and I felt like a real man. The only negative was that my Dad was not there to share in it.

The name of the play was The Young Guards, and it was about a boy who heroically defied the Nazis, a common theme in the arts in postwar Europe. Basically, it was typical communist propaganda, sponsored by our saviors and new masters, the Communist Party of Hungary. I played Rodik Yorkin, a heroic young commie who defies the tyrannical fascists. I was not the main character, nor did I have a lot of memorable dialogue, but I made a great impression just the same. And opening night lives still in my memory. The months of rehearsal had taught me to memorize my lines and learn where to stand, but it did not prepare me for my first round of applause. Its reverberation took possession of my soul. After each performance the cast comes out from the wings, stands center stage, bathed in the warm theatrical lights, and accepts the adulation of the masses. The audience slaps the palms of their hands together and the sharp report lands on the ears of the actors as sweet music. Approval, love, and admiration flood over them as their chests swell with pride. And I was no different. I loved the roar of the crowd, and floated on a pompous cloud of self importance. And the premiere party made my head swim. I was no longer the potato thief, scrounging for crumbs, or hacking away at frozen horse flesh. I was an important thespian, the cynosure of all things artistic, the darling of Budapest. My ego swelled to such proportions they might have built a newer and larger theater just to accommodate it. Clark Gable? Gary Cooper? Small fries! I was Ivan Gabor, star of The Young Guard. Watch out world, here I come!

Our opus of theatrical communist propaganda opened to rave reviews from the communist controlled newspaper, and within weeks I was a celebrity. The public adored me and people recognized me everywhere I went. My fame spread to school where I signed autographs for fellow pupils which Janos found exceptionally amusing. The cast loved me too, and Hilda Gobi practically adopted me, always inviting me to sit on her lap. I was pretty big for such shenanigans, and in retrospect I think I might have passed up a chance at life lessons from this grand dame of the Hungarian theater. One thing we did share though was billing. We were both on the advertising posters.

There is a unique artifact found in European cities, the likes of which I've not seen anywhere else. Wherever you go on the continent there are these peculiar iron cylinders with dome tops that resemble giant bullets, about seven feet high, and which seem to serve no purpose other then to post advertisements. Politicians use them in their campaigns, and they're also used to promote movies and concerts. During the war they were used by the fascists to spread their propaganda. They pasted up endless edicts, most of which were dedicated to anti-Semitic warnings: Beware of Jewish Spies. Don't Help Jews. Turn in Jews. Inform on Jewish Sympathizers. And now, on these very same giant bullets were splashed posters with a new young Jewish actor's name, Ivan Gabor. The communists found my nickname Freddy too western sounding, so I ended up changing it to the most common Russian name of all, Ivan, their equivalent of John. Thus Freddy Gabor, nee Alfred Grossman, was now transformed into Ivan Gabor, sweetheart of the Hungarian theatrical crowd. I not only shared the poster with Hilda Gobi, but also the most renowned actor in all of Hungary, the star of The Young

Guards, Miklos Gabor. The irony of those iron advertising mediums being used to spread my fame strikes me as maximum incongruity. First, they promoted my infamy as a subversive Jew, and now they promoted my fame as a beloved entertainer. The giant iron bullets, quite ugly in and of themselves, peppered amid Europe's classical urban landscape, created a surreal visage unmatched by any artist's imagination. Life slaps me with the sharpest contrasts, always turning me on my head.

During the war I was terrified of being recognized. Now, I was worried that people wouldn't recognize me often enough or fast enough. Growing up I never thought about what I wanted to be when I was an adult. After all, I was only five when the war began, and once that started everybody's fulltime career was survival. And when the war ended I went back to school. I was only ten, and discussion of future employment was still premature. But of all the possibilities that might've loomed in my future I certainly never entertained entertainer, much less star. And I would have stayed with the play, and perhaps gone on to star in more productions, but cruel fate yet again imposed itself on me. Of course destiny gets the blame, but I was the one who actually made the decision that was to forever and irrevocably shape my life.

It was early 1949, and The Young Guard had been playing for several months. I was back stage, getting ready for a performance, and Judah Winter, my Shomer Hatzair counselor, stuck his head in my dressing room door. Since starting the play I hadn't had any more time to attend Shomer Hatzair meetings or take field trips, so it was quite a surprise to get a visit from him.

"Hi Freddy. Or should I say Ivan?"

"Judah! What are you doing here?"

"Just came by to see the play. I can't wait to see you on stage."

Having stroked my ego to the appropriate degree I invited him in. We chatted about the club while I changed, and he suggested he chaperone me home after the show. Somebody always did that, because it was dark after the evening performance, and I was still just a youngster of fourteen. I agreed, and he got the prerequisite permission from the stage managers. Then he took his seat out front. After the show he massaged my ego with more critical praise which put me at ease, and we left the theater together. As we walked through the crisp winter air he asked questions about the play and my schooling, but eventually guided the conversation to Israel. We passed a small tea shop and he invited me to have some cake. It was right next door to one of the best cinemas in the city, and they were playing Laurence Olivier's Hamlet which I had recently seen there. "To be or not to be" still resonated with me. During the war just the actual state of being had been a real challenge, plus I now aspired to be a big actor like the famed Brit. Little did I know that I was about to be set on a course by Judah Winter that would make my life far more reminiscent of the melancholy Dane he portrayed. Anyway, I appreciated the synergy of the proximity of the tea shop with the movie house, and it seemed an appropriate venue for Judah Winter to chat with an actor. But as we enjoyed our snack Judah began talking to me in an uncharacteristically serious tone.

"Freddy, why do you want to perform for people in Hungary? What'd they ever do for you? I'll tell you what they did to us. They cooperated with the Nazis and sent half a million of our people to the gas chambers. And twenty years from now maybe they'll turn on us again. That's the history of Jews here in Hungary. One moment they love you for acting in a famous play, and the next they're out to lynch you for being a dirty Yid."

I was in shock! This rhetoric was far stronger than any I had ever heard from him or anyone else at Shomer Hatzair. Judah was impassioned with a Zionist fervor, and words flowed from him in a zealous torrent.

"There are theaters in Israel, Freddy. You can act for Jews in the Jewish Homeland. You don't have to live under a fake name with a false identity. You can throw away this phony life and live as what you are, a proud Jewish youth in the ancient land of your forefathers. Every moment you act here you're living a lie. You're fourteen, a man. That means you've already wasted twenty percent of your life. Reclaim your birthright Freddy, with Aliyah!"

I had never even thought about any of this. I was an assimilated Jew like my parents. We weren't atheists or anything like that, but being serious about being Jewish had definitely been pushed to the Gabors' back burner. Had father survived he probably would have been on top of things, like getting me Bar Mitzvah'd on time, but his absence obligated my surviving parent to dedicate herself to making ends meet. She was working and grandma was busy with domestic concerns. Religion was out of the loop, but now Judah made me suffer pangs of guilt over it. I was overwhelmed! Every word Judah said seemed to make perfect sense, and there was nothing to offer in rebuttal.

"But what am I supposed to do?"

"Follow your destiny."

"And what is that destiny?"

"Can't you see it?"

I was stuck. I was so confused that my power of speech, such a vital component of my new artistic persona, now failed me. Just as my tongue betrayed me so did my brain. My senses refused to cooperate. But I shouldn't have been surprised by any of this. Of what service had my cognitive powers been thus far? My parents made every decision for me since birth. And the war itself forced upon me every step I took. And now, even as free as I supposedly was, I could not find my own way. Judah was asking me if I could see clearly, and I had to confront the fact that I could not. Just as my father had done for me before, and my mother thereafter, I again needed to be told what to do. But I couldn't even ask that with any conviction. I just sat there, mouth agape, embarrassingly mute. So Judah filled the void, and spoke for me. He slid his chair closer to me, lowered his tone, and looked me straight in the eye.

"Your destiny Freddy is the destiny of all Jews, to return home, to Eretz Israel."

I lowered my eyes, contemplating his words. This felt like the most serious moment of my life. Judah could see that I was on the brink, and he pushed me over.

"We've been waiting for two thousand years, wandering from country to country. Now God has seen fit to give us back our native land and ancestral home. We'd be insane not to take Him up on it. I tell you Freddy, it's more than an opportunity, more than a right. It's our duty to populate Israel and raise her up among the nations of the Earth. The time is now!"

Such Zionist fervor permeated the atmosphere that I thought I heard Hatikvah in the background. He was relentless, and I was beginning to feel as if I were a traitor to the entire Hebrew Nation for not already living there.

"Israel needs you. They need actors as much as anyone, and they'd be thrilled to have a famous star like you join their ranks."

Thespian egos are notoriously susceptible to flattery, and I was a classic case study of that malady. The fact that I would be honored in my homeland as an artist was tempting.

"You'll be beloved among your own. *Chaver,* my brother, this is your true destiny."

As each moment passed Judah's rhetoric seemed more and more reasonable and appealing. Yet, I remained incapable of making a decision of my own.

"But what should I do?"

"It's simple. You come with me to Israel!"

"Just like that? What about the play, my family?"

I started to panic. I had never done anything on my own, without parental approval, and I was scared out of my wits to make such a decision. My stomach was churning. Is this how destiny feels? A momentous event was staring me in the eye and I was unworthy. But Judah was resolute and decisive enough for both of us.

"Freddy, tomorrow I'm taking a group of kids on a field trip. But I will share with you what nobody else on that trip knows but us counselors. We're telling the kids it's another field trip, but it's really Aliyah! We're taking them out of Hungary and we're fleeing to Israel. And Freddy, you're going with us! I'm telling you, because you're so attached to this illusory theatrical world, and would never sacrifice it for just another hike in the woods. But for the sake of Aliyah you would. Plus, you'll be such a huge star in Israel. But you can't tell anyone. Later, the parents will come after, and they'll all be glad we did this. You'll probably be saving their lives. Who knows how long before the communists start arresting Jews? Stalin is no friend of ours!"

Now I was practically having an anxiety attack.

"But what about my mother?"

"As I told you, you're saving her life. The commies are atheists and soon they'll make it illegal to practice any religion."

I thought about my religious grandma. The idea of her being arrested and persecuted for her religious beliefs made me feel outrage. Judah's right. I must save her!

"But shouldn't I at least tell my family?"

"There's no time! Anyway, if anyone finds out maybe the Russians will get word, and stop us. You cannot tell your mother or anyone else. Don't worry. They can join you later. And they'll be so proud of you.

How thrilled they'll be to have a son return to Israel to claim his birth right. And, as I said, you'll be saving their lives!"

I was dumbfounded, but I could not deny this freight train of fate that was dragging me along. The air in the shop froze and was caught in suspended animation.

"Freddy, if you decide to come you'll never regret it!"

Imperceptivity I tilted my head back up and found myself nodding my mute assent. We rose to leave the safe confines of the tea shop.

"Freddy, we'll meet at the train station tomorrow morning at six."

I still could not speak. We left the tea shop and he walked me the rest of the way home. This protective gesture reinforced in me the feeling that he had my best interests at heart, and he gained my trust. And when we got home he closed the deal.

"Pack some things and get some rest. Your real life starts tomorrow. Shalom."

Everybody was already asleep when I entered our apartment, so nobody heard me as I quietly packed my little suitcase. Along with a few pieces of clothing I stuck in photos of my mother and grandmother, and then lay down to get a few hours rest, dreaming of becoming a big star in Israel.

Chapter XI

Miami 6

Our love affair was like a dream. Eventually though everyone wakes up from such a state. In this case it was a small army that took up the task of rousing us from our idyllic romantic slumber. After a few months her family en masse came looking for her. She had told her mother where she was, and the whole truth. As an adult she had that right. I was out when they arrived, and when I walked through the door I could feel daggers shooting out from their eyes. Doubtless, they were all filled with loathing for the man who deflowered their innocent baby. Her mother led the attack.

"What's wrong with you? Don't you have children almost the age of my daughter?"

I was prepared for this, and answered her as respectfully as I could.

"Señora, you have to talk with your daughter, not me."

And talk she did. I waited outside while she and a cadre of other family members harangued and browbeat Rebequita into recanting her decision to leave home. After about a half hour they invited me back into my own apartment. As soon as I walked in I knew it was bad news. Rebequita was staring down at the floor, unable to meet my gaze. Her mother announced a well rehearsed speech, "Promise me you'll never call this man again! Tell him that your family is more important!"

Without lifting her eyes off the floor she whispered, "Sí, mama. I promise. I'll go home with you."

I said, "Okay! And I promise you Señora that, if she doesn't call me I won't call her."

Then she told Rebequita that I would get over her. I wanted her to stay, but I thought of her welfare and said okay. I said it but I didn't really mean it.

After that there was nothing left for anyone to say. They left. What else could they do? I stared at the floor and listened to their receding foot steps down the marble hallway. Then I went to the window to watch her car drive away. I understood her mother, but I was devastated. But I started mending my broken heart by admitting that it was for the best that she went home. I convinced myself that her mama was right, that I would get over it. I took the classic point of view that it was better to have loved and lost and all the rest. This romance had enriched my life immeasurably and it was selfish to feel bitter. So, while the truth had yet to penetrate my consciousness, that I had lost the love of my life, I numbly went back to work on my paintings. Years earlier I had discovered the soothing therapeutic value of putting oil on canvas, and I sought that refuge now. I sat at my easel with brush in hand, hoping for some muse to rescue me. But I just froze. Almost at once tears began to muddy my view. She was gone five minutes and already I desperately missed her. It was five minutes, but soon it would be five days, then five weeks, then months and years, and a lifetime without her that I could not bare. I remained in a stupor until I collapsed on my bed fully dressed. I hadn't slept with my clothes on since World War Two.

The next day I awoke to a bright orange Miami sunrise. It sharply contrasted the deep blue mood of my fitful sleep, but it all came into sharp focus when the telephone started ringing. My ears lit up with hope that it was Rebequita, and the sunlight flooded both my room and mind with good omens. I desperately lunged across the bed for the phone, praying that it was her. Sure enough, her sweet voice answered my augury, pacifying every aching emptiness that had intruded upon my soul.

"I love you! I'm coming back! I want to marry you!"

Overnight I had managed to convince mechanically myself that this was all for the best. So, I related to her my philosophy on romance.

"Life is like a string of pearls. Our experience together is like one of those pearls. Your memory of me will always be like a beautiful pearl on your necklace."

My wisdom fell on deaf ears. She was certain of her feelings, and determined.

"No," she insisted! "Marry me!"

I countered with the same corny argument that had so many times failed me.

"But I'm so much older than you!"

"So what?" was all she used to counter my insincere logic. Love conquers all was a more powerful cliché than mine. But now I brought out the heavy ammo, a dose of reality that was sure to wake her from her romantic dream state. Up to that time I had been living with my two sons. They previously were living with their mother, and were now shuttling between the two of us. Soon though we'd have to make a permanent arrangement to complete their upbringing.

"You understand that if you marry me you'll have to deal with my sons. It's a package deal, Rebequita. I'm never going to abandon them.

I may only have them on weekends for now, but I'll always be their father. And this is no good for you!"

Love not only conquers, it's blind too! She simply steamrolled everything.

"Don't you love me?"

I couldn't really bring myself to say that I didn't, and the next thing I know she was back in our love nest at Bay Park Tower, this time with a lot more belongings. And when the first weekend rolled around, and my sons Gabriel and Adrian came over, I was amazed at how comfortably they fit together. Rebequita is so attractive, and I don't mean that in a merely physical sense, that they couldn't help but take to her. She opened her heart to them, just as she had to me, and the boys liked her at once. She was like an instant sister to them. They knew she wasn't responsible for the divorce, because she hadn't even come on the scene until long after our separation. Gabriel was thirteen, and he had known for a long time that his parents lived in a continual state of tension, and was grown up enough to know that our separation was for the best. Adrian was well adjusted and could also deal with these changes. Of course, just being in America might have had some bearing on the whole situation, because we were not focused solely on our domestic situation. Back in prewar Baia-Mare for example, where everybody knew everybody else's business, a couple's marital discord would have been the topic of conversation for miles. "Oh, Bela and Rivka aren't getting along." "I hear she's a constant nag." "That man has a roving eye, I tell you!" Part of the reason for that was simply because there wasn't much else to do. Besides providing entertainment to strangers in the whole region, squabbles at home took center stage. Even Israelis and Argentineans can obsess on these things for lack of alternate activities. But first world countries offer a fuller agenda. Coming from the third world the United States can be pretty mind boggling. I have to admit that even as a supposedly mature adult I couldn't help but be fascinated by the myriad distractions of the opulence of a developed nation, such as supermarkets, superhighways, Dunkin Donuts, and Disney World. So, we were all a bit beguiled from focusing solely on our domestic issues. We were having too much fun to get depressed over personal problems. Anyway, it was obvious that Rebequita wasn't going to replace the boys' mother, but rather became an adjunct parent and friend. And she took to these roles so naturally it was astonishing, showing interest in everything they did. She nurtured and supported them, becoming older sibling to Gabriel and loving aunt to Adrian. They called her by her name, but respected her like an authority figure. They could confide in her, go to her for advice, and even get help in their homework. Rebequita was likewise attracted to them, and was prepared to do anything for them. She cooked and cleaned for them and was their playmate. Her relationship with the boys demonstrated how truly extraordinary she was. She could be both adult and child, relating to all three of us simultaneously. But Rebequita's ultimate personal conquest was becoming friends with the boys' mother, my ex-wife, Hassida. All of the elements of a classic Latin soap opera were present, such as a man taking up with a younger woman, the estranged ex-wife, and the children bouncing back and forth between homes. But thanks to Rebequita's ample heart none of the typical melodramatic scenes were played out. There was no friction, and peace and blessed tranquility fell on us all. This young Cuban woman was prepared to love me and my whole family. It was amazing! In spite of that I felt guilty that I was robbing her of her youth. Many men would be jealous of my situation, having a gorgeous teenaged lover on my arm, and I must admit that our age difference was evaporating little by little. Her maturity was the equal of anyone my age. Of course, I persisted in trying to convince her that it was best for her if we separated. I loved her, but I felt guilty over our affair and tried to coerce her into going back home. Though every moment with her was heaven I steadfastly maintained my antipathy toward a canopy. I had to fight my desire for her, because lurking beneath my happiness was that old conditioned response to a much younger woman. Like a cornball robot I repeated all the reasons why it supposedly couldn't work. "Our age difference made common interests impossible." "She'd ultimately tire of the fling with the man with the distinguished gray." And the good old reliable, "It was just not meant to be."

If I adamantly refused to marry her, I figured she'd just go. Never mind that it would break my heart. So what if my sons became disconcerted with me. The heck with her feelings! I would hang tough, and she would get the message. She'd throw in the towel, leave me, turn to the quarterback of her college football team on the rebound, get married, move to Akron, and have six blond babies. She'd be a fond memory, but I'd have a clean conscience. My primary tactic toward that guilt free mental state was to continually remind her that I would never marry her. Despite the heated intensity of my no-marriage campaign I felt it was not bearing much fruit. I persisted however, with the hope that enough water falling on the rock would eventually erode her affection for me.

After a few months of us living together like an old married couple I came home one day to discover Rebequita's entire family once again in my apartment. On the floor in front of the whole *mispucha* were two large, black, plastic bags filled with what could only be her belongings. This was the culmination of another campaign very similar to mine called Operation He'll-Never-Marry-You. It had been waged for months by her mother. She had been calling her daughter at every opportunity to drive home this point, so we were allies without even knowing it.

"Rebeca, this man has two kids your age. He's old enough to be your father. And he will never -do you hear me Rebeca?- never marry you!"

Her mother chanted this lengthy litany in her daughter's direction every chance she could, either in person or on the phone, and it finally wore her down. In reality, Rebequita was starting to think the same. For all her talking about the subject of marriage my persistent resistance to it finally made a dent in her bridal armor. It broke her heart to come to that realization, but she had to agree with her pestering mother. At last, she stood up straight and confronted me before her whole clan.

"Ivan, I want to marry you. I want it more than anything! But if you won't have me I'll do the honorable thing and go back to my family. I'm not some common girl of the streets. I will go away. Mother is enrolling me at the University of Perugia in Italy to study art history. Maybe a large separation will cure me, though I doubt it. I will always love you. Goodbye, Ivan."

Though I had waged my own war against marriage, and really thought it in her best interest to live without me, being faced with that reality enraged me. The real prospect of losing her was truly unthinkable. That which gave me life was going off to Europe, and I lost my mental equilibrium. Emotion overcame me and manipulated my arms to pick up the television and fling it on the ground. The crash shocked the room into silence for a moment and gave me the floor without compromise.

"Now please, leave at once."

I said nothing else to keep her there. She left and I was as shattered as the Sony Trinitron. Was I out of my mind? Why didn't I fight for her? Why was I being so selfless? Did I doubt her love so much that I had to test it by letting her go yet a second time? I was insane to go along with this! Of course, her mother wanted her to stay at her side forever. That's what mothers do. But how was it possible that this girl's true love aided and abetted this sentimental crime? Maybe she couldn't be mine because I didn't deserve it. Faint heart fair maiden never won. If I was alone now it was my own doing. Truly, I must have been nuts!

That night she called me begging forgiveness, and I explained that I had already gone through a lot in my life, and I'd be able to get over this too. Crying, she hung up.

The next day, after a sleepless night, I went to my office. In front of it was parked Rebequita's car, and she was inside. She hadn't gone to Italy after all! I ran to the car.

"Rebequita, you didn't go!"

Then I discovered that it was just a similar looking car with someone else sitting at the wheel. I was shaken and I stumbled into my office. Feeling faint I had to sit down to keep from falling down. My head was spinning, and everything went dark. I couldn't breathe and I was nauseous. All control left me and I slipped down onto the floor and passed out.

Chapter XII

Aliyah

I woke up before dawn and slipped out. I left a lying note that said I was going camping for the day with Shomer Hatzair and would be back at night in time for my next performance. I also removed my father's Omega watch which I had been wearing since he died, and left it on the dresser. I always did that when I went on field trips so it wouldn't get damaged. Plus, I was terrified I might lose it. Anyway, if mom saw that I left the watch behind like I always did she wouldn't think anything was unusual. It was all part of the subterfuge, and not even Zsuzsi woke to spoil my clandestine exit.

I walked into the lobby of our apartment building, taking great notice of every detail, as if remembering them would somehow enrich my life. Goodbye hallway. Goodbye apartment. Farewell mama, grandma and Zsuzsi. Adieu Hungary.

I walked outside as I had done countless times, but this time it was completely different. I was now setting myself on a course from which there was no going back. This exodus would reverberate forever. Had I known I might've rushed back inside and hid under my bed.

Instead, I strolled leisurely along the wide boulevards of the ancient capital, illuminated by the new street lamps installed by the Soviets. I passed posters advertising The Young Guard, and my chest swelled like a peacock imagining the same iron obelisks in the Holy Land graced with news of my latest triumph. I pondered if they'd use my new professional name or prefer something more authentically Hebraic? As I was going over these possibilities in my mind, and as the sun began to spread its light over the city I came to the train station. There were over a hundred kids there, and every one had a backpack, anticipating a fun day in the country. I stuck out with my little piece of luggage, and a few of the kids poked fun at me. "Lose your backpack?" "Oh, the big shot actor is too good for a plain backpack!" I searched out Judah who immediately took me aside.

"You didn't tell anyone, did you?" he asked.

"No. Just like you said."

"Freddy, today a new life begins for you. A real life. Your true destiny."

I nodded dumbly in response. I was not as clever in conversation as I was when reciting dramatic dialogue written for me. Anyway, I didn't have much more opportunity to interact with Judah. He had little time to pay any special attention to me as he was busy getting us all on the train for the first leg of our trip. He did take the time to stow away my valise. He didn't want to make anyone especially curious before it was time to divulge the truth of their journey. There was no special mood of jitters, because only Judah, I and the other counselors knew where we were going. On the train the counselors led us in Hungarian folksongs, avoiding the Hebrew ones, so as not to attract undue attention to a group on a clandestine mission. The boisterous chorus of clueless pioneers intensified my pangs of remorse, because it called into sharp relief the differences between their consciousnesses, out for a day in the country, and mine, cutting the apron strings for good and going off to a foreign land. When we got to our destination the kids poured off the train with their usual eagerness to play in the woods. What they didn't realize was that they wouldn't see that train again as was the custom in returning. We were deliberately walking north toward Bratislava, Czechoslovakia.

The forests in Hungary, like most in Europe, are verdant and beautiful. But just as lush is the dense population of the mighty continent, meaning few sectors of nature have gone unexplored. So, the counselors had to take special care to guide us along the least frequented paths. Everyone though was gleeful, unaware of their true agenda. I was uncomfortable, not just for knowing what was up, but for having to schlep my unwieldy suitcase. We got to a campsite, and the counselors instructed us to take out the picnic lunches that our parents always packed for us. As I had been secretive about my field trip I didn't bring the usual picnic lunch from home, so Judah gave me a sandwich. At that moment I tried to speak with him, but he was even busier there than back at the train station, and after a hurried lunch we resumed our trek northward. Besides being ignorant about Israel most of the kids were also naïve about the political situation at that time. The elation of the Soviet victory over the Nazis had slowly given way to the tensions of the cold war, and crossing borders, especially in Eastern Europe, had become anything but routine. Of all the freedoms taken from us, the most restrictive was having our frontiers closed. Hungary was, as most Iron Curtain countries were, like one giant jail, and nobody, regardless of religion or social class, could leave without maneuvering through a labyrinth of red tape. Of course, being a Jew would ultimately cause complications. The Reds were hard core atheists, so anyone with an avowed religious affiliation was considered subversive. For the time being though, due in large part to the recent Nazi genocide, the Soviets weren't cracking down. But enjoying the freedom to discuss *Aliyah* was one thing, while putting it into practice was something that required stealth and subterfuge. For us it was more than just a matter of Zionist fervor. It meant getting past the Iron Curtain, a bona fide covert activity. The cold hard truth was that we'd have to be smuggled across the border. A battalion of kids would have to disappear from Hungary and materialize in Czechoslovakia. Unaware of this our children's crusade trudged on.

A few of the kids became concerned that we had not turned back even though the sun was already low in the sky. Others wanted to know where the tents were, as it was by now obvious that this was no afternoon picnic.

"Don't worry young *chaverim*; we're having a special adventure today."

This seemed to encourage some of the kids, while making others nervous. And here's where part of the tactic of the forced Aliyah kicked in. Peer pressure. Any kids resistant to the big adventure were branded whiners and practically traitors to our esprit d' corps.

"Come on young pioneers, we didn't get our own country by lollygagging!"

When the sun started to set some kids got serious and demanded to know when we were turning back. It was finally time for Judah to make the big announcement.

"Okay kids, listen up. You know how we always talk about Aliyah, returning to Israel, our homeland?"

At this there was the usual supportive cheering.

"And I know it's something that, deep in your hearts, you all really want to do."

More cheering.

"Well, now we're really going to Israel. This is Aliyah!"

Confusion replaced enthusiasm, and most of the kids stood silent, waiting for clarification.

"What do you mean, now? You mean we're actually going to Israel right now?"

"Yes," replied Judah. Isn't it glorious?"

Many of the kids were sill incredulous.

"Today? Tonight? Now?"

Now Judah had to deliver the speech of his lifetime and convince a hundred and forty kids to leave their families and go to a strange and foreign land.

"Listen chaverim, Israel is our destiny. Not Europe. This place will never be our home! The whole history of Jews in Europe is the same. Some king invites us. *Come on Jews, you can live here!* Twenty years go by, and a new king stages pogroms, kicks us out, and robs us of everything in the bargain. It's like that all over. Even in America, Jews can't go anywhere they like, and the big important schools have quotas. Anyway, what did wonderful America do for us when Hitler was locking us up? Did the Statue of Liberty open her arms to us? No! They turned their backs on us too! The whole world turned a blind eye. Wake up! When the chips are down, nobody cares about the Jews but Jews. And now we have our own country, Eretz Israel. There are cities and farms and ports and hospitals and schools. We don't have to fit in, and we're not banned from anything. The leaders are Jewish, and the citizens too. And we have our own army to protect us. We speak Hebrew, our traditional language, and we are one hundred percent free. No one will ever beat you again or take your mother away. We've waited two thousand years for this, and it was paid for with the blood of six million Jewish martyrs. Tomorrow we'll be outcastes here. But in Israel we'll never be outcasts again! Israel is our home, our destiny!"

After a few moments of reflective silence some of the bigger kids broke into a cheer.

"Yeah! Aliyah! Israel today!"

The chant of Aliyah got stronger and louder, and finally peer pressure took over completely, and any dissenting voice was scared of showing its timid vibration. But Judah had to protect himself from possible future retribution, so he made another well rehearsed speech.

"My fellow pioneers, Aliyah must be voluntary. So, if there are any among you who want to turn back, now is the time to speak up. We have a truck waiting to take you back."

Shomer Hatzair did indeed have a truck waiting to take back any of the kids who wanted to. But Judah gave such a stirring speech only one girl spoke up.

"My mother is deathly ill in the hospital, and I'm all she's got. If I go she'll be utterly alone. I absolutely have to go back!"

As for the rest of us that moment was like that the moment in a wedding when they ask if anyone has any reason why this union is not such a good idea, and to speak now or forever hold your peace. Rarely do people speak up at weddings, even if they want to. Nobody has the nerve to open his mouth due to peer pressure. It just seeps into your mind and grabs hold of your free will. Probably a lot of future divorcees take the plunge out of pure peer pressure. Maybe it worked at the Alamo too. And that same mob mentality now held us all under its hypnotic sway. No one dared to be first to flinch. I thought about my mother and grandma and how much they counted on my salary from the theater. I thought about my poor baby sister, and how much she needed me. I was bursting to call out and join that girl, but peer pressure sat on my chest and I dared not be the only boy to call it quits. A girl quitting was one thing, but a boy would be labeled a sissy forever if he turned back now. So I kept my mouth shut. As it turned out though, out of our whole group of one hundred and forty pioneering zealots, only that girl turned back at that stage. The truth is that girl probably had more courage in refusing to go than the rest of us had in going. And once she went back we were all considered to be committed. Any further talk of returning was limited to its definition as it pertained to Aliyah. Then I shared the truth about my suitcase with the other kids, and they were impressed that I had been privy to the whole plan but had kept my mouth shut about it. As we were all now of one mind, Judah spoke more openly with us, sharing plans, and involving us in its implementation.

"*Chaverim*, we have limited funds to get us to our homeland, and we shouldn't risk it all in one parcel. So, we're going to divide it among us all. That way, if one of us has our money confiscated by a Soviet official, or one of us gets robbed, then the rest will still be intact."

This seemed to make perfect sense, and even sounded shrewd. Furthermore, it involved us to a more intimate degree in the great adventure. We were flattered that we were considered true partners, and proud to be considered equals with the adults, entrusted with the precious financial backing of our shared journey and common destiny, and we resumed our trek northward with a renewed spirit of mutual determination.

The kids knew for sure that they had made the right choice for high adventure when a mysterious man appeared out of nowhere who turned out to be a professional smuggler hired to guide us across the border at night, far from the vigilance of Soviet border authorities. There was some haggling between him and Judah, with some heated rhetoric. Judah asked us to return the funds that had been entrusted into our safekeeping, and he paid it all to the guide. But this did not satisfy this *momzer*, and the counselors had to take off their watches and hand them over. This act spoke volumes about their commitment, and witnessing it

Echoes Of My Footsteps

impressed us no end. But characterizing our stealthy border crossing as a great adventure was hardly accurate. We had survived the war, either in a ghetto, in hiding, or in a concentration camp, so this hike through the forest was literally a walk in the woods for the likes of us.

When night overtook us we were still marching, sand the counselors were busy keeping us enthused. They were like Israeli cheerleaders and they had to constantly excite us with images of the Holy Land, freedom, sunshine and orange orchards. They had to do this if for no other reason than to beguile us from our fatigue and hunger.

"Come on pioneers. Be of stout heart! We're going through the woods, across the river, and over the sea to Eretz Israel, our homeland. What's this little hike when we've been wandering in the wilderness for two thousand years? Every step you take delivers you further from the hands of tyrants. We're leaving the land of *goyim*, strangers, for the land of our *landtsmen*. March on, my darling pioneers. March on!"

Judah and the other counselors were really only about eighteen, but we looked up to them as adults. They were little more than children themselves, and who knows what they had lived through during the war. Surely they must have worked like slaves for the Gestapo, and witnessed such barbarity as I can hardly imagine. Their resolve and dedication to Israel were forged in Auschwitz, Dacchau, Treblinka and Bergen-Belsen. Like many of their generation they had lost religious faith and replaced it with nationalistic zeal, more often than not tainted with old fashioned socialist doctrine. But they believed absolutely in what they were doing, and were willing to make any sacrifice for that cause.

After some hours we came to the river. This was the border between Hungary and Czechoslovakia, and our stealthy guide assured us that he had selected this part of the river to cross because it was so shallow. It was a bit nippy to get wet, but Judah steeled our nerves with one of his impassioned Aliyah speeches, and we took the plunge. Many of us could barely keep our heads above this supposedly shallow water, and the counselors had their hands full shuttling us across. I had a particularly tough time due to my valise. Thanks to their backpacks the other kids had their hands free to battle the current, while I had to hoist a suitcase over my head with both hands. Judah helped me, but it was tense going, and I thought I wasn't going to make it more than once. On the other side some Czechs were waiting with towels and food. These men had probably been earning their living doing this since the Soviets started imposing their closed border policies. Clearly, the whole trip had been well planned months in advance. Only the river crossing proved risky, but that was based on misinformation from our rascal guide. Crossing that river was like crossing the Rubicon. There really was no going back now.

It was dawn when we left the river and continued on through the forest. Shortly we came to a small fleet of trucks which had been arranged by our resourceful counselors. They were relics from the war, now pressed into peaceful service. They might once have been used to transport German troops, or in an even more macabre irony, they might also have been the very trucks used to transport our relatives to their deaths. They were open but with canvas tops to shield us from prying eyes. The whole operation was clandestine, and the less we were visible the better. They furtively drove us to a suburb of Bratislava where Judah had rented several houses. Here we rested for several days and got organized for the rest of our journey. They gave us a grand meal which included some of the best bread I ever had in my life. It was fresh, soft and delicious. After eating our fill we bathed and went to sleep on clean beds.

We spent about five days there, relaxing, eating, playing, and being interviewed by a Rabbi to make sure we were all really Jewish. So many kids were hid during the war anything was possible. And the last thing this forced Aliyah wanted was to kidnap a gentile kid. Such a thing would have destroyed Israel before it had a chance to get going. A Rabbi was there to question us and discern if we were who we said we were, and if we were really of Jewish parentage. When he came to me he discovered I had no Hebrew name, so he suspected that I might not be Jewish. To make sure he asked me to drop my pants. This brought back the memories of my Nyilas beating and I refused. It was really quite traumatic. Judah came over and assured the Rabbi that I was indeed a Jew. Seeing my distress he likewise assured me that nobody would bother me about such nonsense again. After the interrogation the Rabbi wanted to give Hebrew names to those of us who lacked them. Actually, my pious grandparents used to call me by a Yiddish name, but I couldn't remember it. So Judah handed out names with a clever game.

"Do we have a moishe here?"

A kid raised his hand.

"Do we have a David here?"

Several kids raised their hands.

"Do we have a Zev here?"

Nobody raised his hand.

"Freddy, you're now Zev."

I had already changed my name so many times it didn't matter to me. So I was now Zev Gabor, though not a syllable of these names was on my birth certificate. Besides, I thought I'd still use Ivan once the first Israeli theatrical production was under way. After all, I was only famous with that name.

The day after our renaming we were off to Vienna, the next leg of our Aliyah. The Soviets controlled those borders as well, and our crossing into Austria was another secret passage through the forest. Subsequently, the Iron Curtain was drawn tighter, making such flights impossible. As it was we had run-ins with the police, but the counselors were always able to calm the situation. Considering that none of us had proper documents it was quite a feat.

Once we rested in Vienna we were taken to a hospital for examinations to determine if we were all basically sound and fit enough for a short boat ride to the Holy Land. It was at that time that I was diagnosed as suffering from stress. Though I'd never heard my condition described in clinical terms I was almost glad to learn that modern science recognized it, and I wasn't as odd as I secretly presumed myself to be. Then we were taken to a building that had formerly been the Rothschild hospital, but was now being used as a processing center for refugees. There I had the most surreal coincidence of running into Bobbi, the daughter of Nandorbaci, the uncle who worked with Raoul Wallenberg back in Budapest. She was there doing the paper work to go to America and she invited me along.

"We're going to America. Come with us!"

"I can't! I'm off to Israel to be a pioneer!"

"Does your mother know?"

Apparently they had some knowledge of the activities of Shomer Hatzair and thought it wise to inquire. Finding out the truth she took me to an office where there was a telephone and made me call home. Of course, by now mother and grandma had gone out of their minds with worry. When I didn't turn up after the alleged picnic they went looking for me at the theater, but they were equally in the dark. Of course, my understudy was utterly unconcerned, and he became the next big star in Budapest. Anyway, it was daytime, so I called my mom's office.

"Rapid advertising."

"Hello mom, I'm okay."

"Oh, thank God. Where are you?"

"I'm in Vienna."

"What in God's name are you doing there?"

"Mom, I'm on my way to the State of Israel. I'm a pioneer."

Her scream was so loud and piercing, and close to the telephone mouthpiece, it practically shattered my ear drum. Clearly, she was not quite as proud of me as I thought she would be. I tried to sound like Judah, talking about our future in Israel, but I didn't have that flair. My memorized words were no match for the red hot fire of her tirade.

"How can you leave us? Have you no feeling for your poor mother, for your family? Israel doesn't need you. We do! You get on the next train back to Hungary. Mr. Major came over, looking for you. He says you're fired if you don't show up by tomorrow night. Freddy, who put this *mishagos* into your head? You come back at once. Do you hear me? At once!"

I tried a few more feeble words, but I was not being the success I had been on stage.

"You've got some *chutzpah* young man, leaving me like that! Listen to me well. If you don't come back at once......."

There was a pause, and I thought the line might have gone dead. Then I heard her voice again.

"Freddy, if you don't come back at once I'll never forgive you. Are you listening? Get yourself onto a train and come home. Return now or I'll never forgive you. Do you hear me, Freddy? Never! Ne..."

As was typical of postwar European technology the phone line went dead in mid-word with "Never" ringing in my ears.

Guilt washed over me like an emotional tsunami. How could I abandon three generations of women, especially after all we had been through together? My mom and grandma saved my life a hundred times. What an ingrate I was! I ran to Judah to demand to go back.

"Zev, they all say that. Next thing you know they join you. Don't you see? You're breaking a cycle. Every generation we European Jews get less and less Jewish. We gotta fit in. Let's cut and dye our hair. Let's dress like goyim. Let's change our names and get nose jobs. And you know what? None of that helps. Most of the victims in the camps looked like typical Poles. Truth is, you can even convert to Catholicism if you want, but when they find out you were a Jew -*were* a Jew!- they still treat you like dirt! No, Zev. Israel's the answer. You'll see. Once you're there your mother will want to join you. Be strong. That's something we Jews are good at."

I was certain I heard Hatikvah in the background that time. Stocking the young state with young people was obviously a major endeavor for the Zionists, and they were determined to do so by any means possible. And, even if the other kids didn't think about it at that moment there were many anguished parents left behind in Budapest. We were all of one culture, and our reactions to stress usually tended to express itself with the same behavior. If my family was upset theirs were too. Apartments all over my neighborhood resounded with cries and wails for their missing darlings. And had this honest parental emotion penetrated our selfish egotistical armor we would have been destroyed by remorse. But the bulwarks against such an assault were strongly braced by distance and Shomer Hatzair brand guilt trips and peer pressure that kept us in line all the way to Bari, on the Adriatic coast of Italy, the threshold of the last leg of our journey to the Promised Land. We enjoyed the warm climate, played soccer, and became enamored of Italian culture. Everywhere you looked was another statue or fountain, and the buildings were ancient and ornate. Budapest is a remarkably cultural capital, and I was proud to be from such a beautiful city, but sunny Italy was far more captivating. I ate plenty of pasta, and expanded my culinary horizons experimenting with new and exotic foods. But though I loved many things one thing in particular truly disgusted me. I saw some fishermen eating oysters and I asked them what it was. They laughed and gave me one drenched in lemon juice. I eagerly slid it out of the half shell into my gluttonous mouth, as they demonstrated, but almost gagged, making them laugh all the harder. Fonder in my memory is my first ever orange. And when they told me that they grew like weeds in Israel I became eager to get on the boat. Drinking orange juice every morning before rehearsals sounded like a great life to me.

The idle mind of the Aliyah child is the devil's playground, so the counselors got me to organize a production of the Young Guard with some of the other kids. We set up a stage in the open air and I taught the parts to our volunteer actors. This pepped up my morale, and I again felt confident in my decision to press on to Israel where my greatest success surely awaited me. When I saw the words Holy Land I looked at the first part and it reminded me of Hollywood. For me Israel and stardom were two words intrinsically entwined. I couldn't wait to set sail for my next venue of artistic triumph. Enigmatic sages warn us to be careful what we wish for, and my being anxious to get to sea proved to be a prime argument in favor of that mysterious maxim.

It was hardly the glamorous cruise I had envisioned. Our little vessel, the Galilee, constantly battled a stubborn Mediterranean current, and I spent half the voyage, leaning over the rail. After a couple of nauseating days I finally got my sea legs and was able to appreciate how picturesque it was to sleep on deck out under the stars. This particular romantic detail was due solely to the unaffordable cost of the cabins. But the beauty of the heavens at least served to distract me from my anxiety over leaving home. And after four days of bobbing up and down I finally beheld the ancient hills of Carmel beyond the port of Haifa. It looked primitive, but in a friendly way, like the pictures in my childhood story books in Baia-Mare. I had been told so much about Israel that my heart was now racing to finally be here. I couldn't wait to explore its countryside and every holy town. Also, being on the verge of so much attention actually gave me a case of the jitters. Would there be a big reception for me? Interviews? And when would we begin our first big Israeli production? Every second that passed the Galilee was closing the distance between the high seas and the high water mark of my career, stardom in Israel.

It was around ten in the morning, and we were about to make port in the Holy Land of Eretz Israel. I would dwell in King Solomon's ancient homeland and walk the same hallowed ground where Abraham and Jacob trod. I'd sit in the shade of an olive tree where David played his lyre. The land of the Bible was now home, and my troubles were about to begin.

Chapter XIII

Miami 7

I lay on the gurney in that emergency room in Miami Beach with my eyes tightly shut. Every time I opened them I took off on a swirling merry-go-round, both sickening and frightening. Everything flew by me, but I couldn't get a firm grip on anything. I saw with the eyes of a ten year old Hungarian, then through the glare of the Israeli sun, then the theater, Debrecen, Buenos Aires, the Suez, the river. I couldn't focus on any one thing. But I called out one name and one name alone, Rebequita.

We began our relationship as friends, not as lovers, and that made all the difference in the world. Though I might have first noticed her for her lovely eyes I soon saw beyond them into her lovely soul. Blinding passion did not forge our union, but rather concern for each other as individuals. Looking in the rear view mirror at the events leading up to that fateful traffic light is clearly a glorious life lesson. To dispel this enigma I will reveal the full truth of how I came to be cruising through Miami Beach in my Cadillac in such a romantic mood so many tropical moonlit nights ago. I just thought it best to open my life to you before exposing such a lusty episode as I will now relate, lest you prematurely judge me.

One week before that night of sweet destiny I was hard at work in my office, preparing for the American debut of my line of teen apparel. Although I was already savoring the sweetness of early commercial success in my newly adopted country I was planning on insuring its prolonged growth by hiring another designer. And as my English was practically nonexistent at that time I was hoping to find someone not only talented but fluent in that language that I was finding so hard to learn. The truth is I totally depended on my bilingual secretary, Connie, as a buffer between me and the outside world. None of the languages I spoke could help me in Miami except for the one I had learned in Argentina, where I most recently had came from. In that respect I was like any other immigrant from South America, hiding behind the security blanket of the Castilian tongue. Miami is such a linguistic cocoon for Spanish speakers we tend to venture outside of it only when all other verbal alternatives fail. Then sultry Loretta walked in and burst that bubble.

She was responding to our ad for a designer, and she made an amazing first impression. She was about thirty and was possessed of all the attributes of a seasoned professional. She was impeccably dressed, and carried with her the aura of experience.

I rose from my desk, grinned, and then exhausted a hefty percentage of my English vocabulary on her.

"Hello. Niz to mit you. I yam Ivan."

Whether she found my accent charming, or was merely being tactful with a potential employer, she flashed a smile that was at once friendly and sexy, and then forged ahead.

"I saw your ad in the Herald for a designer, and I would love to show you my portfolio. I think you'll find that we could be a good fit."

For all I know she could have been talking about the space program, such was my mastery of English at the time. But more than that, her demeanor was charged with that brand of female confidence that I associated with women in the movies. She was the first example of a cinematic kind of feminine mystique that I had personally confronted since immigrating to America, and it totally captivated me. It was as if someone had stepped off of the silver screen and into my office. Foreigners think that all Americans are like Gary Cooper and Marilyn Monroe, so it's always a little disappointing to move here and discover that there are no cattle drives down Main Street, or that broadly smiling buxom blonds do not exclusively populate the landscape. So now my expectations were finally met by this zaftig beauty whose communication skills were enhanced by her striking body language. Connie coughed a slight wake up call, and I had to drag myself down to Earth and back to business.

Besides being impressed by her physique her resume told me that she was just what we were looking for. Her drawings were as beautiful rendered as her make-up, and her designs looked like the very thing that would help our company compete in the American market place. I told her that she might be right for us and then asked the big question, how much she was looking to make? Her answer did not require translation. After all, when you do business in a foreign country practically the first vocabulary you acquire is how to count. And though I couldn't pronounce it as well as she did I understood quite clearly that she was asking for one hundred thousand dollars a year to be our new designer. And now I had to make her understand just as clearly that we simply couldn't afford her. In any language, that kind of money was out of the question, regardless of how much she resembled a movie star.

Though I would have to tell her no I didn't want to be harsh about it, and detoured into personal territory with her. Just because my company's budget made a business relationship with her impossible I saw no reason to stifle other categories of union. She was as shapely as any woman had a right to be, with a mane of luxuriant hair framing an oval face with pouting red lips, high cheek bones, and heavily lidded blue eyes. Passion replaced thoughts of commerce, and her inviting smile aroused in me images I'd blush to describe. Being aroused did not improve my English however, so I relied on the other present female to translate our flirtation. I told her I was Hungarian and not in the states long. While not on the highest level of subtly or sophistication this mundane datum seemed sufficient to seduce her onto the personal plateau as well.

"I just love Hungarian food! You know I'm quite a cook in my own right."

I praised her for her adventurous culinary expertise, and thanked her for coming in. Connie rolled her eyes heavenward and exited. Loretta left too, but her perfume was a calling card that stayed in the office the rest of the afternoon. And though I wouldn't allow lust to persuade me to go over my budget I couldn't help but think of her at least as long as her costly French scent hung in the air. As it happened that sensuous cloud would very soon engulf me again, because the very next day Loretta called to invite me to her place for a home cooked meal. As I had the resolve to make business decisions on an objective basis I had no fear about dining with this fetching creature. On the contrary, she was the most exotic woman I had thus far met in the land of the free, and as I was free as well, besides being white and twenty one, I eagerly accepted.

The following day happened to be Friday, and though I did not follow in the tradition of my old world grandparents by observing this evening, I certainly hoped it would be a *gut shabbos* of a different sort. It hadn't been overly long since last sharing the pleasures of the flesh with a woman, but enough time had lapsed to make me as enthusiastic as any red blooded male, whether she served me a hot meal or not. So, I rushed home, scrubbed up, and dressed myself in the style of the day, a flashy leisure suit. Ready for combat I jumped into the bucket leather seat of my gleaming white Caddy chariot and zoomed off to my date with the American bombshell.

She lived in Brickell, which is an exclusive enclave of high end condominium towers on Biscayne Bay, nestled between the banking center of downtown and bohemian Coconut Grove. Her address told me that she was probably accustomed to earning the six figures she asked for, and if that honesty carried over into her coquettish smile and batting eyes I was sure to enjoy my meal. To add to the romance of the evening I stopped off for some flowers and wine.

When she opened the door my expectations were met to an overwhelming degree. She wore a dress, or at least some small percentage of one, that exposed a critically high percentage of that part of her anatomy that could have easily fed quadruplets. It was all I could do to drag my eyes upwards when I said hello. I managed a passable, "For you," as I handed her the flowers, then went back to leering at her ample bosom. As if that wasn't enticing enough, when she turned around she displayed her completely exposed back with a bare hint of another kind of cleavage all together. She made some verbal sounds that I took to mean that she had to check on things in the kitchen, or maybe look for a vase for the flowers, or maybe something to do with the space program. Whatever it was it didn't seem essential to the agenda at hand. As she briefly disappeared, leaving me with nothing to ogle, I took in her apartment. It was expensively decorated in elegant taste, and candles and incense created an exotic atmosphere. Of course, as a typical man,

I had been in the mood since three o'clock that afternoon. Actually, at that time in my life, not being in the mood was a rarity.

Almost as soon as she departed she returned, allowing me to compare the unique aspects of both her coming and going. She carried a menu which she proudly presented to me, with more than a hint of suggestion in her gaze. I found this quite impressive, and it actually took my attention off her body for a moment. She'd hand painted it and it featured a drawing of her in an outfit that made her present attire look like deep sea diving gear. It was one of those frilly French maid uniforms, and she was bending over with her totally naked *tuchis* protruding at a pleasingly generous angle. On her bare butt was a tattoo of half of a bright red heart. Ironically, my English was too crude to appreciate her beautifully handwritten bill of fare. It listed some kind of meat, a vegetable, wine, and the last item was, "Me." She didn't realize it at the time, but I actually couldn't read her titillating efforts. But the evening looked so promising I didn't need any verbal instructions to understand. None of it was any too subtle.

She offered me champagne which I gladly accepted. Then she served me the meal which I felt obliged to eat, at least in order to fortify myself for what I hoped would soon be *gut shabbos*. Actually she was a pretty good cook. Of course, she could have served me day old pizza and it wouldn't have mattered. I was three steps ahead.

As it turned out she was already four steps ahead. We drank every drop of that champagne then enjoyed some cognac on her sofa. She put on some romantic music and invited me to dance. In a moment I had her in my arms and as we moved to the rhythm we locked lips deeper than mouth to mouth resuscitation. Next thing I know we were in her bedroom behaving as if the future of our species depended solely on our behavior. And during the exploration of some of her more interesting destinations I discovered a unique treasure, the other half of the heart that was on her artistic menu. It was stuck to her nicely rounded *tuchis*, and she peeled it off and handed it to me, adding with a laugh, "Here's a souvenir."

Without bothering to speculate on what she used to paste it there we continued testing each other's stamina. And when Saturday night rolled around we called it a day, and a night, and another day. From sundown to sundown if had indeed been a very *gut shabbos* for me. I felt *muy macho*, having as my conquest an American woman who fulfilled all my erotic fantasies. Twenty-four hours in the arms of such a femme fatal left me with a self satisfaction bordering on hubris. Of course, at that moment I didn't see that it was she who had me, and not vice versa. But ignorance is bliss, and I, the king of my illusory world, was sailing through the sultry subtropical night in my deluxe status symbol, feeling like cock of the walk. America was paradise! Better than Hungary, Israel and Argentina rolled into one. My horizons were unlimited. And here at this traffic light on the corner of 79th Street and Harding is yet another beautiful American woman, smiling sweetly at me! *In my life I love you more*! But where is that sweet smile now? *Let me see you smile again!* Again, I was left alone. *Oh, how I've been alone!* And when loved ones depart from my life it's always bad, because it's always for good.

Chapter XIV

On The Streets Of Haifa

We all gathered on the deck of the Galilee and watched Israel draw nearer. Details became clearer and its sights and sounds and smells filled our senses. We could see Arabs in traditional dress, carts drawn by donkeys, and swarthy dock workers running all over. This was a whole new world for European kids, and most of us were jumping up and down with excitement. I, on the other hand, was filled with dread. I had been talked into this in a moment of weakness and regretted even being here. The more zealous kids were overcome by emotion and were crying. Judah Winter and the counselors were waving toward the shore, and their greetings were returned. Seeing the waving officials on the shore I assumed that my welcoming committee got its cue and was now getting ready to receive me. Would there be flowers for me? Would they be from just the newspapers, or was radio going to interview me as well? I was a little apprehensive over the possibility that the press might have brought photographers, because I was a mess. The accommodations on our Aliyah had been quite Spartan, and my clothes and body were not at their cleanest. I hadn't shampooed my hair since the day before my last performance, and my clothes were soiled and wrinkled. I couldn't wait to soak in a hot tub and relax in whatever plush hotel suite they had reserved for me. Contemplating all this made me excited to get to shore. To add to the excitement I could hear singing. Above the industrial clamor of the activity on the dock resounded a choir of children singing a welcome. It was a song we ourselves sang at Shomer Hatzair meetings and field trips, *Avenu Sholem Alechem. We will bring peace to you.* They sang it boisterously, and it leant real emotion to our arrival. My previous regret and misapprehension was replaced with the excitement of another opening night. Soon though I realized it wasn't meant specifically for me, but for all the hardy Hungarian pioneers on Aliyah. It was my first disappointment of many to come.

They tied the Galilee up to the pier, but it stubbornly continued to bob. I grabbed my little briefcase and negotiated the unstable plank to solid land. *Avenu Sholem Alechem* was now loud in our ears. I was all smiles for the cameras and I waved enthusiastically to my fans. But I was pushed along by the hardy pioneers, and shuffled off to one side. I was disoriented and confused, because I couldn't find the gentlemen of the press. And no doubt they were just as frustrated at not being able to locate me in the press of bodies. I looked every which way, but I couldn't see any reporters or cameraman. There was nobody bearing bouquets of flowers. No giggling adolescents approached me with open autograph books. My broad smile faded as I came to the harsh realization that there was no reception for me at all. There were no reporters to hang on my every word. No orchestra heralded my arrival. And not a single camera snapped my likeness for the afternoon edition. Worse, I was being jostled by the crowds and totally ignored. Judah Winter was nowhere in sight either, and I couldn't find any of the counselors. The whole atmosphere was incomprehensible, and I retreated back into the thick of pioneers who were a mix of emotions as well. Some were jubilant while others sobbed over having set foot in the Holy Land. Others, like me, were confused and uncomfortable.

Some tanned strangers were herding us onto a caravan of old buses, and I calmly assumed that I would meet the press once we got to our destination. By now the jolly children's chorus had subsided, replaced by an incessant cacophony of Hebrew and Arabic shouting on the dock. We were practically dragged onto the buses, and they took off as soon as we were in our seats. I looked around for Judah, but he wasn't on our bus. I supposed he was on one of the others, and I'd see him once we got to wherever it was that we were going. Then he'd straighten things out once and for all. For now I couldn't even think about any of that. I was distracted by our speeding through narrow streets, practically rubbing up against the ancient mud hovels. This was nothing like Europe. To me all these ancient buildings looked like the Stone Age. As we careened around each curve in the road I held on for dear life and hoped we'd get to the theater soon. Nobody knew me, and nobody waved. How was this possible? Didn't they realize that the biggest child actor in Hungary was in their midst? This was not what I expected at all. But I shrugged and thought it'd all get sorted out at the end of this wild ride.

The bus was no less rocky than the Galilee, and we were going through country that reminded me a little of Italy, but was ten times as arid. Europe was green everywhere, but this place was like a different planet. It was all sand and dust. How could they grow oranges or anything else here? It was hard to tell which was worse, my disillusionment or depression. I couldn't wait to tell the authorities about their mistake. With this resolve in my heart we arrived at some place called Kiriat Shmuel.

The buses slid to stop, and they announced that this was the orientation center. As far as I could see it was just a mass of tents in

Echoes Of My Footsteps

the sand. We were still on the coast and you couldn't walk three feet without stepping on ten stones. There were some old houses like the ones we had seen on the way, and some of the land was furrowed like it had been planted with something. Strange languages buzzed in my ears as we were taken off the buses and led to those tents. Some kids were greeted by people they knew, and their welcoming hugs and kisses made the rest of us feel glum.

Rather than an orientation center they should have called Kiriat Shmuel an alienation center. The strangeness was intimidating, and made me feel as uncomfortable as I ever had in my life. Even though I had just crossed Europe and the Mediterranean I had done so in the company of kids of my own culture. The strangest thing I had to contend with on the whole trip was Italian food. Now, I was surrounded by an astounding variety of kids who were all from somewhere else and spoke something else. There were Asians with funny eyes like I had only seen in books, blonds like I had briefly seen in northern Italy, and I laid my eyes on my first African. In one sense Israel was just as Judah Winter described, a melting pot, filled with people from all over. There were Moroccans, Yemenis, Syrians and Siberians, and every single one of them seemed happier than me. Young pioneers had stood on the deck of the Galilee, weeping over their first sight of Eretz Israel, but I was crying now for a totally different reason. Nothing was as I was led to believe. Or perhaps I had expected too much. Close to hysteria my body could barely cooperate with my mind. My senses were out of control and I was paralyzed with stress. Searching for Judah Winter produced no relief, because he was nowhere to be found. I felt truly alone. It was as if I had been plucked up by an unseen mystical force and dropped down into a bizarre nightmarish landscape. It was the carnival of the macabre! Allowing Hungarians as mankind's standard, it seemed as if the human race didn't even belong here! The atmosphere so overwhelmed me I couldn't breathe. My chest was heaving and my air came in short gasps. I was light headed and saw distorted clown faces with ghoulish smiles everywhere, and an invisible circus band played off key. My mind was on a spinning carousel and hallucinations ambushed my consciousness. The cacophony of foreign voices was a jumble of indistinct noise. I was reduced to a floundering life form of some lower species, incapable of cognitive thought or action. And the knot in my gut was so big and tight I felt like I was made of solid lead. How did I end up here? This can't be real. That's it! It's a dream! Surely I'll wake up any second. I'm supposed to be in Hungary, sitting on Hilda Gobi's lap, joking about the matinee. My grandmother has my lunch waiting for me. I must go! Someone help me pleeeease! Listen to me! I'm Ivan Gaboooor!

I had shut my eyes tight to block out the unwanted scene, and when I finally opened them I found myself staring into the face of some kid who was looking at me with an expression of worried concern. He asked something in a language I didn't understand, but his calm tone momentarily pacified me. He gestured with a plate of food in his hand, and then shrugged and walked away. I looked back to where he had indicated and saw that they were serving food in a line. The only normal thing I felt at that moment was hunger so I got in line, still desperately scanning the horizon for Judah Winter.

My first Israeli meal was soup with some kind of beans I had never seen before, and some thin, floppy bread. Even though I had starved in the war, and was always grateful for any edible scrap, I had since become spoiled, and now picked at my ethnic platter with indifference. And as soon as it was over I found someone who looked authoritative and tried to set things right. This man was so unlike the people back home he seemed unreal. He was shorter, had a tan, and wore an open collar shirt with his sleeves rolled up. Everybody here was tan and had their sleeves rolled up. They even rolled up the legs of their short pants which were worn by both men and women. In Europe short pants defined a male as a child and long trousers as an adult, and no girls wore either. The radically different appearance of these people made me feel all the more alienated. I stopped one man and tried to explain my situation.

"Hi! I'm the well known child actor from Budapest, Ivan Gabor. I'm starring in the Young Guard. You've heard if it? Well, I was told that…"

He listened patiently, especially considering that he didn't understand a word I said, but stopped me short, holding up his hand as if to say, "Wait. I'll help you in a moment."

He went off, and soon returned with another man, who also had his sleeves rolled up. This guy spoke Hungarian, but made no fuss over our common bond. He just wanted me to get to the point, and remained passive upon hearing of my notoriety.

"Listen *boychic*, we got no use for actors here. We're building a country. That's what we're doing. This ain't Hollywood."

I was furious and I unloaded all my frustration on this poor guy.

"You guys cheated me! Judah Winter is nothing but a liar! I was supposed to be received here and taken to your national theater. But it's all lies! Nobody here knows who I am or cares. You're all a pack of liars! This is the worst cheating I've ever heard of! I demand that you take me back to Hungary at once!"

They just looked at me like I was crazy, shrugged their shoulders and left. I stood there with my mouth wide open, speechless and bewildered. All my dreams and illusions evaporated in the arid desert air. There was no theater. My acting career was over. It was all a lie. My body ambled along in a trance until it reached a solitary spot and plopped down on the ground. I could not have felt more isolated had I been flung onto an alien planet. There was nothing to do but weep.

And as my tears gushed my mind raced. I went from feelings of suicide to revenge, and slowly it dawned on me why this was happening. It was obvious, but I didn't want to face it. So, before swallowing that bitter pill I considered every other alternative. Aliyah recruiters were liars, Israel didn't have its priorities in order, or God was making a mistake in punishing me when he really meant to be socking it to someone else who happened to look a lot like me. Of course, there was no escaping the truth. This so-called betrayal, supposed deception, and faux fraud were all forms of true justice, proper punishment for abandoning my family. Every fast one pulled on me was well earned. I had forsaken my mother who had sacrificed herself endlessly for me, seeing me through encounters with the barbaric fascists, going without food to see that I was fed, and protecting me from certain death like a ferocious lioness. This woman supported, nurtured and sustained me through every travail, no matter how terrifying and intimidating. She was unconditional love and encouragement, and I deserted her. The love of her life, her husband, had died, leaving me as the man of the house, and I abandoned my post. I just up and split! Three generations of women put their hopes in me and I let them all down. My poor old grandma who had rubbed my feet, and scrounged the no-man's-land of war torn Budapest to find food for me, was now out of my life forever. My baby sister, counting on her big brother, was likewise left in the lurch, and must now grow up an only child. And my mother who would have given her blood for me was now more alone than ever! I quit on them all! No amount of punishment was sufficient. Whatever came my way I had coming. I had freedom and abused it, and ended up making the worst decision of my life. I utterly betrayed my family. How could I do such a thing?! How could I sink so low, be so selfish, turn out so rotten? My guilt and remorse were immeasurable, and panic overtook my consciousness. Furthermore it was clear to me that, as long as I remained here, regret and misery would haunt me. To impress upon me that reality my well deserved punishment was right at hand in the form of poverty, loneliness and rejection. No family, no friends, no money, nothing. This epoch of my life would torture me forever. The war was a horror, of course, with death around every corner. But I would've died in the bosom of my family. Here I could die like a rat, and nobody would know or care. I was totally and completely on my own. I couldn't catch a train or a trolley back home. Hitching a ride was out of the question. I left Europe, and I was stuck in another continent. I might as well have been on Mars. I no longer had a home, just this tent in the middle of nowhere.

Nowhere turned out to be my home for almost a week, during which time I was the most homesick kid in history. I cried from loneliness and despair, sometimes vomiting from the shock of isolation that now enveloped me.

Although I was still with my Hungarian Aliyah group most of them were beginning to act differently toward me. Some of them were homesick as well, but most accepted being there, and they were running around like normal kids, exploring and playing. They were even interested in meeting some of the strange new kids from other places. Instead of being horrified by the situation most of them were charmed by this incomprehensible conglomeration of foreign peoples, customs and languages. The only mixing I did with them was at meal time. At those times the hodgepodge of strange tongues made for an Aliyah Tower of Babel, and caused friction among many of the kids. There were shoving matches in the lines, and it just made me all the more depressed. The food itself was another source of antagonism. We all sat at these long tables, but couldn't stomach the same food. European kids liked the Ashkenazi dishes, while the others preferred the Sephardic. Finally we worked it out so that we simply traded with each other until we all got what we wanted. Even then I was forced to experiment with weird new delicacies. I recall my first olive. It made me want to throw up my very soul, and I was glad to trade my second one for a herring with a boy who was equally glad to barter. In retrospect, I have to admit that the food was abundant, and most of the other kids were probably as frustrated as me. However, I was totally unsympathetic to their cause, focused as I was on *numero uno*. That was the real cause of my problem; I thought only of myself. I was so busy feeling sorry for number one, and singing my sad aria *O Sole Mio*, I didn't have empathy for another living being. If I had I would've reflected on my family before gallivanting off to Israel. But it would be a long time before I really learned my lesson.

Odd cuisine and a lack of notoriety I could survive. My greatest trauma was home sickness. Until now I had been with my mother since birth, except for a week with my father in Debrecen and a few days camping with Shomer Hatzair. Even through the war I always had the security of that indomitable maternal presence. There were ghouls out there waiting to kill us and bombs falling from the sky. Death, cold and hunger were our constant companions, but I always had the aura of protection provided by Ilushka Gabor. She was life, and wherever she was it was home. We were nomads in Budapest, roaming from building to building, but as long as I was with my mother it was a constant level of comfort and familiarity. She was the commander in chief, quartermaster, negotiator, and personal body guard. As far as I was concerned she knew all. She was the sun of my solar system. As long as she was there, and she always was, I didn't have to make a decision or plan. This beautiful, intelligent and confident person was there to guide and protect my every waking moment. Until now. On the Aliyah I had temporarily projected the faith usually reserved for mother onto

Judah Winter. Now, even he was gone, and the void was unbearable, being an unnamed asteroid floating in the cold void of space.

I had it all and I blew it. I left the one person to whom I should have been true. I could have double-crossed anyone, but not the woman who had given me life and nurtured and protected me. I would've felt guilty abandoning someone under normal circumstances, but my mother had been my protection from the holocaust, the most threatening juggernaut of mayhem ever to crawl the Earth. She had not only done the expected of a female parent, but ran interference for me from World War Two. How did I repay her? By leaving her cold. And all because some guy I hardly knew sold me a bill of idealistic goods. It was his dream, not mine. My mother was right. It wasn't Israel that needed me, but her, and my grandma and sister. As fledgling as this place was there were plenty of other candidates for the pioneer position. I was the only man left in my family. The Nazis had seen to that. My mother had no other male relative upon whom she could rely. Her father died just prior to the invasion, and her husband right after. Uncles, nephews and cousins all perished in the camps. I was it, the leader of the clan, and I didn't realize it. How could I not relate to her and share her feelings? Anybody but a spoiled child, which is what I clearly and sadly was, would have seen the similarities between us. She was raised an only child, as was I up until just a few years ago, and we had both relished being the focus of familial attention and affection. Had I simply followed the Golden Rule, and treated her as I would have liked to have been treated myself, and as she surely would have treated me, I would not be in this dilemma. But I could not see beyond my own childish wants and needs, and ended up making the stupidest decision of my life. Sadder yet, I had yet to learn just how irretrievable that Rubicon crossing was.

Depression took control of my soul and I moped around like a delirious madman, unaware of the needs of my body, walking in a trance. I ceased bathing, and my appetite withered. Every day it got worse, but nobody seemed to take notice. Everyone else had their own agenda, leaving me really and truly on my own. My head was reeling from confusion and alienation.

After what I calculate must have been about a week a glimmer of hope appeared on my desperate horizon when they announced that we would spend the afternoon at Kibbutz Dalia, the communal farm that had been our true destination since leaving Budapest. Well, maybe this was what Judah Winter had been talking about all along. Perhaps I had prematurely panicked. Of course! I should have realized that a mere orientation center would not have all of the facility of a major kibbutz! Hadn't we seen those photos at our Shomer Hatzair meetings? These communes had everything! Surely, a functioning theater would be at this new place. Maybe there'd even be a group of theatrical students waiting for me to address them. Doubtless they'd have a drama club presenting plays like the one we did in Bari. Now it made sense. And from there we'd go to the National Theater. I was utterly deluded, but newly enlivened. And while in this good mood the adults with the rolled up sleeves invited us on a beach excursion. The weather was warm, and as most of Israel seemed to be beachfront property, why not take a dip? Encouraged that things would soon improve I playfully romped in the surf and posed for a photograph to capture the moment. I happen to run into some Hungarians on the beach and they were kind enough to snap me.

The following day another fleet of rocking and reeling buses brought us to the Kibbutz where we were enthusiastically greeted by more tanned people with their sleeves rolled up. Even though the place looked greener and more tranquil than Kiriat Shmuel it did nothing to instill any pioneering spirit in my soul, focused as I was on the theater project. They fed us and gave us a tour, explaining that we'd work in the fields half a day and study academics the other half, including intense classes in Hebrew, our new mother tongue. But nowhere on the grand tour was there a theater or drama club in sight. The young man who led the tour was going to be our counselor so I spoke to him.

"Excuse me, but Judah Winter told me that I'd be doing plays here in Israel. But where is the theater? Where are the other actors? I don't understand any of this!"

He stared at me with the same quizzical look I got back in Kiriat Shmuel.

"Chaver, I'm not sure I know who Judah Winter is, or what he told you. What I can tell you is that we're building a new country here. I'm afraid acting and playing dress up are not very important to us just now. We're building a nation! Come join us!"

He turned and walked away, leaving me with my mouth hanging open.

My depression was now so great it drove me to sneak off alone and weep. I prayed to wake up from this nightmare and find myself in my private bedroom in the chic exterior apartment at Csengery Utca, number fifty-one. What had I been thinking? What madness was this? I just wanted to go back. I wanted my momma.

On the bus ride back to Kiriat Shmuel my ears pricked up when I heard a couple of the other Shomer Hatzair boys complaining about kibbutz life. Apparently, I wasn't the only kid less than thrilled about Aliyah, and I enjoyed hearing their grumbling. Misery loves company, and I felt my angst was validated by these boys' protests. They vowed not to return to the kibbutz or even Kiriat Shmuel if they could help it. What's more they even had the chutzpah to declare it to some adults. I decided to join them, but only after one more stab at establishing the Ivan Gabor National Theater. Once back in Kiriat Shmuel I found an adult who spoke Hungarian and pled my case. After taking the full brunt of my industrial strength whining he gave me the same obtuse stare as everyone else.

"Boy, please get this *fakatka* acting idea out of your head. It's Eretz Israel, the land of Israel, not the theater of Israel. Now we got work to do. Stop making such a fuss!"

"But I didn't come here to work. That's just the point. I came here to act!"

He was clever and got rid of me by saying, "Don't worry. We'll discuss this later."

Discouraged at not being put in charge of the national theater immediately I went to my secondary position, that of reverse Aliyah to Hungary.

"But….my family…I want to…"

He cut me off with a stern, "Please!"

I took that as my final rebuff, so I sought out the other rebels from the bus. Together we plotted to stay behind when the rest of the Shomer Hatzair pioneers took off merrily for the kibbutz. This plan of inaction gave me solace, and I thought it a logical first step in my master plan to return home. And sure enough, when the last packed bus of singing Hungarians receded into the distance I felt as if I had escaped the gallows. After a few hours though I was gripped by a queasy uncertainty. The army with whom I had marched for so long was gone, leaving me feeling oddly alone. They might have been naive fanatics, but they had been my close friends for a month, and now they were history. We had hiked through the Hungarian forest, forded a river, snuck across several international borders, explored the pleasures of exotic Italy, braved the mighty Mediterranean, and landed in a foreign land, together every step of the way. They had been my surrogate family across two continents, and now they were out of my life. Adding to the minus column, their absence greatly reduced the ever shrinking pool of people who spoke my difficult language. The microcosmic society that had been my reality was gone with the wind, and I was now more alone than ever.

With the usual buzz of activity at Kiriat Shmuel now muffled, the minutes dragged by like hours, and I was anxious over what might come next. So, it was no small gesture when a benevolent counselor observed our stress and calmly offered us a solution.

"Okay, not everyone's born to be a pioneer. Israel takes some getting used to, I admit. Maybe you boys need to relax a little. If you like I can take you down to Carmel where we have a place just for kids like you. It's called *Ahuza*. It'll give you a chance to calm down and think things over. What do you say?"

It was a most merciful offer, spoken in the most reasonable tone I'd heard since being in Israel. Without hesitation I accepted. We all did.

Ahuza, it turned out, was an orphanage. The war had produced a lot of parentless kids, and they often suffered from psychological problems. There were French, German, Russian, Polish, and even a few Americans. They were all special cases, and a sincere attempt was made to deal with them. Actually, the people at the kibbutz were kind and friendly. Some might have been zealous, but they were earnest and well intentioned. The farms were lovely too, and represented great sacrifice. There's no doubt that Israel was a bona fide phenomenon, but my blinders prevented me from seeing any of it. It's true I had been tricked, but nobody had put a gun to my head either. I was basically a naïve, self centered child, unprepared to deal with the world beyond my mother's kitchen.

When we got to Ahuza I found it to be an attractive enough place, and if I had bothered to notice I would've seen that the attention was considerate and gentle. But it was all lost on me and my self-centered agenda. It could have been the mystical land of Shangri-La, and I wouldn't have appreciated it at all unless it had a sign pointing to Hungary. What caused the worst suffering was loneliness for my family. I had only known the actor's life for a few months, so the absence of theater was bearable. What was unbearable was the utter lack of Gabor women. I had been attached to my mother since birth, so the demands of my theatrical ego were nothing compared to the primordial need for maternal love. Hungary topped my wish list. Only there were both of the things I craved, family and stardom. Budapest would restore my lost life.

The new and less demanding surroundings allowed me to imagine that my family would come for me, or that I'd finally be free to start a theater. But I was so impatient even one day's deviation from that vision put me on edge. Perhaps they recognized my anxiety, and conjectured that a change of scenery might do me good. So, they offered to take me and the other two homesick Hungarians into town for a brief visit.

As theorized, the change was therapeutic. After all, we were urban kids, and we'd been thrust into nothing but rural environments since getting off the boat. Though we had enjoyed brief stopovers in the familiar looking European cities of Bratislava, Vienna and Bari, most of our entire Aliyah had been a series of rural sights. We longed for a touch of urbanity, and while Haifa was no Budapest it still felt good to stroll city streets and feel a hard surface under our feet. It was primitive, but charming, and we relished the freedom to stroll around. While wandering aimlessly along one of the narrow streets the other kids were talking about splitting off to go and visit the distant relatives that lived there. They were lucky to have family there, and I felt jealous. Mostly though, I felt betrayed that they would go off and leave me alone. As they chatted about these plans I was unaware that we were being tailed by another boy. Just as they were about to depart, leaving me trembling and aching with sadness, this kid who was following us came up and boldly spoke to me.

"Hi, I'm Ivan Schindler. Why don't you come back to my house and meet my family?"

It was like an angel came down and relieved me of my depression. On the one hand he distracted me from my melancholy simply by appearing, speaking Hungarian with the same accent as my family. And on the other he was so genuinely friendly I had to accept. It was the kind of big hearted innocent act that might never have occurred in the hustle bustle of big city Budapest. Hearing his own language he had become intrigued with our presence. His casual eavesdropping revealed to him that I was about to be abandoned, and his kind and empathetic nature took pity on me. He appraised the situation accurately and offered me exactly what I desperately needed, family. And that's what really disarmed me, the notion of being with a family. I missed it far more than any impersonal theater proscenium or back stage dressing room. It's what I truly pined for. Belonging with someone feels so natural to me, and is so vital to my welfare, that all other existence seems uncomfortably surreal by comparison. So, I couldn't refuse this kindness, even from a total stranger. To be part of a family, even someone else's, and even for a moment, was irresistible. The other kids were off on their own, and now I too had somewhere to go. My anxiety dissipated, replaced by curiosity about my new friend from home with the same name.

As it turned out he and his family came from Transylvania as well, and he was as excited as me to meet someone from the old country. As we walked to his neighborhood, chatting all the while, I took in Haifa and confirmed that it was indeed a far cry from the great urban centers of the Austro-Hungarian Empire. Most of the buildings along its narrow streets were one or two stories, with an occasional sky scrapper of three. It was well worn around the edges, slow moving and totally devoid of iron obelisks to display my posters. But it wasn't exactly a hick town devoid of character either. People had lived there thousands of years before Attila the Hun swept into the valley of the Danube. The prophet Elijah dwelt in the caves above its hills, and the whole atmosphere was imbued with a serenity I would have been wise to perceive. But I would have to endure a lot more bashing before any part of ancient Israel penetrated my thick skull. For now I needed to take a break from everything, including my tenacious ego, and accept the generosity of my first Israeli friend. Of course, my ego was in the driver's seat, so I didn't question why a stranger would befriend me. I was still the spoiled brat from Budapest, darling of the theater set, and accustomed to people, including strangers, making a fuss over me. I basically took it in my stride. I didn't recognize this as a magnanimous act of open hearted love. I thought this boy was yet another fan of mine when I was actually just an object of pity. In any case, it certainly saved my emotional life. I was actually close to losing my marbles when Ivan Schindler came along.

The Schindlers had only been in Israel about a year and a half, and their living circumstances were quite common for that time. Like most Israelis they were poor, but enthusiastic. They occupied half of the second story of a house that had been abandoned by Arabs. When Israel declared its independence it was attacked by their Semitic cousins, both from within and without. When that aggression failed most of those faithful to Allah felt compelled to flee, abandoning their homes in the process. Most Arabs houses were simple, but their immigrant Jewish occupants were glad to have any home after what they'd been through in Europe. Ivan's second story apartment had two bedrooms separated by a central kitchen. A family of four occupied each bedroom, and they each had their own table in the kitchen. The one vestige of luxury was the balcony which afforded its residents some tranquil privacy now and again. Ivan warmly introduced me to his parents and brother, and they were all smiles and kindness. Ivan's father worked in a shoe factory and didn't earn much. Their hospitality, though genuine, was sparse. They shared their meager lunch with me, and I felt a bit guilty about taking any of it. Observing their humble surroundings, the unadorned walls and simple furniture, I could see just how different their existence was from the high society I knew back home. The whole place was smaller than our apartment at Csengery Utca, number fifty-one. Actually it was more like Csengery Utca, number sixty-one. Of course, for all I knew they may have enjoyed the same middle class life we did back in Europe before the war. Who knows what misery befell them and prompted their flight to Israel? But I was so self-centered and immature it never crossed my mind to inquire. I just saw their present station in life, accepted it as the way they had always lived, and felt guilty for taking any small part of what little they had. Accepting their food also seemed unnecessary on my part, as I could have stuffed my belly back at Ahuza. But they were happy to be able to offer me a little chicken. One thing they clearly had in abundance though was love. They smiled at me and looked me in the eye as I regaled them with tales of my artistic triumphs in Budapest. They sincerely seemed to care, and it was a cherished escape from the frustration I had known since arriving. They understood my agenda, but let me know that as long as I was in Haifa I was always welcome to visit them. And, to avoid the confusion of having two young men with the same name they dubbed me Big Ivan because I was all of six months older than my new friend. But what a relief it was to visit there and have a home, even if for just a few hours. I might've gone crazy if it weren't for them. Despite their open heartedness I still longed to go back to Hungary, and I didn't hesitate to let them know.

"I want to meet someone to help me return to Budapest. Can you help me?"

They confessed they were unable to help directly, but suggested some offices that might. Getting to those offices however was difficult. I was supposed to spend my weekdays at Ahuza, and I could only get out on weekends when government offices were closed. Also, the orphanage was far and I had no money for bus or taxis. Talking about that reminded me that I was supposed to get back to the bus station and Ahuza. Still unfamiliar with Haifa little Ivan walked me back. On the way he made a suggestion.

"Look, if you come back into town hang around this bus station. I'll look for you there on Friday nights just before sundown."

And the very next shabbos that's just what I did. Ahuza was actually kind enough to give me bus fare and I eagerly made my to the bus station and waited for Ivan. True to his word he wasn't long in coming. Though it was shabbos he took me around to find some secular fun. The Schindlers were like a lot of Israelis, culturally Jewish, but not so religiously inclined. They were committed to their homeland and their people, but not their God. This is surrealism of a primeval nature. It is incongruity incarnate to live in a land named for Biblical roots, but with scant echo of that sacred foundation. They enjoyed the greatest degree of freedom of religion they'd known in two thousand years, but showed little interest in exercising it. In essence, the chosen people chose to ignore He who chose them. Maybe it's precisely that identity, of being within such a special group, which gave them the license to ignore, rather than adore, God. But if they weren't gung ho for God, they definitely were for His nation. They created Israel for their security, even if they felt estranged from the Almighty. Such a cavalier attitude toward religion in a land so closely linked to God is the ultimate surreal context.

As for myself my lack of religious upbringing stuck. But while I'm not an out and out atheist I can't claim to be a true believer either. I admit that I wish I had faith, and I admire those that do. The impression my religious grandma made on me suggests the possibility that there's something of a higher nature out there. I do have an open mind regarding evidence that might lead me toward a spiritual path, but I definitely lived my days in the Holy Land in a less than holy mood. In other words I fit right in with most Israelis. We were more concerned with the welfare of our bodies than our souls.

One of the less than divine pastimes in which we engaged was ping pong. We discovered it while exploring the old Arab quarter of town where he lived. It was actually just a couple of blocks from his house. I played back in Hungary, and I recognized the familiar paketa-poketa emanating from the second story of a building we were passing. We went up and asked if we could play and they agreed. But it turned out the venue for playing this innocent game was yet another slap in the face to the Almighty Lord. It was the local branch of the atheistic communist party.

While not completely in synch with the Russian version of socialism, many Jews still clung to Marxism as a political model for ruling their new homeland, regardless of its disdain for the opiate of the masses. When Lenin introduced this political philosophy to Mother Russia he made it clear that the Hebrew Nation was not to blame for the inequalities which plagued their woeful lives, and that anti-Semitism was a regrettable vestige of that old way of thinking. Naturally, this endeared the Bolshevik revolution to many of Abraham's tribe who saw life without organized religion and pogroms preferable to life with limited religious expression and having your mother and sisters routinely raped by Cossacks. Of course, the idealistic Jews embraced communism in its purest form, bemoaned the distorted Soviet version,

Echoes Of My Footsteps

and clung to the hope of implementing Karl Marx' pristine dream somewhere sometime. The new State of Israel, imbued with altruism, and modeled along modern democratic values, tolerated all credos. Ideology of course was not at the root of my visit to the communist party headquarters, but rather my dual primordial needs of hitting a small white plastic sphere with a paddle and going home. I reasoned that if Hungary was now ruled by the commies then this socialist organization would feel duty bound to help me get back there. As poor as, or poorer than, any other organization in the Holy Land, the unholy Commies could ill afford to sponsor a trip to Europe. But while our trip bore me little fruit beyond recreation, it initiated a lifelong obsession for Ivan Schindler. He took up the banner of Marxism with all his heart, though it's never intruded upon our friendship. Actually, I couldn't argue with a philosophy that professed total equality for all, but I really could not come to live it. After all, if we were all the same than ping pong matches would go on forever. Someone has to be better in order to win. That, by the way, turned out to be me. I'll admit that this bastion of Bolsheviks managed to accomplish the nearly impossible. It actually brought together some Jewish and Arab youths. That's no small feat. But, while not swayed to adopt Marxism as my credo, I enjoyed our visits there. I liked the games, occasional free refreshments, and social outlet. There were, after all, commie girls too. And after a few visits I made another bid for help.

"So, you're Hungarian? Well, maybe we can help you. First, you gotta get away from that orphanage. Once you're free we can get to work on getting you back."

"How?"

"Well, here in Israel, kids like you who are fourteen or fifteen, are practically treated like adults. But as long as you're in the orphanage you're under government control. The only way out is if a relative asks for you to be released."

"But I don't have any relatives here."

"No problem! We'll send someone pretending to be your uncle. He'll sign your release, and you'll have no more obligations there."

I barely knew these people, but I was so determined to go home I heard them out. And sure enough, a few days later, the orphanage administrators came to me.

"An uncle is here looking for you."

I was lying on my bed staring at the photos of my parents. If it was possible to wear something out by looking then it would've happened. I looked at them as a constant ritual, closing my eyes, and envisioning home. I was so delirious with sadness I actually imagined myself at home. It was like a hungry man staring at pictures of food. I so longed to transport my body home I traveled there at the speed of mind. So, when they came to tell me my uncle was looking for me it was completely confusing. I was so absorbed in my fantasy life I had forgotten about the conversation back at the Karl Marx social center. I dumbly blurted out, "I don't have any uncles in Israel."

Then, just as I was about to ruin everything, my phony commie uncle burst in.

"Hello my darling little nephew, Ivan. How are you doing?"

I shook the stupefied lethargy from my head and took my cue, giving my first performance in a long time.

"Oh yes, uncle! So good to see you."

"Little nephew, your worries are over. I believe I can help you get back to Budapest."

"Oh, I'm glad to hear that, uncle! But how do I get out?"

"Well, as your relative, I can sign to release you."

"Oh, I understand. Then, let's do it!"

My performance didn't have to be as heartfelt as it was, but considering I had no prepared dialogue or rehearsal I was convincing enough. In retrospect I am outraged that they didn't even verify if this stranger was my uncle or not. Anyway, he told me to pack my things, and before I knew it I was ushered out of the orphanage. I couldn't even imagine why this individual would want to help me, but I was grateful just the same. He was a friendly gregarious type whose nonstop patter kept me distracted on our bus journey all the way to the end of Herzl Street in Haifa. We got off in front of a cinema that was playing a western with Glenn Ford. My father bore a resemblance to this actor, and I've never been able to completely enjoy any of his films, because it depresses me to be reminded of dad. Standing in front of the cinema my phony uncle addressed me.

"Well, I hope you are happy, and I am glad to have helped you. Now you just have to find some place to sleep, and you'll be alright. When you have a chance drop by and see us. Goodbye, comrade Ivan."

He left without asking me if I had any money or anything else. He just vanished. The idea I might be on my way back home now evaporated into the dry desert air. In an instant I had hope and then, just as quickly, lost it. Now I had no home of any kind, not even the orphanage. It's as if I was treading water in the middle of the ocean. I was so miserable I was nearly suicidal. Sadness so engulfed me my body nearly ceased to function. I stood there like a dolt with that same damn valise I had been schlepping since Hungary. I was so completely lost I literally didn't know whether to turn left or right. The only people I knew in this city, and the whole country for that matter, were the Schindlers, and though I was absolutely dying to make my way there I had no idea how. On my previous visits I had not taken the care to observe our route, simply letting little Ivan guide me. I was penniless, homeless, and utterly, utterly alone.

I had officially hit my lowest point since the war. Back then I had mom and grandma to share my misery. In my Aliyah I had Judah Winter and the other kids. Even the Israeli government centers had some adults to hold my hand and listen to my whining. So, factoring in my isolation, this truly was my official nadir. It was the street, abject loneliness, hunger, and a complete lack of resources. To make matters worse there were no prospects to improve any of my conditions. The bitter icing on the sour cake? Night was approaching and the temperature was dropping.

I roamed around aimlessly, looking for somewhere to rest. I had no idea if I was walking south, north, east or west. I tried to speak to some people, but I couldn't speak Hebrew, and no Hungarians happened along. My gimnazium French found the same failure. With exhaustion gnawing at my bones a pile of sandbags, remnants of the recent war of independence, invited me to lie down. I put a few together to form a bed and passed out as soon as my body hit them. After what must have been only a few minutes, as I still felt dead to the world, somebody shook me awake. They asked me something in some foreign sounds, and I responded in Hungarian. To my surprise they actually recognized my gibberish well enough to send for an interpreter. I sat there groggy until someone finally came and asked me in broken, heavily accented Hungarian what I was doing there. I said simply that I was tired and wanted to sleep. To my surprise they were not at all upset, and after a few minutes they got me some food and a blanket. But before I had time to thank them they disappeared as mysteriously as they had appeared. At least I had something warm in my stomach and on top of my body. I drifted off to sleep but it was no escape. Now, I was tortured by nightmares. And, as it would turn out, they were here to stay. For months, my nights were so restless I practically feared going to sleep.

I dreamt of my parents. They floated in and out of my dreams like the haunting images of a Chagall painting. I wanted to speak to them, to apologize. But time and time again the vision of my mother confronted me. She was always dressed in black.

"Mama, why are you in black? Papa's been gone so long."

She looked at me with piercing eyes and intoned, "I'm not mourning him, but you!"

"No mother, come back. It's Freddy. I'm here."

"No. You are dead to me. I have no son!"

"Noooo!"

These nightmares persisted for years. As my days now consisted of barely surviving, and my nights were plagued by Kafkaesque visions, my life had descended into a hellish nonstop cycle of torture, regret and despair.

When the sun rose on that first morning of sleeping in the street I awoke to a new epoch of my life. I was on my own, homeless in Haifa. No Kiriat Shmuel to exercise my complaining talents. No Ahuza to mope around in. No tents or kibbutzim. Those commie bastards had completely screwed me. They took me out of a warm nurturing orphanage with psychological counseling and set me adrift on the mean streets of Haifa. No family, friends, money, bed, food, or affection.

For days I roamed around, first this way, and then that, my cumbersome valise making this odyssey even worse. I kept switching it from one hand to the other, and it was incredibly annoying. I cursed Judah Winter for the suitcase, for bringing me here, and for everything else. How could an organization like Shomer Hatzair do this to a kid? A month ago I was walking on cloud nine at home. Now I aimlessly wandered around a squalid town in the Middle East, devoid of friendly faces. I was like a desert nomad with filthy nails and badly in need of a haircut. My feet ached and I stank. An eerie and familiar feeling came over me that reminded me of the war. No bullets, bombs or thugs plagued me, but I felt almost the same. Asleep or awake my life had become a nightmare. Every night I found another pile of discarded sandbags and passed out. I always made sure to place the bags in a doorway, hoping for a repeat of the pity I received my first homeless night when the kind strangers brought me food and a blanket. Sometimes it worked, but mostly hunger and cold were my steady nighttime companions. Then, out of the blue, I got a tremendous surprise. A kid from my Shomer Hatzair group happened to run into me. His name was Tomy Blau.

"Tomy! What are you doing here?"

Tomy was older and bigger. I always saw him as more mature than me, so I thought I might get some help from him. Tomy explained everything.

"I couldn't stand that damn kibbutz! So I took off and made my way down to Haifa. What are you doing here?"

"It's a long story. Have you got anything to eat?"

"Not on me. Hey why don't you join us?"

"Us?"

"Yeah. Ernie Weisz came with me when I left the kibbutz. We both started working this job in Haifa. It's lousy, but it pays enough to eat, and the boss even lets us sleep there. Come on."

I was ecstatic to find someone I knew, and I figured any job would better my situation. Just getting some reliable food and a place to sleep seemed like a wonderful improvement to me, and having Tomy's company again dispelled my loneliness.

His place of employment was in an ancient, decrepit building across the street from Haifa's old derelict train station. The station itself was out of service since they built a modern depot, and the businesses around this old one were mostly boarded up. But a few humble enterprises that did not rely on pedestrian traffic took advantage of the low rents. They were usually run by immigrants whose lack of language skills did not impact their bottom line. One such man, a red haired Pole, had devised a business out of little more than thin air. Nearby furniture manufacturers needed cheap fabric as backing, so the resourceful refugee collected discarded burlap bags used to ship grains, and employed low paid unskilled labor to open their seams. Then he sold the resultant crude cloth to the makers of sofas and chairs. Tomy, Ernie and I qualified as that low paid unskilled labor. We took a gunny sack from one huge pile, opened its seams, and then tossed it onto another huge pile. It was menial and awful, but better than the street.

The immigrant entrepreneur was a humorless fellow who never tired of working, and expected the same level of effort from his employees. For us it was good to have somewhere to work and sleep, but our boss locked the doors at ten o'clock at night, so we were practically prisoners there. I was afraid there'd be a fire, and we'd be trapped inside, but Tomy pointed out a window in the back comer to squeeze through in an emergency. Our boss opened up just after dawn and didn't lock up again until ten at night, and we were expected to toil the entire time. It was mind numbing tedium, but we stayed because it just edged out the street. Occasionally they let us into the old train station bathrooms to bathe. And while the bags were comfortable enough for sleeping the residual bits of rice and corn attracted armies of rats, and they swarmed over us as we slept. I was often woken by rats running across my face. The pay was a lira a day. This was not an Italian lira, but its Israeli counterpart, and it was barely enough to get a plate of food which was always bean soup with hummus. My life was reduced to mere survival, and the persistent sadness plagued me.

It turns out that this humble trade had competition from yet another Polish immigrant doing exactly the same thing, in exactly the same building, over in another corner. Despite all their similarities they were mortal enemies, and mutually antagonistic whenever possible.

One night I was going mad from tedium and had to get out, so I squeezed through our emergency escape window and walked around. Thinking of my parents I was overcome with homesickness and wept as I walked along. I was too depressed to be anywhere near the train station so I kept walking. The rhythm of Haifa was a far cry from my home town which only came to life once the sun went down. There were countless cafes, nightclubs, and theaters, and I didn't even start work until it was dark. But in this Mediterranean town sunset meant sleep, and now I roamed its deserted walkways, accompanied only by the feint echo of my footsteps. In European cities the reverberation of our shoes bounced off the walls of the cement canyons with a sharp report, betraying our presence. Here, it was a bare hint of that eerie sound, and I would not have been aware of it at all but for my solitude and the lack of competition for the attention of my ears. But even these puny whimpers took me back to when we escaped the Nyilasok. That escape was more successful than this one, because the sound of my steps only reminded me more of my mother's sacrifice, making it impossible for me to get that source of sorrow far from my mind. There was no evading the depression, so only utter fatigue dragged me back to the train depot and my vermin infected boudoir.

After some days of opening gunny sacks I lost track of time and missed my bus station rendezvous with my Israeli pal, Ivan Schindler. That bitter realization triggered an even greater depression within me. I'd never find their house on my own, and the warmth of a family, even someone else's, would be denied me for good. Just at that precise moment however, I chanced to turn around and saw Ivan Schindler pass by right in front of the train station. By blessed coincidence he had to go by this building on his way to school. I ran out to him at once.

"Little Ivan!"

Happily, he was just as glad to reconnect with me.

"Big Ivan, I thought you got lost. My mother was asking about you."

This was music to my ears. He even called me by the nickname they had invented for me, which made me feel even better, like one of the family. I blabbed on.

"Hey, this Friday let's go back to that communist social center. Those sons of bitches screwed me! They took me away from somewhere safe and left me alone on the street without helping me at all. Please, take me back there so I can see if there's any chance of getting some real help from them, like they promised."

From that moment on it was a priority never to lose contact with Ivan or his family again. And when Friday rolled around he took me down to the commie ping pong club and I gave them a piece of my mind.

"You bastards talked about helping me, but all you did was to ditch me on the streets! What kind of a thing is that to do to a kid? You're just like everyone else here, liars. I thought socialists cared about people. But you don't care about anyone. You're nothing but a bunch of silly, useless bureaucrats!"

My last word to them was the single greatest insult you can hurl at a communist. However, to be offended you have to care, and they truly did not. All they could feebly offer was to try and find the office of someone who could help me.

After I got that off my mind Ivan and I hung out and chatted about Hungary. Doing so had the dual effect of comforting me and making me homesick. But it reminded me that I should be writing home, so using the Schindler house as a return address, I began a consistent campaign of writing my mother.

In my letters it was important to always sound happy and positive, assuring her that I had decent employment. But that part backfired when she answered and explained how much they needed some extra income after losing my theater salary. She also reminded me how ill my baby sister was. And the communist government there didn't exactly appreciate her son fleeing their socialist paradise for Israel. And when I asked for help to get back home it was always the same. "Freddela," she wrote, "you should have thought of that before you left us high and dry. Where am I going to get money to bring you back? You made it there without my help, so you can figure out how to make it back. You thought only of yourself Mister Pioneer. Keep thinking of yourself!"

Each letter left me more demoralized. If there's one thing I was not, it was a pioneer. I had none of the spirit that characterized Israelis. But one thing I always did when I wrote home was to send my warmest greetings to my grandma. Had I not I would have eternally endured even worse guilt. She was a saint, and I'm glad I always remembered her in my letters. Of course, remembering her made me feel lonelier yet. I was also very careful not to tell her of my true situation. I had already done quite enough to make her suffer. If she knew my low station it would've made her feel worse.

Loneliness, nightmares, lousy food and the invisible and inexorable element of time had all become my enemies, rotting my mind, my spirit, my body and my clothes. I was plagued by holes in my shoes, and I tried putting cardboard into them. But they became wet and I felt as if my feet were festering. Actually, I felt as if my whole body was rotting. I had developed a cavity in one of my teeth off to the side of the two front ones, and it caused this handsome matinee idol no end of humiliation. In my mind lived yet the dashing actor, and any diminution of my striking countenance was a horror not be tolerated. If I had an opportunity to talk to a girl I'd hold my hand over my mouth.

Out of desperation I rolled up a piece of white bread to fill the hole in my tooth, so I wouldn't look so pathetic. But the whole situation was just that, pathetic. I was merely surviving, with barely enough food to keep body and soul together, and I had only a few articles of clothing. I was filthy and I literally slept with vermin. Added to this was the heartache of being rejected by my mother. I was incurably depressed and racked with guilt. She was right to reject me. I left her, and her mother and her baby. I had been the big bread winner and man of the house, and I dropped them without as much as a word of goodbye. No wonder she wouldn't forgive me. What I had done was truly unforgivable.

Tomy Blau was a little older and street wiser. Back in Budapest he was one of those kids who constantly hung out at the flea markets, looking to make some deal. It was his second nature to have his ear to the ground in search of anything easy or free. That's how he found about ration books. If I had stayed on the kibbutz, or even the Ahuza, I would have learned about them earlier, but my negative attitude kept me out of the loop of Israeli society. As it turns out the government issued ration books to all its citizens to help them get the basics, such as food. It was such a staple of Israeli culture it was glorified in a folk song which we had all been singing since Shomer Hatzair days. It was called Tzena Tzena Tzena, and was actually a hit song in America, recorded by some folk singers. But the people who sang it phonetically in the west weren't aware that it was just about ration coupons. Anyway, they were as good as money, but goods could be purchased with them for lower prices than market value. People also bartered for things not on the approved purchase list with them, and Black Marketers paid a premium to get their hands on them. I'd been living on the edge of Israeli society so I was ignorant about such things, but as soon as Tomy told me about them we went down to the government office that issued them and received our first ration book's worth of coupons.

To get the ration books was remarkably simple. All you needed was to be an Israeli citizen. After all, wasn't that why we had come here? Aliyah provided, and still does, that all Jews have a right to be Israeli citizens. And this government office was going to issue me my citizenship papers and an identification card in addition to the ration book.

There was a short line of refugees ahead of me, most of them bearing some kind of documentation. I had none and was momentarily worried I might be rejected because of this. While I was reflecting on all of the technical reasons why they might reject someone like me my turn came up. I stepped forward and they asked me my name. They looked at me with innocent eyes, patiently waiting for my response. Then it hit me. I realized that I really didn't need any paperwork. I was a Jew in Israel who had gone through the war and hadn't any papers. It was hardly a rare circumstance, but it didn't really matter. The old life in Europe was dead, and the new life in Israel was beginning. I had paid my dues by going through the holocaust and coming out alive, and I was free to re-invent myself and become whomever I wanted. It was a chance life rarely ever gives us. I could've told them my name was Franklin Roosevelt and I was from Tibet, and they would've accepted it. It was a moment of total trust. But who would I be? I was born Alfred Grossman, but have no memory of ever being called that. And was it really a Jewish name at all? Grossman was a German name, and more of an attempt to assimilate than anything else. No, Alfred Grossman lived a long time ago back in Transylvania. Then I was Freddy to my friends and family back in Hungary, but that was a nickname invented to deflect suspicion of being a Jew. So, it hardly seemed appropriate for an Israeli. Ivan was picked to accompany me in my theatrical dreams, and was still relatively new to me. As I still had dreams maybe it fit me a little. And Zev was the first hint I was a Jew. So I forgot about my birth name once and for all and picked one that suited me. Ivan stood for my dreams. Zev was an Israeli. Finally, I couldn't lose the connection with my father or the rest of my family, so I stayed a Gabor. My age and country of origin stayed honest. Fully prepared I stood up straight and looked them in the eye.

"I am Ivan Zev Gabor, age fourteen, from Budapest, Hungary."

"Very well," he replied. And that was that.

He filled out my papers, stamped them, recorded it in a large ledger, and handed me my Israeli citizen identity card. It was that simple. I was now my own man. Previously, I had been someone's son, grandson or nephew. But now my fate was my own. I was Zev the Israeli.

The ration book was even easier, because you didn't even have to request one. It just came with the citizenship. Sadly though, I was still naïve and unaware that these books were better than cash. In my ignorance I made a bad deal to trade my monthly ration card for room and board from a religious Hungarian couple. Tomy Blau made this arrangement before I even got my ration book, and considering his experience at making deals he made a really lousy one for our new lodgings. Ernie Weisz joined us and we all rented meager quarters in another abandoned building in Wadi Salim, an Arab sector of town even poorer than the previous one I knew. The three of us lived in a squalid little room, built into the side of a hill. There was nothing in the room but a pile of dirty mattresses, and we had to use a bathroom in the hall that was shared by everyone else there. The room was dank and depressing, and the bathroom was actually just a smelly latrine with an open cistern for splashing water on ourselves. Our room had no sheets or blankets and we simply covered ourselves with a second mattress to keep off the night chill. The worst part was that we had to pass through our landlord's room to get to our own. The bearded man had an extremely fat wife, and whenever we passed through they seemed to be perpetually trying to increase Israel's population. We shut our eyes, but they were so noisy about it that it was impossible to ignore. I was still a virgin at that time, but this couple did nothing to excite my sexual curiosity. The place was dirty and smelly, as were they, and the woman was obese and sweaty. Our arrangement included Friday night dinner, but it was served on dirty plates and was an affront to God. Calling it shabbos dinner is an insult to the memory of every loving parent or grandparent who ever provided such a sacred feast. In addition to being indescribably gross our landlady was the worst cook in the history of the Hebrew Nation. Also, it was a little embarrassing to sit and eat Shabbos dinner with people whose sex life was constantly on display. Eventually their dedication produced offspring. Actually, she was so fat I was unaware she was even pregnant. But now they had a child who cried as nonstop as was its process of conception. I cannot swear that it wailed twenty four hours a day, but I can attest that it did cry one hundred percent of the time we were present. From my current condition and perspective I can flatly declare that it was without a doubt the foulest, filthiest, most awful place I have ever dwelled in my entire life. On top of all that it was a huge rip-off. The sole detail of not tolerating rats as bunk mates made it tolerable.

We continued to open burlap bags by day and sleep between mattresses at night. And the only sane stability in my life was my growing friendship with Ivan Schindler. He too had been given a Hebrew name, Natan. So, to be good Israelis, we determined to always address each other as Natan and Zev. We passed a lot of time together and often included Tomy Blau or Ernie Weisz. But I only went back to the communist center a few times more. The first time I went back was just to get some practical help to help me in my quest to return to Hungary. They gave me information about various government agencies that could supposedly help me, but they all turned out to be dead ends and wild goose chases. And the bad taste left in my mouth from my dealings with those half hearted humanists took the glow off the ping pong as well. Anyway, by then the better loved pastime was the cinema.

Once we could accept the absurdity of cowboys speaking Hebrew the movies became our favorite pastime. After buying my daily plate of soup and beans I saved the few pennies change for biweekly trips to Hollywood's latest export. As with most social events it's more fun with someone else, but poverty got in the way of that ideal formula. To overcome that dilemma we developed a routine by which two people could get in on a single ticket. I went in and made sure to smile at the usher so he might recognize me if I went to the bathroom, And when I went to bathroom I passed my ticket stub through the window to an alley where Natan or Tomy waited. The usher already recognized me, and didn't require seeing my ticket. And now my friend also had a ticket. Other petty crimes of that period included stealing produce. There was a lot of successful agricultural goings on in Israel and we used to rob whatever we could in order to improve our diet. We were lucky and never got arrested or beat up. Such shenanigans were necessary at that time in our lives. And when money was too tight for even one movie ticket simple cavorting had to suffice.

As we worked near the railway we used to walk along the rails. One time I lost my balance and slipped off, landing on a nail. It went right through the hole in my shoe into my foot, and I had to go to a clinic for a tetanus shot. I limped for a week, but my greedy boss threatened me with dismissal if I missed even one day. This callous behavior made me so lonely for my family I often cried myself to sleep. And worse yet, I was having nightmares full of wartime terrors. Visions of Nazis and everything horrifying had come back to haunt me. Nazis, explosions, my beating at the hands of the Nyilasok, and the shooting by the river all made nightly reappearances. So, my days were awful and my nights unbearable. I even recalled how Judah Winter had lied to me. I envisioned him saying, "Just try a year. If you don't like it we'll send you back." Then I envisioned myself strangling him for saying it. All of this filled me with a new resolve to try and get back, so I contacted a Jewish agency and begged them to help. But their response was the usual gung-ho slogan that I was destined to become an integral part of Israel's future.

"We're fighting for our existence, and need young men like you!"

They had such huge important things to worry about they couldn't pay much attention to a whiner with emotional trauma. After all, half the country was made up of people like me, orphans and immigrants. I understood it, but I was still inconsolable. So, out of desperation, I found myself going back to the commie ping pong club to demand they do something to help me. Either to help me, or just get rid of me, they suggested that I go to the Hungarian Business Association in Tel Aviv to plead my case. Naturally, they were not prepared to finance my trip, so I learned to hitch hike.

To get to our fondling nation's largest city by thumb took a couple of hours, and I had the opportunity to see a lot more of Israel than I had seen since my arrival. Basically, it just looked like more of the same, more sand and rocks. My frame of mind would not allow me to enjoy any part of the Holy Land. And when I got to the great metropolis it was too late to go to any office, obliging me to seek out somewhere to pass the night. As my resources were still nonexistent I spent the night on the street. I found a park and a vacant bench and lay down for the night. In the morning I was shocked to see that all night I had been across the street from the Habima Theater, home of the Israeli National Theater. I had finally made it. Thank you Judah Winter! I couldn't help but marvel at the twisted irony that brought me there. By now there was not so much as a thought within me of reviving my acting career. All that was now just a vague and distant memory. Did I ever stand on a stage? Was I ever celebrated for it? Such reflection only depressed me more as I ended my brief visit to our country's great beaux art venue.

I made my way over to the hotel that housed the office of the Hungarian Business Association. In those days there were no fancy office buildings in Israel, and visitors did business right out of hotel rooms. In one such suite I made the acquaintance of the commercial attaché of Hungary in Israel. I told him my situation and begged him to visit my mother and plead my case. He often traveled to Budapest, so he promised to see my mother and do as I wished. He agreed to see me on his next trip to Tel Aviv, and I finally felt like there might be some light at the end of my dark tunnel.

I hitched back to Haifa and continued to work at my gunny sack career. Hour after hour, day after day, I opened the seams in those burlap bags until my fingers ached. I didn't know it then, but eventually that activity would one day serve me in a most unexpected way.

Although I was not motivated to reignite my artistic career in Tel Aviv, there was a Hungarian social club in Haifa that invited me to recite some poetry at one of their cultural nights, briefly beguiling me to tread the boards anew. I really wanted to, but I was too embarrassed by my ragged attire, and bowed out. That's when I knew for sure that any dream of an acting career was absolutely and totally dead. But what really killed it off was when I finally came to the realization that I couldn't act here due to my accent. I was such a puffed up rascal that I never thought about the fact that I was a foreigner with a thick accent. They would have boo'd me off the stage. No doubt about it; I was utterly unqualified for the life of an Israeli thespian.

As I continued to open gunny sacks I prayed for the commercial attaché to convince my mother to take me back. My concept of an attaché was some lofty individual possessed of great powers of persuasion. Surely, he would not fail me. And, after opening about a thousand more seams he finally returned. I hitch-hiked to Tel Aviv and ran to his office, anxious to hear the good news from home.

"When I can return to Budapest?"

I had assumed that he would bring me nothing but good news. After all, why wouldn't my own family be as eager to have me back as I was to return? I had learned my lesson. Time heals all wounds. Surely, they missed me too.

"No! There is no way for you to return to Budapest."

No way to return! That's what he said. Not 'in a few weeks.' Not 'in a few months.' He said 'No way!' My mouth dropped open, and I stood there with it, staring at him, and didn't blink for a solid minute. All he added was that he was sorry, and then he gave me some chocolate. He had bought it with money my mother had given him to get me a present. He couldn't help but notice how despondent I was, and said that we might be able to talk in another two or three months. Then I had to leave. In utter desolation I managed to hitch hike back to Haifa.

Chocolate was a poor substitute for my family, and my desperation to get back now took a mildly criminal turn. Tomy Blau and I boldly decided that we would try to return to Budapest ourselves. We checked out the port and found out that there were Turkish freighters that embarked from Haifa bound for various European countries. Even though Hungary was landlocked, if we could at least get as far as the continent surely our families would help us get the rest of the way. So, we determined to become stowaways.

We tried to pass ourselves off as laborers just to get onto a ship. We mixed in with the other laborers, picked up some crates and bundles and carried them on board. It seemed to work, and we were congratulating each other when they found us and kicked us off. Two days later we tried again, and this time they didn't find us until the boat actually left the pier, which made them all the more irate, being forced to dock up again. They told us they'd just toss us overboard next time and called the cops. Deciding that we were not really criminals, they took us to a center for problem kids. But we escaped from there and made our third attempt. That failed too, as did our fourth and fifth. Finally, the authorities threatened to treat us as real criminals if we persisted. So we gave up and returned to the burlap bags. It was the same awful situation, but still a full half step better than an Israeli jail of 1949. We even felt lucky to have our employment back.

Two winters came and went but my life knew no improvement. I was still knee deep in burlap, a return to Hungary was no closer, and any thought of becoming an actor was dead. All this time I had been writing home once a month with the hopes of a cordial response, but my mother's wrath knew no quarter. Her rebuff was as fresh and committed as the day I abandoned her. And my sentence would not be commuted regardless of good behavior. Only the Schindlers offered me respite from my travail. Thank God for them. They were my family in Israel.

As grotesque as our landlords made sex appear we were still at that age when meeting girls was an obsession. Being as ragged as I was though, it was an embarrassment for me to try and even talk to a regular girl. Therefore, we concentrated our efforts on irregular girls, females whose conditions were so tough that they would never reject a boy because of a shabby wardrobe. Israel was so full of impoverished people back then that even some nice Jewish girls turned to a life of easy virtue, including more than a few Hungarians. I was quite totally naïve regarding the world's oldest profession, so Tomy had to take me aside and patiently explained this age old custom. It was short and sweet.

"You pay money and you have sex!"

Just like the movies or any other entertainment? You pay and you enjoy? I was amazed and delighted by the sweet simplicity of the arrangement. So, armed with this information, Natan and I decided that it was time we became men once and for all.

We investigated the going rates for the services of women of the night, and then made the commitment to sacrifice movies for a whole month in order to accrue the necessary funds to finance our first taste of the pleasures of the flesh. Tomy turned us on to a reliable address in Haifa where sexual fulfillment awaited the properly funded, and we were off. We boldly approached the door of this house of ill repute, took a deep breath and knocked. Soon a robed lady came out and spoke to us. I was sixteen, but looked like a nervous fifteen year old.

"What are you doing here?"

We were too embarrassed to properly reply to her inquiry, and she just laughed and invited us in. Though unfamiliar with the biology of the occasion we were both eager to learn. She told us to sit down and wait, and then she vanished into another room. Moments later a detached siren voice beckoned to us. To this day I don't remember who went first, but Natan and I passed this rite of passage on the same night with the same partner, within fifteen minutes of each other. But not all of us had to pay for it. Tomy sought romance elsewhere and ended up with a bona fide girlfriend named Cathy. He even moved in with this pretty Hungarian girl.

Women symbolized family to me, and I couldn't help but envy him the solid relationship he had with a girl. Anyway, now that Tomy had a domestic situation of his own he was basically out of the picture. About that time Ernie Weisz vanished as well. Ernie had disillusioned his family with his secret Aliyah as I had, but his folks relented and financed his return. Learning of this drove me into the deepest doldrums. I took it as proof that I was now officially unloved. Ernie's mother cared enough to bring him back, but not mine. The door that had already slammed in my face now felt bolted shut.

By attending Hebrew classes we were getting more in tune with Israeli culture, though it did nothing to appease the poverty that was still our ever present companion. Occasionally stray jobs came our way to augment our miserable burlap curse. I got to know other businesses in the neighborhood and frequently got extra employment with them for a couple of days here and there. One man distributed milk and bread to the houses in the area, and he hired me to help him whenever his usual helper took sick. I had to get up at four in the morning to do it, but I didn't mind, because I wanted that extra income. He picked me up in his car and drove me around on the delivery route. He stopped at every customer, and I jumped out and delivered the order. At the end of the route he gave me a loaf of bread and a bottle of milk besides my meager pay. The milk and bread were breakfast, and the extra income went into the movies fund. In this epoch the cinema was my salvation. Of course, I couldn't understand them at all. They were never in Hungarian, and the sub-titles were always in Hebrew. Anyway, it's just as well I didn't understand them. I loved the westerns, but I think it would've spoiled everything to hear or read, "Shalom, Tex!" We also got jobs helping in a garage that repaired motorcycles. This made me especially glad, because I thought being a mechanic was a more useful occupation than what we were doing with the gunny sacks. But nothing ever lasted and the pay was always awful. Whenever I went for a job I'd ask, "How much are you going to pay me?" And the answer was invariably, "Not much. Just enough so you can eat!" The garage owner was slightly kinder than my other employers in that he invited me to his house for lunch. But I always ended up back with the damn burlap bags, eating the same crappy soup and hummus.

Natan started to learn a practical occupation which seemed right in line with his typical proletariat thinking. He decided he would take his place alongside the workers of the world as a welder, and I could easily picture his torch replacing one of the implements on the classic hammer and sickle emblem. But a steady occupation eluded me, and I continued to do such menial tasks as the unschooled must. One such job was offered to me by another Hungarian, a paint manufacturer. I cleaned out large industrial painting machines, which was hardly less monotonous than opening the seams of burlap bags. Worse, I used to get covered in paint. Every day I came back a different shade, and endured endless kidding, "Hey, red boy! Hey, blue boy!" Once the boss asked me to cut some metal with an acetylene torch. I had only gotten basic instructions with this dangerous tool, but I figured if Natan could do it so could I. With more confidence than brains at the helm I ended up hurting myself badly. The torch cut through the bar quicker than I thought it would and I had no time to grab it before it crashed down onto my foot. I didn't know how badly my foot was hurt until I took off my shoe and saw that it was filled with blood. Screaming in pain they rushed me to a clinic.

My recuperation was slow and agonizing. I lay in my dank apartment on a bare mattress, agonizing, terribly alone, and generally lamenting my whole existence. But it gave me a lot of time to think things over. At first I just felt sorry for myself, comparing life in Haifa with Budapest. The last time I had something wrong with my leg was when I froze my foot and had my loving grandma to rub them. Now, I was on my own with nobody to kiss the boo boo and make the pain go away. I was not a baby any more, and I came to view my wound, like my whole predicament, as completely my own fault. But now I resolved to do something about it. This was a bold and maturing step for me. I also realized that blue collar occupations were not for me, and I would one day have to do something to improve my status in life. Maybe I wouldn't be an actor, but there were certainly other things to do besides break my back, burn my skin and shatter my bones. For now I was a high school drop-out with no formal training, and my prospects were poor. Someday though, I'll do better. After all, I have no where to go but up. Just that feeling of determination made me feel better.

Meanwhile, good old Natan continued to bring me food whenever he could. And when he couldn't manage that he took some old clothes or other things to the flea market to get some money to buy me medicine. The kindest thing I could wish for anyone is to have a friend half as selfless and loyal as Natan Schindler. If it weren't for him and his family I can't imagine what a desolate emotional landscape Israel would have been for me. I surely would have become a basket case without them.

When I could finally stand I returned to the gunny sack factory. My usually greedy boss, in a most uncharacteristic manner, actually behaved halfway human toward me. He expressed a bit of sympathy for my condition, and even went so far as to promise me a better salary and some vacation time. I was stunned by such generosity, and most appreciative of it. I needed time off to visit a few agencies about getting sponsorship back to Hungary. In spite of becoming more acclimated to Israel it still seemed best for me to somehow make my way back. I felt that if I could only contact a government office or private business I'd find someone to back my return trip. Naiveté still had possession of my soul, and I thought that another Jew somewhere out there would take pity on me and help out. After all, back in Hungary it was normal to expect one Jew to help another. Of course, back in Hungary only about one percent of the population was Jewish, so we tended to stick together. Israel, on the other hand, was wall-to-wall Jews, and I was hardly a rare commodity. My benefactor never surfaced, but it took me forever to come to understand why. In any case, looking for my mystery landtsman was time intensive, so it was a real blessing to have my old boss grant me this freedom. Previously, he had perpetually threatened to replace any us for being absent too long. I was actually quite lucky to still have my job there after such a long period of recuperation, so it was like an extra act of mercy to have the liberty to search for outside support without the threat of unemployment hanging over my head. Or so I thought. As it turned out all that magnanimous talk about higher pay and time off was a pack of lies. When it came time for him to make good on these promises he played dumb. That man made me a promise just like Judah Winter had, and my phony communist uncle, and the commercial attaché. It was the proverbial straw that broke this camel's back. All of my frustrations boiled over and I went berserk. All the lies and hunger and nightmares came exploding out of me and I grabbed a stick and whacked him. But I wasn't just hitting this pathetic Polish burlap merchant; I was hitting every person that had disappointed me since leaving Budapest. And I didn't just hit him once. A lot of people had disappointed me, and I had gone through a lot of anxiety. I totally lost control and hit him repeatedly. Soon he was bleeding profusely, and the sight of it caused me to come to my senses. Panicking at the sight of his blood I dropped the stick and ran. Everyone stood around in shock as I fled to Natan's house.

"Ivan! Natan! I killed a guy! I killed a guy! "
"Who did you kill?"
"The Polack I work for."
"What are you talking about?"
"I hit him and he fell down bleeding."

"Oh you probably just hurt him a little. You're no bruiser. But you better get back."

I did go back, and discovered him wrapped in bandages. I had hit him so hard he needed stitches, but I was greatly relieved that he was going to be okay. It was a further relief to learn that he hadn't called the cops. Oddly enough he didn't seem to be taking it all that seriously, and being the workaholic that he was, he didn't even stop production. All things considered I was pretty lucky. I had taken out all my frustrations on this poor guy, yet I wasn't going to have to face any harsh consequences over it. Furthermore I got rewarded for it. Of course the reward came from somewhere else entirely. It turns out that my boss' nemesis, his fierce competitor down the street, was thrilled over what I had done, and he gave me a job where I got to sit down. He even taught me how to sew the bags together with an industrial sewing machine. These working conditions were far superior, and he doubled my salary to boot. I took it all as a good omen, and when the cops didn't come to arrest me I felt as though I had been given a second chance.

The whole beating and getting a better job experience defined a time of transition for me in which I was able to save a little money and, along with two new friends –a Moroccan and another Hungarian- find a nicer place to live. I even made it to the flea market to buy some clothes. Old, worn, and unwanted by their previous owners, they seemed new to me, especially compared to what I had been wearing for months, which was hardly more than rags. I had a picture taken of me in my new flea market outfit to send to my mother to show her that I wasn't doing so badly. Of course, I also hoped it'd inspire her to reconsider and bring me back. Sadly, that was one situation that was not about to change any time soon.

My new job also gave me enough money to allow me to escape the cellar of the Israeli economic scale and make it to the second lowest rung on its economic ladder. All in all I was starting to feel something we now call self esteem. No longer mired in mere sustenance survival I sought out more social interaction, and I started to attend gatherings of other immigrants. Among them were concentration camp survivors and I heard about their experiences in such places as Bergen-Belsen, Dachau and Auschwitz. After hearing about their lives I could see that my own didn't look quite so bad after all. Even my toughest times in the streets of Budapest and Haifa were mild by comparison with what they had been through. Even though my story seemed less traumatic than theirs it was still a great release for me to be able to talk about it. In all the time I had been in Israel I never had the opportunity to completely reveal my heart and mind as I did at those meetings, and it was at least a partial panacea for my solitude.

Growing to manhood, whether in Europe or on the shores of the Mediterranean, is all the same to adolescent men, and Natan and I were always girl hunting. We wanted something more fulfilling than women of the night, so we were always trying our chances with nicer girls. And when we were lucky enough to find a pair of young ladies we'd go dancing and share some refreshment. And double dating produced the comfortable result of an instant family of four. It was cozy and reassuring to be in the company of my date along with Natan and his date. Sex wasn't a prerequisite as long as I could luxuriate in the company of females. During the roughest time of war it was the gentle sex that had sheltered me from harm, and as far as I was concerned they were all symbols of security. Depression and anxiety had no chance when a woman was around, and I was continually attaching myself to one girl or another, at least emotionally. They enjoyed my visits and always listened patiently to my stories. But some detail always prevented us from maintaining a relationship. One of us was always too poor or lived too far away, or something. Thus, my subconscious need to create a family was always foiled. I also lacked confidence due to my shabby overall appearance. Despite improved employment and language skills my second hand wardrobe, inferior to what I presumed constituted a sharp appearance, and imperfect smile, got in the way of meeting girls. Regardless, some well meaning parents tried to help, introducing me to some proper and eligible young ladies. I had blabbed so much about my acting fame back in Europe they saw me as someone of worthy potential, and didn't mind my associating with their daughters. But my low economic and social condition caused me such embarrassment I was hesitant to accept their well intentioned invitations. One immigrant girl with whom I was allowed to associate had the same name as my sister, Zsuzsi. We had a lot in common, and we liked each other. Having already lost my virginity I was always on the lookout for any possibility of repeating the experience, and I tried my utmost to convince her. I'd go over to her apartment after work and whistle for her to come down. I never wanted to go up, because my clothes were ill fitting and threadbare. We would chat as I plotted taking our relationship to a more intimate level, all the while trying to hide my imperfect smile. But our conversations always ended with the distant call of her mother, "Zsuzsika, come up!" When her birthday rolled around she invited me to her party, casually mentioning that everyone would be dressed a bit more formally than usual.

"But this is all I have," I told her.

She thought for a few seconds.

"Well Zev, I don't want you to feel uncomfortable. So, if you want to come a little later and whistle like usual, I'll bring you down some birthday cake."

Actually, wearing second hand clothes was quite common for a lot of people in the early days of Israel, but I suffered terribly over it, remembering as I did the example of my chic father. Zsuzsi felt sorry for me and brought me that cake which I fondly remember. Of course, it was absurd to stand on such formality. All of our circumstances in Europe had been better before the war, and yet we still let those ridiculous middle class affectations prevent us from finding some happiness together.

Three birthdays had passed since I had disembarked from the Galilee, and although I continued to think about Hungary I was slowly evolving into an Israeli. Hebrew hadn't come so hard after all, and I had made a few good friends. I was poor, but my eyes were starting to open up to the opportunities that this new society offered a young man like me. It had taken a good long while, but I was finally maturing. Then, an idea dawned bright within the darkest dankest regions of my mind, and I suddenly realized that there was indeed a way for me to have that family, stay well fed and clothed, get my teeth fixed, be socially acceptable, and even get an education in the bargain.

Chapter XV

Miami 8

I opened my eyes for a moment to see if the hospital room stopped spinning, but everything was mottled, blurry, and frightening, and I had to shut them tight again to escape the nausea. My breathing was labored, and I was broken out in a heavy sweat. I was seriously afraid I was having a heart attack, and panic engulfed me. The nurses were running around trying to find the proper medication for me, but I knew it was hopeless. Supine, and at the mercy of cold hearted fate, I knew their pharmacology held no cure for me. Their shelves were stocked with every federally approved potion available in the west, but not one of them could affect me for the better. No pill, elixir, salve or intravenous drip offered relief from my torment. The panacea for me was thousands of miles away in Italy, and I was going through heavy withdrawal symptoms from lack of it. Without her by my side I couldn't even breathe! I finally realized that this sweet, young, Cuban-American woman was my soul mate. It's true that I was old enough to be her father, and had kids nearly her age, but she accepted all that and still loved me. I just couldn't put up the act any longer. No more pretending that I didn't love her. No more theater of the absurd. I went over the love affairs I'd had with other women, and none had the deep significance of what Rebequita and I shared. We cared about and respected each other. Women like Loretta had affairs with me out of pure lust, but torrid passion is no substitute for real caring and affection. Those women are control freaks who ensnare men with their sensuality. Real love vanquishes such base considerations. It's the difference between dreams and nightmares. My object of sincere innocent affection abided solely within Rebequita, and her absence was driving me insane. Complicating my anxiety was the stress I felt over providing a secure emotional environment for my sons. I had uprooted them and we were still in the process of transplanting them when I had met Rebequita. The weight of responsibility was so dominant in my life that I even felt guilty for robbing time from them with this emotional breakdown of mine. The boys deserved an oak, and I was behaving like a weeping willow. And even though she gladly accepted the package deal of three male Gabors I had continued to hold Rebequita at arm's length. I really was out of my head. The history of matrimony is full of scary tales of second marriages that suffer from envious second wives and wicked step mothers, but our situation was the opposite. I had it all, yet I wouldn't commit. Truly, I was nuts. I could not distinguish sweet reality from bitter illusion. I was like a man with jaundice. In that condition the taste buds don't function properly and sugar tastes sour. But by eating candy the condition improves. Sweet Rebequita was the cure, but like a crazed lunatic I denied myself the ease of its application. I didn't even need a prescription. The dulcet remedy was over the counter and in reach. So, why fight it? Illusion imposed itself on reality. Imaginary guilt smothered innocence. Like a Freudian text book case I assigned blame where there was none. I characterized myself as a sinner, offensive to all moral codes and ethics just for loving an adult chronologically inferior to me. But the truth was that she was far more mature than me. How else could she have tolerated such a goofy Hungarian?

I don't think that the dream like surrealistic state that I inhabit is unique to this world. What makes my case unusual is that I occupy this terrain as an adult. Children almost always experience this planet as a verifiable surrealistic event, understanding almost nothing that's going on, while being fascinated by it at the same time. My plight is that I never outgrew it. The entire universe, especially my personal encounters with it, looks completely insane to me, and I can't do a thing about it. I see madness everywhere, yet I'm powerless to impact it for the better. I've felt this way since before I could properly express it, and it's never lost its grip on me. In my hospital bed it was all becoming clear to me, but too late. Rebequita was gone, and all that was left was pain. The agony washed over me and transported me back to that source of greatest pain and how I struggled to overcome it.

Chapter XVI

Army Life

In 1952 in Israel it was a common sight to see girls in military dress. Their uniforms were identical to what the men wore, with their khaki pants tucked into their boots, shirt sleeves rolled up to mid-bicep, and rakish berets. This had nothing to do with a fashion craze, but was the practical result of a nation with a small population being faced with the dire need to defend itself. Absolutely everyone between eighteen and forty-nine had to serve a term in the army, officially known as the Israeli Defense Forces. The women served too, replacing men in almost every noncombatant position, and even fighting when the need arose. But I must tell you that the women looked far sexier in those uniforms than the men ever did. If you'll forgive a double entendre I must tell you that I wanted to get myself into one of those uniforms too. I was a few months shy of eighteen, and I figured that they would ignore that detail to get another man under arms. But I was devastated to be rejected for being too young. They gave me an interview to determine if I could speak Hebrew well enough to follow orders and I passed, but the age rule held. I had already terminated my employment, such as it was, and I asked them to waive the restriction. Again they refused. I wasn't about to give up, so I begged them. "I'm alone, hungry, and have nowhere to live. Let me join!" Still they said no.

I roamed Haifa with the solitary thought of coming up with a fool proof ruse that would convince them to let me in. I had to do something, because at that time I was no better off materially than when I had started opening gunny sacks. But after two more weeks of Spartan drudgery I couldn't think of anything clever or logical. So I marched back there and, not being possessed of any particular plan, applied pure persistence to persuade them. Such patriotism, or whining, had seldom come their way, and after contorting their faces and scratching their heads, they finally put aside the regulations, turned a blind eye, made an exception, and let me in. It was the moment that changed everything, the absolute dividing line of my life, the mark against which I calculate everything. Now if anyone asked me where I lived I had one proud answer, "The Israeli Army is my home!" No more crumby jobs or flea bag hovels. I gleefully surrendered my miserable minimal independence to the all consuming commitment to military life.

Ecstatic over winning my first military engagement, that of overwhelming blind adherence to rules, I left word with the Schindlers where to find me, and made my way down to the Haifa recruitment Center. I was the only fellow there under eighteen, but my grit was no less ripe. I was physically the match of any of them, and my life experience made me no less prepared than them either. There were parents there to see some inductees off, which caused within me momentary melancholy, but along with my oath of allegiance to the flag I made my own silent declaration to replace my persistent gloom with an enthusiasm to change my life. I eagerly leaped into the back of the truck to boot camp, and never looked back.

Even though Israel was in its infancy she had well established military bases that had been abandoned by the exiting British. They were complete in every way, from barracks to officer's clubs with bars, and were a valuable strategic boon to her early defense. I was assigned to base number four, which was one of the most prestigious. It was inland, between Tel Aviv and Jerusalem, in the small town of Sarafend, and it was enormous. There was a training area for new recruits, a motor pool for tanks, and a modern communications center. Its barracks constituted the cleanest domicile I'd inhabited since leaving Budapest, and its bunks, with clean blankets, made me feel civilized again.

Everything about the base was attractive to me. I loved the order, because my life thus far in the Holy Land had been unholy chaos. The first thing that was put into good order was my diet. It finally became scheduled and dependable. I ate like a condemned man, though I certainly didn't feel doomed, and I finally got to fill out my frame. Height wise I had grown to manhood in Israel, but poverty had prevented me from putting any bulk onto my skeleton. Having already swallowed a thousand portions of poorly prepared hummus and beans, army chow tasted like haute cuisine. Of course, every moment of every day was spent burning off those calories and molding that new bulk with calisthenics and physical exercise, the most intense military training anywhere. Much later I learned of the reputation enjoyed by the Israeli army, that it was respected everywhere as the best in the world. With dedicated enemies at our every border we had no choice but to be the best. Anything less and we would have been overrun by our neighbors. We got up every morning at 5:30 and ran around the entire two mile perimeter of the base. And that was before breakfast. The object of such rigorous training was to produce men of steel. And that was just the start. Besides putting us in peerless physical condition our minds were well honed too. I'm not bragging that we were smarter because we were an army made up mostly of Jews, but it's a fact that we had more than our fair share of college degree holders among our ranks. Unlike America and other developed nations that gave student deferments, Israel drafted everyone into military service at the age of eighteen, regardless of social status, educational level, or gender. Surrounded as we were by hostile powers, and always on high alert, we had to be both physically and mentally sharp. As part of my basic training I got advanced classes in Hebrew, and a variety of other subjects to improve my mind. Like a sponge, I soaked up everything they had to teach me, from making up my cot to strategic tactics. I woke up with reveille and went to bed with taps, and fell into the rhythm of martial life like I had been born to it. It was a challenge every moment of the day, and I loved it all. I took whatever they dished out and begged for more. It made me tough and it took care of every one of my needs to an unlimited degree. There are things in my life which I regret, and would love to have the mystic power to change. But, given the choice, my life in the Israeli army is something I would gladly do over again. I went into the service a directionless, bitter, sickly, ignorant, confused child, and came out a fulfilled, confident, content, healthy, educated and motivated man. My comrades stayed friends for life, and a day doesn't go by when I don't find myself following some guideline taught to me at base number four. I'm grateful they took me in, and I did my damnedest to see they didn't regret it. I'm not prouder of anything in my life than having served in the Israeli National Defense Forces.

Besides training my mind and body the army provided me with the perfect opportunity to do something about my appearance. For the first time in over three years I got to dress in something other than rags and, being every inch my father's son, I kept my uniforms immaculate. Whenever I went out I had a crease in my trousers, and my shirt was clean, starched and pressed. My boots gleamed, I was cleanly shaven, and my hair was always trimmed. I was a proud soldier, determined to present the ideal image of an Israeli fighting man. And now that I belonged, my sleeves were smartly rolled up. The only vestige of my pre-military life, and the one constant of my Israeli journey, was Natan Schindler. We were still friends, and I was always glad to see him and whip him in ping pong. His whole family was important to me, and I never let too much time pass without paying them a visit. They had sustained me psychologically through my roughest times in Haifa, and they shared in my pride as I progressed.

Another benefit of being in the army was the blessing of getting my teeth repaired. The Israeli army provides free dental care to its troops and I finally got that cursed hole in my tooth filled in. I had been a vain boy, and for nearly thirty anxiety ridden months I had been forced to endure an imperfect smile, making me feel like a deformed troll. I had been bereft of youthful charm and confidence. Everyone had looked upon me with pity, or so I thought. Now I was reborn.

The army was my home to the exclusion of all else, and I even stayed in the barracks when the other troops went on leave. Not that I had anyone to visit. I only knew the Schindlers, and if I had gone to see them there wouldn't have been any place for me to stay. I visited them of course, but only for a few hours now and then. Any longer would have been an imposition, so I mostly stayed on the base.

Mail-call was a rare reminder of sadness. Letters came for others, but rarely for me. I was expecting to hear from my mother, but it was always a long wait. It seemed as if her vow to never forgive me was in earnest. But I was determined not to let it get to me. Ghosts of the war and Aliyah still plagued me, but I was in a program now that let me deal with all those issues. I had long since learned that I was not alone in coming to Israel along a bumpy path. All the Israeli pioneers had stories that would tear the heart out of a stone. We had all run the gauntlet, and I felt great camaraderie with these brave men and women. The decision that had brought me to Israel in the first place was born of guilt and peer pressure, but now, as an adult, everything seemed to be making more sense to me. I really had made the right decision. Israel was my home, and the army, at least for now, was my role in it. The sum total effect of all this on my consciousness was that I was finally ready to confront the psychological trauma inflicted on me from growing up during the war and cope with it.

My superiors recommended me for a special course to learn combat tactics. We trained with live ammo, and I became a marksman. It was amusing to think of myself, someone loathe to harm another being, as now being possessed of the ability to personally render someone dead or wounded at a great impersonal distance. Finding this niche reminded me of my eternal connection to all things surreal.

Once I had absorbed all the specific theoretical techniques involved in hostile engagement I was assigned to patrol the border. That's where conflicts were most likely to occur so it was part of routine training. I climbed miles of rocky barren landscape and scanned endless Arab horizons through my binoculars until my stint was up. While Israel has the reputation of constantly enduring attacks I report that my own time on the frontier was blessedly tranquil.

I celebrated my first anniversary in the military, but I was such a gung-ho soldier I wasn't even aware that an entire year had flown by. Soldiers the world over make it a habit to gripe about army life, and they love to complain about getting up early, the bad food, and a thousand things, but not me. I was such an eager beaver they made me a drill sergeant and put me in charge of training new recruits. What pride to be awarded those three stripes! I was assigned to F Company where I remained for the rest of my career in the army.

I applied myself to mold my charges into spit and polish defenders of Israel. I met Jews from all over the world with different levels of education, and helped train college graduates, as well as teens that had been forced to drop out of school to hide or defend their families. In some of my dealings with these guys it was like looking in the mirror. I could relate extremely well with them, but I also studied psychology to give me a more objective understanding of them. I loved them like brothers, but was as hard as nails on them, and merciless in my demands. Anything less would have let them down. Being a drill sergeant for the Israeli army in the early fifties meant that the defense and survival of this infant nation, the homeland of these recruits, was in my hands. Did we want to live and die at the mercy of Nazis or Nyilasok or Cossacks again? Were we to keep assimilating within a bunch of arrogant, eternally latent anti-Semitic dilettantes, begging like puppies for a bone of respect? Or were we going to stand on our own two feet, the equal of any, and demand it? To do that meant uncompromising self-determination. There was no question about it; we had to be tougher and more motivated than any soldiers anywhere. And it was my job, my responsibility, my mission, to be blacksmith to their iron. I had to stoke the fire, fan the flames, pump the bellows, hammer the anvil, and forge these landtsmen into Israel's first line of defense. If nobody was going to come and take our mothers away it was my solemn duty to make them ready to take on all such comers, even if my methods made them hate me for it. Some of my charges went on to become majors and generals, and they appreciated every stern order I gave and every task I set them to. But once basic training was over I lowered my defenses and we all became friends. They often invited me to their homes for Shabbos or High Holidays, and I was always happy to go. Of course, I always showed up in my uniform, because I still didn't have any presentable civilian clothes.

The first three years of military service were done as just that, service. It wasn't a job and, except for minimal vital expenses, there was no salary as other armies offer. So, chic civilian wardrobe had to wait. But I didn't care, because I always felt dapper in my uniform. And like soldiers everywhere, I was not averse to attracting young ladies with epaulets, beret and swagger.

As I trained my charges I too became tougher, more dedicated and self confident. I was following in the footsteps of my own drill sergeant, and I had to do him proud. What a miracle he had performed. It was by now impossible to reconcile myself with the scraggily ragamuffin who had begged to be let in before his eighteenth birthday. What happened to that pathetic kid? I physically did not resemble him, and I didn't think as he did at all. I was content as a soldier and hardly ever reflected on my brief career on the stage. Also, homesickness was nearly forgotten. Naturally, I still wanted to make amends with my mother, but the misery of the rued Aliyah was decidedly on hold.

Army time is busy time so the months and years flew by. I felt like I had barely worn off the first polish on my boots when I celebrated my third year in service with a promotion to Sergeant Major. In the Israeli army the rank of Sergeant Major is highly respected, and my word was obeyed without question by F Company. I was second only to company commander, Captain Massa. I now had a private room inside the barracks, and I was finally allowed a rare luxury in the Israeli army, a real pillow and sheets to go along with the blankets. For three years I had shared the Spartan simplicity of three blankets per bunk. We slept between two, and rolled the third up as a pillow. Actually it was the fist time I had slept between sheets since my actor days. Now, as one of the privileged few, I rated this refinement. In addition to all this finery an office with a secretary was at my disposal. But the real coup de grace was the salary. After all my time in the military I finally got paid. All in all, being a Sergeant Major was a big deal, and it was the pinnacle of my life in Israel thus far. On my wrist was the special khaki bracelet that indicated my rank, and I was determined to honor the trust my new country placed in me.

During this period the Fedayin guerrillas were making sporadic raids into Israeli territory, mostly to try and put fear into the hearts of the population. They also attacked lookout posts on the frontier. But these incidents were far from Sarafend so weekend passes were the norm for everyone, including officers. As I always stayed behind I was left in charge of my sector of the base. There were no military obligations with which to occupy my time so I busied myself on the phone trying to talk to whatever females were left on the base. We would chat about everything, from politics to sports, and I always tried to end the conversation by making a date. Then, one day I needed to make a long distance call to Tel Aviv, and I heard a new operator's voice on the other end of the line. It was a particularly lovely voice, and I knew at once that I had to know her. I totally forgot about the long distance call, and after blabbing for an hour she agreed to meet me at the main gate. She was as lovely as she sounded, and we sat and talked for hours. Her name was Yona Costello, and she had an angelic face with the eyes of an innocent doe. Her laugh was captivating, and she was the sweetest person I had ever met, and by the end of our conversation we were head over heels in love. She was my first real sweetheart, and she brought me greater happiness than I had ever known before. Besides my parents she was the first person to ever tell me she loved me, and I was so moved by it I felt like the hole in my soul was finally mended as well as the one in my tooth. Actually, I could not even recall ever being told such a thing. Probably my parents and my grandmother must have said that to me, but I had no specific memory of it. So, when sweet Yona made that pronouncement it finally made me feel like someone of real worth. And the fact that it happened while I was in the army rounded out my training in a most unexpected way, giving me self esteem on a level never anticipated.

Yona and I absolutely adored each other, and my delirium made me forget any pangs of guilt hidden within me. With Yona in charge of the heart department, and my body taken care of by the military, fulfillment was mine at last. She and I were both soldiers with many duties to perform, but we sought out every possible opportunity to be together. She used to bring me home cooked meals, and we slept in a tent in the countryside. Though I had been with my share of young ladies this was the first time in which sentimental affection was on an equal par with physical intimacy. When we were not in a passionate embrace we were in rapt conversation. She patiently listened to me describe my whole life, laughing at the happy times and weeping at the sad. Her musical voice delighted me as I heard her recount her own history. Dad was a British soldier, also a sergeant major, stationed in Palestine, and as is so often the case, he was one of those members of the occupying forces that falls in love with and marries a colonial. She was a pretty girl, originally from Yemen, and they settled in a town near the base where Yona was born, and he became a part of Israeli society. He was an old fashioned military man with a handle bar moustache and ramrod posture who was a musician and became administrator of the Israeli army band. I was thrilled to go to Tel Aviv to meet him, and being accepted by Yona's family made me feel as if I was immersed in an ocean of love. After meeting Sergeant Costello a lovely destiny gave us occasion to work together, putting on concerts for the troops. I had impressed my superiors enough to be given many responsible assignments, including those not directly related to national defense. The most memorable of those were the shows we staged at the base.

Many well known international artists came there, with audiences of a thousand soldiers for each show. I was in charge of organizing them and I had a small army under me, setting up the stage, sound, and lighting. It was exciting to have Yona's father directing the band, and an immeasurable thrill to be able to work with the big stars that came to entertain our troops. One of my favorites was Danny Kaye. A landtsman, he kidded with everyone in Yiddish and brought the house down. The highlight of the show was when he took over directing the orchestra, which gave me the double joy of being entertained by one of the most charming performers in memory and involving my sweetheart's dad all at the same time. Etched in my mind is being warmly greeted in Hebrew by another great star who came to entertain our troops. Frank Sinatra shook my hand and said, "Shalom." Old Blue Eyes was at the peak of his career at that time, and it was certainly not an artistic or commercial necessity for him to travel so far to sing for such a tiny audience. But his trip there said to the world that he supported the Jewish State, and his presence meant more to us than having America send over a fleet of tanks. At one show we had a guest in the audience bigger than any entertainer, our commander in chief, Moshe Dayan. I saluted him, thrust out my hand and identified myself.

"Sergeant Major Zev Gabor, my general."

He returned my salute sharply and cordially gave me a nice firm handshake. Meeting him was naturally a great thrill, but it paled in comparison with the brief audience I was granted with David Ben Gurion. This man was Israel's George Washington, and he was held in the highest esteem by every citizen. When he finally retired from political life he moved to a Kibbutz in the Negev Desert. He always maintained that Israel would not make the progress it needed to unless this arid place was properly irrigated, and his presence there was a statement to remind us to make that dream a reality. It was called

Kibbutz Sde Boker, and some of us who had been working at that time to raise funds for cancer research were selected to have a little chat with him in his modest bungalow. We would each be allowed one question, and when my turn came I first told him that I was from Hungary which he seemed to consider noteworthy. Then I asked him, "How can we deal with the growing Arab population? There are so few of us and so many of them. And they keep having more babies. What can we do?"

He patiently regarded me and said, "In time quantity will submit to quality."

His answer seemed satisfactory, but it was his charisma that was most convincing. Although he was in his eighties at that time his eyes were as clear and bright as a child's. When he looked at you it was as if his gaze could pierce you to your soul. With such leadership surely we would prevail.

The army had matured me, so I was able to keep a level head even while floating on cloud Yona. So, while it's normal for a young man in love to consider marriage I knew that it was absolutely impossible in my financial condition. Israel was poor, so even paid soldiers such as myself didn't make very much. And, having already struggled through Israeli poverty, I didn't want a repeat of it, much less subject someone I loved to it. And sure enough, Yona brought up the topic of matrimony, and was devastated to hear my practical and intractable position. She let me know that her military obligation was ending and that she wanted us to get married. But how could I marry anyone? I was a pauper, and couldn't afford to leave the army!

Although I felt great affection from Yona's family there was a lot of friction for her at home. Her dad, British and gentile, married a Yemeni Jew, and despite his love for her, and his decency, and willingness to participate in Israeli society, there was just so much cultural difference between them that they were always squabbling over something. Yona wanted to break away from that, and the only way she saw to do it was to get married and have her own home. She'd been waiting to do it since she was twelve, and with her army obligations finally coming to an end she just couldn't stand to wait any longer. She wanted to get married and get out of the house, and she even became aggressive over it.

"You're only interested in my body! You don't want to spend your life with me!"

"I can't provide for you. You know what a soldier makes!"

"Don't use that as an excuse! If you loved me you'd think of something!"

I couldn't make her see how difficult our lives would be. Part of my motivation in joining the army was to escape abject poverty, and there was no way I was going back to that, even with a lovely lady on my arm. Yona knew all about my pre-army suffering but was blind to it when it interfered with her agenda. She wanted to flee her home, and saw matrimony as the escape route. Arguing about it didn't do any good, and she finally stopped taking my calls. I even went to Tel Aviv to dissuade her from her plan, but it was no use. Things deteriorated rapidly, and she finally sent me a letter saying we were through. If I wasn't the marrying type, she wrote, then I wasn't the one for her. As it turns out, there was an officer who had been after her, and even though she loved me, she married him. She left me for another, someone who would give her what she needed. It was lonely at first, but I really didn't feel so bad when it was all over with. After all, she had brought me so much happiness it would've been ungrateful of me to feel resentful. It was at this time that I formulated string of pearls philosophy. I learned to treasure every pearl on life's necklace, and Yona is one of that strand's loveliest. Ultimately we became friends, and I even accompanied her on her initial visit to the doctor when she was expecting her first child.

Echoes Of My Footsteps

I ran into her on the street and she told me about her life and her marriage. The way she looked at me made me think that she still loved me, and if I'd have been able to commit to marriage, then this child would've been ours.

There were many more pearls, but one stands out, not just for its romantic memory, but because it actually effected the course of my career. Our base commander was Colonel Dov Yermiyahu, a hero of our war of independence, and a personal friend of General Moshe Dayan. He had the respect of every man on the base, but he was still just a man and had feet of clay. Despite the fact that he was married with children he couldn't take his eyes off his knockout of a secretary. Every soldier on the base shared the colonel's lust, including me, and it kept the colonel in a constant state of high jealous alert. She herself was no stranger to amorous liaisons, and her wild reputation frustrated the colonel no end. He knew I liked her, but he wanted her to himself and was determined to thwart my plans. When my last Hanukkah in the service rolled around I got an unexpected present when she let me know that she wanted to be with me. There was a party at the officer's club to celebrate the Festival of Lights and the noncommissioned officers, like me, were invited. She was there and we snuck off to the apartment of a friend of mine. Later someone knocked on the door, and when I opened it to see who it was he got a glimpse of her over my shoulder in the bedroom. Of course when he went back to the party he blabbed about what he had seen, and it wasn't long before Colonel Yermiyahu got wind of it. That was that. My military career took a nosedive. From that point on I could do nothing right, and was reprimanded for the slightest imperfection in the performance of my duty. And if I actually did something worthy of a reprimand he tried to escalate it into a court martial charge. On one such occasion I landed in hot water over a bird.

Echoes Of My Footsteps

We had been instructed in the technique of firing at low flying aircraft with a rifle by judging its speed and aiming slightly ahead of it so the bullet would perfectly intersect with the speeding aircraft. It's called leading your target. I learned it and stashed it away in my brain, never really knowing if I'd ever put it to use. Sometime later I was driving around the base on a security check with a few other soldiers when I spotted a high flying bird and decided to put that leading theory to the test. Without getting down from the jeep I asked one of my comrades to pass me his rifle and I took aim. Drawing a bead on a patch of air about a foot in front of the bird I squeezed the trigger. A second later the bird and the bullet met, and my men cheered my eagle eye as the dove plummeted earthward. When we got back my comrades spread my fame. One officer heard the story and said he was going to nominate me for crack shot of the base. I was feeling proud and happy when another jeep roared up. A soldier got out carrying a small dead bird in his hand, and that same officer called him over to examine it. After taking a good look at the avian corpse he looked up at me with a frown, and went straight to Colonel Yermiyahu to make a report. Shortly, I was summoned.

"Is this the bird you shot, sergeant?"

I was starting to feel apprehensive, but I had to tell the truth.

"I believe so, sir."

Looking down at the tiny cadaver I knew I was in it deep. The bird had a tiny metal cylinder strapped to one of its legs. This was a carrier pigeon, an old fashioned battle field mode of communication which the Israeli army had successfully brought back into service. Had it been war time I would've been guilty of a serious crime. But even in peace time I was in for it.

"You know what you've done soldier?" he bellowed. "You've destroyed an important member of the Israeli national defense system!"

"Sir, yes sir!"

"Who knows what vital information our winged comrade was carrying?"

"Yes sir!"

"If this had been under real combat conditions your senseless act of wanton destruction could have doomed a whole regiment, maybe the whole base. Now, are you or are you not aware of the level of calamity you might have precipitated?"

"Yes sir!"

"I have every intention of recommending you for a court marital. Do you understand?"

"Yes sir!"

Indeed, I did understand what I had done. It was barbarically stupid. And I was truly grateful that we were not at war. But Colonel Yermiyahu had it in for me, and he actually had the power to court martial me. Fortunately, cooler heads prevailed, and he was convinced by other officers to let it pass in light of my previous excellent record.

Before the carrier pigeon incident I had been considering making a career in the army. A big general personally tried to convince me to stay, and it was tempting. After all, the army had given me so much, and I was grateful beyond evaluation for that experience. But my love life had so badly sabotaged my chances of advancing I knew that it was time to move on. I sadly tendered my resignation and it was accepted. But a few weeks later, before I could assimilate to civilian life, the Suez conflict broke out, and I was recalled.

At first I just trained recruits, but soon I was sent to the Sinai front and assigned to a combat unit to capture ambushers. The Arabs used to hide behind rocks and wait to ambush small reconnoitering units. Basically we were taught to outflank them. Doing so we could have easily killed them, but they were useful to trade for our own prisoners.

Their population was vast, but we highly prized every one of our soldiers, so it was a normal tactic to take Arab prisoners with the eventual goal of swapping them. We captured so many we could afford to release ten of theirs for every one of ours. Such odds were irresistible and assured the release of many of our troops. But it was risky, because we couldn't spare many troops to guard those prisoners. Just one other comrade and I, armed with submachine guns, would guard an entire column of thirty or more of the enemy. We carried the famed Uzis, and counted on them not to jam in any terrain. The Arabs knew of their reliability and were afraid to jump us. So, I never had to use the Uzi up close. I saw combat, but I was always shooting across a wide battlefield. If any of my bullets hit pay dirt I was unaware of it.

    I had been in the military over four years now, in both war and peace, and I hadn't suffered a scratch. And it looked like I might make it out of this conflict in one piece. We were on the offensive, poised to thrust deep into enemy territory, and everyone was talking about our rapid progress and success. In high spirits some comrades and I were pushing forward in an armored personnel carrier when we hit a land mine. The explosion flipped our vehicle and threw me twenty feet into the air. I came down hard, and my shoulder and head were badly hurt. My eyes were filled with blood, and I was bleeding from my mouth and nose. The medics couldn't stop the bleeding, and only my strict training kept me from panicking. I was evacuated to a field hospital where they kept me alive through a series of transfusions. Finally my condition stabilized and I was transported back to our own lines where I was put in a hospital to recuperate. By the time my wounds healed the conflict was over. I survived that explosion, but one of my best friends died in it. I grieved the loss of my buddies all, but having done my duty to my country I felt free to retire to civilian life once and for all. I lost some precious friends in the fighting, but many more were alive, and we've stayed in touch to this day. The allegiance of men who experience combat together is immeasurable and unbreakable. I recall Sergeant Yitzhak Gibli, whom it was an honor to know. He was as famous in Israel as Sergeant York and Audie Murphy are in America. He was in the legendary Commandos 101, under Ariel Sharon, and performed one heroic act after another. And when he was captured, becoming the first Israeli defense fighter to be taken prisoner, Sharon led a raid into Jordan that captured twenty Arab military officers just to be able to trade them back for Gibli. I was also honored to serve with General David Eleazar, or Dado as he came to be called. He was the heroic defender of Jerusalem during the war of independence and later a hero of the Yom Kippur War. Eventually he became Commander in Chief of military operations. What a lady killer he was. He looked like Gregory Peck on steroids and enjoyed a reputation that made Warren Beatty look like a monk. So many incredible men of destiny crossed my path it dims any thought of life in the theater as worthwhile. I treasure the friendship of these men of destiny and value above estimation the organization that put us together. With a lump in my throat I walked out of Base number four.

The entire time I was in the army I had accepted whatever I was ordered to do, and go wherever I was sent. Not one time did I ever request a transfer. Now, my first transfer was to civilian life. I'd miss the army, but I knew it was time to move on.

Chapter XVII

Miami 9

They transferred me from the emergency room to a regular room in order to give me some tests, including checking my heart. I could now open my eyes without having the room spin around, but I was still overwhelmed by anxiety. My mind was no longer my ally, and images of women from different eras in my life invaded and fled at their leisure, all backed up by snippets of Beatle songs about aborted love affairs. Broken hearts in the Middle East, rapprochements from mothers, and erotic nights in Miami. *I once had a girl, or should I say, she once had me.* Was I condemned to live like Ulysses, ever tempted and plagued by the sirens? Maybe I should become a monk and stay away from women? *Ah girl!* Maybe I should just settle down? But look what happened last time I tried that! *Cried for no on. A love that should have lasted years.* Did I love Rebequita, or was I being selfish? I was too old for her! *When I'm sixty four.* Her mother was right! We would never marry! It wasn't fair to her! She was young! *Your mother should know.* But I love her! *And I love her.* No, I must think of her first! But she says she loves me! It isn't right! Love isn't right?! No! *She loves you!*

Use your head, not your heart! It isn't right! *In my life I love you more!* It isn't fair! Rebequita! Rebequita!

The next thing I knew a doctor was gently shaking me awake.

"Mr. Gabor, can you hear me?"

As reserved as he was it still startled me, and I sat up with a start.

"Rebequita!"

"Mr. Gabor, I'm Doctor Madaliago. Can you understand me?"

I slowly became aware of my surroundings. A man in a white lab coat and a tie came into focus with a nurse standing off to his side. Both were smiling.

"Mr. Gabor. How do you feel?"

"Un poco nervioso," I said, still relying on Spanish as my default language.

"He says he feels nervous," said the nurse to the doctor.

"I understand Spanish, Nurse Gomez. I am originally from Colombia."

It was a relief to hear the doctor speak Spanish. Too bad he didn't speak Hungarian.

"Mr. Gabor, your tests reveal nothing abnormal physically. Clearly though, you suffer from extreme hyper tension and emotional distress."

I was glad to hear that I wasn't physically ill, and it was no surprise to hear about my nervous condition. He merely confirmed what that Austrian doctor had told me back in Vienna so long ago. It was no surprise back then either. I've always been emotional and prone to stress. And let me tell you, you don't rid yourself of something like that with pure will power. It's just something you have to learn to live with. But certain stimuli can aggravate or relieve it, and losing Rebequita was about as aggravating as things could get. The doctor's calming tones helped a little though.

"You had an anxiety attack, actually an emotional crisis. I've rarely seen one so extreme. Your blood pressure levels on these kinds of episodes can bring serious consequences. So, we're going to keep you here for a week and conduct more tests. Well, good luck. Adios."

I lay in my hospital bed quietly meditating on life. The doctor was right of course. I couldn't drive myself crazy with all this stress. On the other hand, the cause of my stress, this unresolved relationship with Rebequita, was going to continue to fuel my anxiety. For the moment I was calm, thanks to modern science and tranquilizers, but I had to come to terms with all this in a drug free condition. Such things drive people to drink and dope, and my dilemma with Rebequita was driving me to understand how that can make some people do that. My drill sergeant had trained me better than that, and despite my susceptibility to emotional crises, I was not about to turn to drugs. But I had to find some way to deal with this impossible destiny.

Chapter XVIII

On My Own

After Yona Costello and I had separated I vowed to myself to be frugal. So, having saved up most of salary from my last year in the army, I looked around for something suitable to do with my life. At the invitation of a friend I went to Tel Aviv and stayed in his primitive wooden house near the central bus station. Nearby lived my new girlfriend, though she actually spent more time at my place than hers. I was a red blooded young single man, and I had a series of girlfriends during this stage of my life. This was before the famous sexual revolution of the sixties, but I was definitely in the vanguard of that movement. However, I never felt as if I exploited those women for mere physical pleasure. Passion was there of course, but I always cared for them as human beings, with affectionate consideration. But maybe the lack of family caused me to consider my relationships with these girls as temporary homes. My mother still rejected any chance of reconciliation, so I might have subconsciously portrayed my affairs as more domestic than they really were. I loved them, and had true romantic yearnings for them, but beyond the ardor of young lovers,

Echoes Of My Footsteps

I felt a certain security in their presence that I couldn't get anywhere else. In the psychological evaluation test known as word association I always equate the words girl or woman with family. After all, all of my surviving family members were female. I had a mother, a grandmother, a sister, and that's all. My father had passed away, and practically all of my parents' siblings, cousins, nieces, nephews, aunts and uncles had perished in the holocaust. It all happened when I was young, and my overwhelming memory of family focuses on a single gender. I wouldn't go so far as putting an Oedipal interpretation on it, and not even the most Freudian shrinks dared to suggest that intimacy with my girlfriends approximated any twisted liaison with family. I simple missed the close relationship and confidence that blood relatives have for each other. Even the wonderful Schindlers fell short of that mark. Their affection seemed platonic in comparison with the closeness I yearned for. Looking back on it now, I see that I was blind to the confidence extended me by Natan's kin. They opened their hearts and home to me, but I was so formal and worried about imposing on their hospitality I wouldn't let that wall down. Thankfully time eventually afforded me the chance to become as close as real family with them. Anyway, I had a girlfriend in Tel Aviv.

I read the classifieds and found an ad seeking ex-soldiers to prepare eighth-graders to go into the army. In the Israeli educational system the eighth level is like senior year in high school. In that year there's a program called Gadna, which is like American ROTC. A big difference though is that it's mandatory. So, I applied for it, and with my extensive and recent stint as a sergeant, they considered me ideal for the position. The young men and women were sent to a camp and I showed them what to expect in the army. I even put back on my old uniform. And because they gave me a place to stay and fed me I had no overhead and saved nearly a hundred percent of my salary. In a way it was like being back in the army, so while I performed my duties to the best of my ability I kept an eye out for other opportunities, convinced as I was that a military career was not for me. And after a couple of months a friend invited me to join him running a restaurant on the beach, midway between Haifa and Bat Yam, in an Arab town called Jabalyah. It was a wild unregimented six months, dealing with care free tourists. We had cabanas and served food and drink. Friday nights musicians played and lots of pretty girls came and went. I made some money, but the grueling grind of running a restaurant was not for me.

Next, I heard they were looking for physical education teachers for public school. The job was mine after just one interview and they even gave me a course of study during which time I was also paid. It turned out to be quite a nice position. It paid well and I was back in Tel Aviv where I was convinced a young man could find the best opportunities. I found a small apartment near the school, and before long I had another girlfriend, Pnina. Life was good.

By then it was 1957, and I started receiving letters from my mother with greater frequency, discussing the possibility of her immigrating to Israel. The Soviet regime in Hungary was repressive and life under communism was miserable. Oddly enough, Judah Winter's prediction was coming true, albeit behind schedule. The thought of my mother and grandma and sister coming to Israel was unimaginable to me. I was thrilled over it, but I also knew that I would have to get a stable, well paying position. Finally, after the 1956 Hungarian revolution a letter arrived saying they we were coming. I almost keeled over from the surprise. I liquidated everything to raise cash, and I was in such a dither preparing for their arrival I forgot about Pnina. Doubtless I was in a mental state of regression think about nothing but getting back together with my family. In anticipation over seeing them I was overwhelmingly happy, but also apprehensive as to how she would actually treat me.

After all, she had sworn never to forgive me, and every letter included her mantra, "You left me!"

Besides worrying about how my mother might treat me I was concerned about my sister Zsuzsi. Would she resent me for abandoning her too? When I left she was only three, and now she was a young lady of twelve. Would she feel anything for me at all? One person I didn't fret over was grandma. Above all I knew I could count on her love.

I went to Haifa on my recently purchased motorcycle to receive them, and my frame of mind was such that I forgot to even tell Pnina. I felt selfish and guilty over that, and I suppose it demonstrates just how true my family replacement theory was. Sweethearts were my surrogate kin, so as soon as my real blood relatives were on the way their substitutes were forgotten. Eventually I came to terms with having both.

When their ship got to Haifa I was on the dock waiting. There was no choir, but I received them with a heart full of love. Grandma wrapped me in her arms and smothered me, treating me as if nothing had ever happened. Seeing my grandmother again was a revelation. Actually, my grandma was not like being with just any person. In her case you were in a presence. In spite of the brutally tough life she had led she was always willing to sacrifice herself even more. She was like Gorky's mother character, selfless and dedicated. She emanated love and warmth, and was like an entire family unto herself. Next was my sister Zsuzsi. She was like a stranger but eager to greet me and know me. Then came mother. Now, I would love to report to you that she too wrapped me in her arms and all was forgotten. The truth is though she was different. She did hug me upon arrival, but it was with an air of detachment. There was most definitely a wall there. I was its architect, to be sure, but I had to wonder if it would ever come down. It ruined the reunion, but I kept a stiff upper lip.

After a welcome meal and conversations to catch us all up reality sank in. I now had to support my much larger family. I was supposed to have been doing so for the last nine years, but now that we were all together again I had to begin in earnest. In any case it was a great joy to have my family back. It was the last mental link missing in the reconstruction of my character. Not even the army or the Schindlers could accomplish what was now brought to fruition. To help this transition my grandma pulled me aside and told me not to pay so much attention to my mother's attitude.

"She's just nervous. Always been that way! Don't worry!"

Beloved grandma did her best to smooth it over and make me feel better, but it was obvious that the healing process, if it would work at all, would take a long time.

The Jewish agency provided them with a little apartment in the small town of Herzliyya, a little north of Tel Aviv, and I moved in with them. With my experience and connections I got another job as a public school physical education teacher. I worked as hard as I could to tend to my family's every need, but my salary was not enough to provide everything, and my mother had to find a job as a cashier in a supermarket. Zsuzsi felt comfortable in Israel, and she studied in school and took piano lessons. Piano lessons would have been a bourgeoisie affectation back in Budapest, and mother was happy to see her daughter learning music just as she had when she was a girl back in Baia Mare. My grandma was having no trouble readjusting at all. She loved Israel from the moment she stepped off the boat. After a lifetime of enduring anti-Semitism she was finally home, free to practice her religion to her heart's content. I think she must have always secretly longed to live here. Over time Zsuzsi was becoming comfortable with me, though mother was still a little bitter and standoffish. Nine years is a long time, and the memory of my abandoning them just wouldn't die easy. Ultimately she declared she was not happy in Herzliyya and ended up moving to the city of Bat Yam. I followed them there, and we lived together for a short time. But it was no use. We just couldn't get along any more. There was always some kind of conflict. It all boiled down to mother seeing me as an unrepentant fourteen year old kid. That's how she treated me. I was fourteen when I went on my Aliyah, and she had been fuming at a fourteen year old brat ever since. I never aged in her memory. I didn't shave, serve in the army, or change in her memory in any way. And that was the main stumbling block to our relationship. I don't blame her for that at all. It's just the way it was. Anyway, to try and lessen the friction I moved out. Of course, I continued to contribute to their upkeep, and visit daily. Every day I got closer to Zsuzsi and I especially enjoyed hearing her play the piano. Despite the fact that grandma didn't learn Hebrew she fit right in. With so much Yiddish spoken there it didn't seem to matter.

After a few months I found a much better paying and more rewarding position as director of the Office of Continued After School Youth Education and Festivities. The army gave me a nice letter of recommendation which so greatly impressed my immediate superior, a cultured gentleman named Chaim Toam, that he didn't even bother to check my credentials. I really should have held a higher certificate of formal education, but that letter cemented the deal. Mister Toam was a bit older than me and became my mentor in this field. He even became sort of a father figure to me. He was the director of Education for the city of Bat Yam and I became his right hand man. They gave me a nice looking office, and an even nicer looking secretary. I had come a long way from sleeping among the vermin across from the old train station and I couldn't help but feel elated.

Bat Yam is Hebrew for daughter of the sea, and it's a beautiful location for such a cultural educational facility. The mayor told us about an unused basement in one of the buildings and we came up with the idea of teaching painting and sculpting in the French style there. We established an academy of art there and produced many fine artists. It's still there, and it's one of the proudest accomplishments of my life. Despite the fulfillment that era of my life gave me, the discord with my mother persisted. We also founded the Rebach Museum, named for an artist who died tragically young. Because of my talent as an administrator Mr. Toam also put me in charge of youth summer camps. In this field I made a real name for myself. We brought the kids from the kibbutz in the mountains to the shore and put them up in the school. We convinced the army to loan us cots and we converted classrooms into dormitories. In turn, we sent Bat Yam school kids up to the kibbutz in the hills. To decorate the seaside summer camps we got one of our most promising young art students, Yankel Ginzburg, to devote his energies to it. He did such an impressive job Mr. Toam made special mention of it, praising me for my astute ability to hand pick staff. Young Yankel even made a gift of one of his paintings to me. When we opened all the kids were happy and everyone was thrilled with the whole operation. The newspapers talked about this novel idea, and I became so talked about for my cleverness I considered going into politics. But when I gave talks to social groups and some people made mildly innocent comments about my accent it threw me into a quandary. Apparently, hovering just below the surface of an apparently calm mental exterior I still suffered from identity crisis. Was I Hungarian or Israeli? Of course I was in no way ashamed to be from Hungary. My fellow Hungarians gave a lot to Israel. Sadly though, the older Israeli generation placed great merit in being born there. They called the native born Israelis Sabras, and greatly honored them. In a way though it was silly. After all, it's just a coincidence of birth and how can anyone take credit for it? If there's anyone to thank it's the immigrant parents who went there in the first place. But I still suffered the stigma of an outsider. Of course, by then I was confident enough to ignore the absurd prejudice of the older generation and I took my chair as the secretary of the local chapter of the young labor party with pride and confidence. My political career did not include a salary, so I continued to work with Mr. Toam. Things were also improving for my mother. Still attractive in her forties she attracted the attentions of a Czechoslovakian immigrant who had been living in Israel for many years. His name was Uri Altman and he fell in love with my mother. He was really a wonderful man, and was coincidentally an accountant, just like my father. Also like him, Mr. Altman was vastly intelligent and a great intellectual, widely admired and regarded for his erudition. So, in 1963, after seventeen years as a widow my mother remarried. We were all thrilled for her. Uri was kind and loving and treated us all like family. He was also able to provide handsomely for everyone, and his prosperity gave me some much needed freedom. They all moved to Jerusalem, and I was able to pursue my own life, free of familial obligation.

Before she left for Jerusalem my mother shared with me a letter she had been holding since the end of the war. It was written by my father, and she felt that I now deserved to read it. He seems to have presaged his mortality and discussed plans for my Bar Mitzvah. Clearly, if he had lived he would have seen to it that it was celebrated. Sadly he did not. This is what he wrote.

"To my one and only son. Today you have reached a significant stage, the thirteenth year of your life. According to our religion and its laws this is the age when a boy crosses the threshold into adulthood to become a man. With this knowledge in your mind you must guide your steps and actions into the future. Even though you are not completely independent yet you must act with seriousness and just contemplation.

Help your parents so that they may direct the vehicle of your life in the proper direction. The best way you can assist them is with good conduct, seriousness, and accepting their good advice. With my deepest heartfelt love, I hope that God will keep you healthy and happy for many years to come."

It filled me with regret to read it, because I had been so lacking the presence and counsel of my father all these years. If my mother would have given this to me back when I turned thirteen the course of my life might have been different. Now its practical value was nil, and its worth lie mainly in its sentimental value. It also served to remind me that the wounds of the past were healing, and I needed to focus on my future.

As part of my responsibilities of administrating the summer camps I had to interview prospective counselors. One day an extremely attractive woman walked in and applied for that position. As you must know by know, I always had an eye for the ladies, and this one particularly got my attention. Her name was Hassida Bar Cohen, and her father was one of the founders of Bat Yam. She was a Sabra, and very popular, and I was afraid that I was not in her social class. But the army had made me brazen, so I challenged myself to ask her out. Of course, nowadays such behavior during a work interview would be considered the worst kind of sexual harassment, but I flirted with her and she didn't seem offended. She simply let me know that she wanted the job, but had another month left to serve in the army. We talked at length about the military, a subject I knew well, and by the end of the interview it was clear there was a mutual attraction. I took a chance and asked her out, and she accepted. We went to a lovely beach, the most common kind of date in Bat Yam, and we talked about our futures. One thing she asked of me was to write a letter to the army on her behalf requesting her early release so she could work with me. Naturally, I was glad to do it. She called me Zev, and before long we were going everywhere together. And after just a few months of romance we decided to get married. Making such a decision so early in a relationship is classically Sabra, and Hassida was a classic Sabra in every way. She was decisive, frank and strong. Her father had been an adventurous Pole who spent years in Turkey before being bit by the Zionist bug. He immigrated to Palestine and became an early pioneer. Still vigorous in his sixties he married a woman thirty years his junior and started a new life. He had three children, with Hassida being the second born. She had an older sister and a younger brother. Though her father had passed on many years before his memory was still well remembered and honored by my generation. That great respect, along with my own reputation as a popular municipal administrator, made our wedding a huge affair. It was like the celebration of some national holiday. Even the mayor came. Of course, my mother, grandma, Zsuzsi and Uri attended, as well as the Schindlers and all my army buddies. What a party! We even had guests from the other side of the world. Grandma had been communicating with her niece, Rozsika, who had moved to Argentina after the war. She had been sent to Dacchau concentration camp, but miraculously survived. Not only did she survive but she went through a kind of experience that was strange, yet not totally unheard of, during that era. She was in Germany after the war and thought her husband was dead, so she remarried. She had actually met her new husband, David, in the concentration camp. His wife and daughter had been murdered by the Nazis. He worked in the kitchen and smuggled scraps of extra food to her. Otherwise she never would have survived. After the war they got married. While she was expecting their first child her first husband, long believed dead, turned up. Peace was made between all parties, and Rozsika and David immigrated to Argentina. It was an honor to have them come so far for my wedding. Most of our family had died in the holocaust, so our marriage was seen as part of a new Genesis for the Grossmans, or Gabors. Rozsika was actually my second cousin, but due to her matronly persona and age I called her aunt. Naturally, I called her husband Uncle David. We chatted at the wedding in Hungarian, and it was a fateful conversation. Rozsika was in seventh heaven to be with so much family, as was my grandma. The war had decimated our clan, so this occasion was like the phoenix rising from the ashes. She called me Freddy, because that's how she remembered me, and she showered love and attention on me. It was like having a second grandma. They stayed two weeks in Israel and I personally gave them the grand tour. They observed that I had interesting work, was respected and loved. But Uncle David wanted to know more.

"So Freddy, what are you going to do to support your family?"

"Well Uncle David, my career as an educator is going pretty well."

"Can you afford to buy a house and car?"

"Not yet, but I also have some prospects in the political arena."

"Yes, but can you afford a house and car? You gotta support your family."

No matter what I said he enumerated the costs of raising children and finally proposed something that I never would have considered in a million years. He suggested I come to Argentina. I didn't even know where that was. The only America I ever thought about was New York City. But he persisted. South America, like North America, he said, was still the New World, and there was a world of opportunity there for a young man like me. Before he left he made me promise to consider it.

Hassida and I rented a house in Bat Yam and I finally felt like a real Israeli. It also seemed as if almost everything in my life was resolved. My family from Hungary was here, I was married to a beautiful woman, and my identity crises seemed quelled at last. The nightmares had long since stopped, and so much happiness felt almost surreal. It seemed as if the past was totally buried, but when I wasn't distracted by the myriad activities and responsibilities of my position, thoughts of my mother crept back in. She was in Israel, and she spoke to me, and naturally she attended my nuptials. But it was not like before. She was reserved, and a cold barrier was firmly in place between us, one that she insisted I had put up in the first place. I wanted to tear it down, but it was two man job, and she wasn't willing to shoulder her half. I had the love and respect of everyone in my new homeland, but my own mother still held me at arm's length.

Marriage is something you have to work at, and my hands were full with mine. First of all, I now had to earn a lot more money. When I opened burlap bags I could survive on one lira a day. But now that I had the responsibilities of married life money was a priority. The other great challenge was the marriage itself. Once the honeymoon was over tensions became obvious, and I thought that more prosperity would ease the friction inherent in our relationship. Her Sabra temperament was making itself manifest now, and she was indeed the proverbial handful. She wasn't doing anything selfish or nasty, but the native Israeli mood is headstrong. Their attitude is the result of two thousand years of being pushed around. Jews, always strangers in a strange land, were obliged to be submissive, and hoped that such behavior would protect them or their rights. But violence, disenfranchisement and murder still plagued them wherever they went. It culminated in the holocaust, and nobody in the world did anything to help them. Thus, they came to realize they were on their own. This epiphany resulted in the abandonment of submission in favor of the acquisition of aggression, even at the cost of tact or manners. In the simplest possible terms, "F*ck you world!" is practically their motto. They go after what they want with tenacity and you have to learn to deal with it as best you can. They're an intense people, and Hassida was no different. My respect for her has never diminished, but day to day living with such a person, especially if you're not the same, can be a challenge. And it didn't help dealing with her whole Israeli family either. It was so difficult I was actually considering divorce.

At that time an historical event occurred that emotionally affected me, Hassida, my family, and all of Israel. The young and popular president of the United States, John F. Kennedy, was assassinated. Israel, a young country, full of youthful people, greatly admired this vigorous leader, and when he was cut down in the prime of his life we felt as if we had lost a close friend. We were all devastated.

Around that time Uncle David barraged me with letters to convince me to visit Argentina. He had bent my ear at our wedding about the opportunities waiting in the west for adventurous young men like me. His propaganda campaign did not fall on completely deaf ears. While I was enjoying my career and popularity in Israel I was also intrigued by the picture he painted of new horizons on the other side of the world. Months went by between letters and I was taking notice of newspaper articles that talked of developments in other places, such as South America. Little by little I was learning that Buenos Aires had been developing successful after school programs not dissimilar to what we were doing in Israel. Also, during this era, it was very much in vogue for Israelis to visit other countries to study foreign technology and methods in order to improve things back home. It was even a bit of a status symbol to undertake such a journey on behalf of the homeland. Considering all my options I took into account my upcoming month long vacation with pay and decided to investigate Argentina's educational methods. Mr. Toam thought it was a great idea too, and we sent a letter to the Ministry of Education over there, extolling my efforts in Bat Yam, to see if they would allow me to visit and learn from them. To our surprise they responded most enthusiastically, and extended a cordial invitation to me to pay them an official visit. I spoke with Hassida and she was also supportive. Then I went and spoke with the other three women in my life. Thanks to Uri I could leave them without any anxiety. He even offered to help pay for my passage. Actually, this man was a blessing. He loved and cared for my mother, Zsuzsi and my grandma, and his presence allowed me to do something I don't think I could have done otherwise. Fifteen years earlier I had left my family, and it was considered abandonment. Now I was leaving them again, but this time with their blessing. They understood my need to progress and wished me well. One thing that worried me though was whether or not I would ever see my mother or grandma alive after I left. They were both fifteen years older than when I had left, and though it doesn't sound like a tremendously long time, the war and post war eras were tougher on the human condition than comfortable middle class life. They had aged and who knew what awaited them in Israel. Grandma was twenty years older than mom, having suffered the same hardships and deprivations. She was tough but not indestructible. Of course, things had become more civilized since the end of the war. Besides, they were in Israel, and as Judah Winter pointed out, nobody was going to come and take my mother away. Thus, in late 1964, at the age of twenty nine, I confidently embarked on a totally new epoch. I had been the survivor, the actor, the urchin, the soldier, the administrator, and now I was off to a blind destiny full of confidence, and with a clear conscience.

1. Yona.
2. My mother and Uri, her second husband, in Israel.
3. Pnina.
4. Capt. Mass'a wedding. You can see the camaraderie we felt for each other. I'm standing far left.
5. Mom and Zsuzsi on their balcony in Bat Yam.
6. Nobody was ever happier to have immigrated to Israel then my grandmother. I'm glad she was able to spend the second half of her life there. Here she is with her great grandson Gabriel and my mother.

1. In front of one of Yankel Ginzburg's summer camp decorations.
2. Another Yankel summer camp job.
3. As a gym teacher with my class.
4. Teaching self defense to gadna students.
5. Dancing with Zsuzsi.
6. In Israel shortly before going to Argentina.
7. Bat Yam City Hall.

1.

2.

3.

4.

5.

6.

1. Arriving in Buenos aires, contemplating my future.
2. Uncle David and Aunt Rozsika. From my first day in Buenos Aires they made me feel at home.
3. Not exactly a gaucho, but I enjoyed riding in el campo.
4. Hassida by same anti-Semitic graffiti at the start of the Dirty War.
5. One of the first newspaper articles about our business, The free advertising was invaluable.
6. Known again as Freddy, I found myself celebrated as a top designer.

Just a smattering of the publicity that swept the country. We were in all the top magazines. All clothing design is by Creaciones Gabriel. Baby Gaby clutches our main model's hand. We always dressed our workers alike. It made them feel they were part of a team.

Hassida with Gaby and Ady.

The boys and me on Avenida 9 de Julio in Buenos aires, the widest boulevard in the world.

Gabriel in the beautiful campo of Argentina

One of hundreds of stores in Argentina proudly advertising that they sell Creaciones Gabriel.

Chapter XIX

Miami 10

Not ten minutes had gone by since the doctor had left when the phone rang. I assumed it was somebody from the office checking up on me. I hadn't told Hassida or my boys yet, because I didn't want to worry them. My kids are the dearest things in the world to me, and I would never do anything to upset them. Besides, I figured I'd be out in just a day or two, so why get them all worked up over a little headache? I grabbed the phone expecting to hear my secretary.

"Oh Ivan, you're in the hospital. What's wrong mi amor?"

I was so stunned to hear Rebequita's sweet voice I couldn't speak. How could she possibly have known? It turns out that, by the rarest of coincidence, serendipity so sublime that I couldn't help but consider it destiny, a friend of hers found out that I was in the hospital and called her up in Italy. To this day I don't know how her friend, a girl named Suzi, whom I had actually met, knew any of this. Who looks such thoroughbreds in the mouth? Even the static charged vibration of her voice coming from overseas was like a jolt of adrenaline, and it made me ecstatic. Sometimes life can be that blissfully simple.

In spite of my bliss I was still possessed by this demon inside of me, insisting she forget me because of this inane age thing. Some devil was putting words in my mouth.

"Don't worry about me, I'm okay. Keep up with your studies and you'll forget about me soon enough."

I recited the words like dialogue from a play, dutifully, but utterly without conviction. The speech emanated from my mouth, not from my heart. What I really wanted was to see her, hold her, feel her silken hair against my cheek, and smell her innocent pure scent. I wanted to know she was there and always would be. But too many dramatic movies were filling my head with melodramatic nonsense. I had to be Rick from Casablanca, nobly telling Ilsa to leave, sacrificing her for a greater cause. I was saying words I didn't believe myself, and knew she didn't either. I said them just the same. But why? There weren't any more Nazis to fight, and the war was a distant memory. Furthermore, I wasn't Humphrey Bogart. We were living in America, free to pursue our happiness. There was no sane reason to deny her. It's what she wanted. It's what I wanted. She was an adult and so was I. Why was I acting so crazy? I should've begged her to fly to my side. Why didn't I give in to her, to me, to my true feelings?

"No," she insisted, "I'll never forget you!"

Still I persisted in pontificating on the mental platform.

"It isn't fair to you! It isn't fair to your family. It isn't fair to my kids. It isn't fair to your mother."

I was running out of victims of injustice, and yet the dripping water of her love continued to wear away at my stone heart. Her sole argument was to insist she loved me. Her heart was in the pilot's seat while my co-pilot was distracted with the flight manual. Maybe it was the drugs they gave me in the hospital? Why was I acting so nuts? Henry Berger, and a thousand other young men would have grabbed at this chance without a thought, and here I was, turning it down. I truly deserved to be in a hospital, only it should have been the mental ward. Maybe it was! Or perhaps I wanted to punish myself in some way.

When you lay in a hospital bed there are no distractions. There's no school, no play, army, business, family, or anything else to dissuade your mind from going where you're afraid it might. In my case that meant the Aliyah and guilt city. It was all coming back and haunting me. Perhaps this is why I was denying myself Rebequita? I had abandoned a woman, and now I wanted to punish myself by forcing a woman to abandon me. It's as if I was trying to orchestrate my karma instead of leaving it up to the invisible powers that controlled it so much better. Did I really want to chastise myself? Was it just? Would it satisfy my mother? How could it? She knew nothing of any of this or the misery that ricocheted around inside my mind. But whether she was aware of it or not, I must have been punishing myself for what I had done to her. Rejecting this young woman who loved me was my sentence. My sin had been committed when I was young, a mere teen. And now I had the chance to be young again, yet I persisted in forsaking that opportunity. It was painful, but I deserved it. This fair damsel made this middle aged man feel as if I inhabited a body in its second decade, the period in which they make so many sophomoric mistakes. I was again in that epoch of life when I committed my great devilry, and denying myself Rebequita was my just deserts. It was a harsh sentence, because she possessed the key to bring me back to life. She was my chance for renewal. I was middle aged, yet she brought me back to the point when I went astray. She was that second chance, but my head would not listen to my heart. It preferred to box with it. The merciless sparring would not stop. My guilty brain threw my heart to the mat and the ref was counting me out.

Chapter XX

The New World

Israel was just sweet sixteen when I set sail for the New World, and she was proud to have a small line of cruise ships. There were just two, the Jerusalem and the Theodore Herzl, the latter of which capably bore me on my journey west. My previous ocean voyage had been plagued by anxiety and nausea. What a difference fifteen years can make! This was a journey of immigration, but it was also my first vacation of more than two days ever. It was fabulous. There was an orchestra on board for dancing, and there was endless food and entertainment. The weather was lovely and the seas were calm. The long sea voyage also let me reflect on a million things. The vast ocean humbles you and you get to see things in perspective. I relived my life a hundred times over in my head, and thought deeply about what I ought to do. Standing at the rail of an ocean liner of even modest luxury it seemed unimaginable that I had ever been hunkered down in the basement of a bombed out building, praying to stay alive. That was a different life in a different world. My existence was like reincarnation, and I had the names to match. Most importantly I reached the conclusion that I was free to do as I please. I had patched up relations with my family as well as anyone could, served my country honorably, and taken my place in society. I didn't owe anyone any money or other debts, so I was free and legal. And now a whole other hemisphere was opening up to me. In some ways it resembled my last big move. When I went to Israel I left behind my mom, grandma and sister, causing a major uproar, and I didn't speak the language of my new destination. And here I was, repeating the scenario. This time though I had my family's blessing. Interestingly enough, Judah Winter had been right about my mother following, though he was drastically off on his timetable. Time had matured me, and I understood what Judah did. He was caught up in the idealism of sophomoric youth and sincerely believed he was doing the best thing for Jews in Hungary. And who's to say he didn't? After all, what he said about history was accurate. Later I learned that Stalin, Hungary's iron fisted ruler after the war, became paranoid of the Jews, as he was of everybody, and was planning on massive repression and persecution. Fortunately he died and such plans were trashed. But had he lived maybe my family would have been locked up in a Gulag, not much better than a German concentration camp. I actually laughed out loud into the sea breeze when I thought about our Aliyah through the woods and across the river, and that ridiculous valise of mine. And I continued to laugh like a madman remembering those burlap bags and my old landlords making babies. What a life I had lived! Thank God I could laugh about it now. And, as for not knowing the language, I figured that Spanish couldn't possibly be half as hard as Hebrew. I was not afraid.

We stopped off in Naples, Lisbon and Madeira, and I got to relax and play tourist. And when we hit the western half of the globe we stopped off in Brazil. I found it quite exotic and the beaches reminded me of

Bat Yam. Next we had a brief stopover in Uruguay where I sampled the food which I was told was similar to that of my new home.

With my voyage, and its accompanying vacation, nearing its end, I got my head on straight and prepared myself to make port and confront reality again. The last time I did that I was totally disappointed and devastated. I had anticipated a warm welcome but was utterly ignored. Now I was to be greeted by my Aunt Rozsika and Uncle David, and I knew they would do everything short of hiring a brass band. Aunt Rozsika was as loving and warm as my grandma, and she was looking forward to seeing the family grow in the New World. I thought it best not to expect anything, so as not to be disappointed, but I knew they'd be there for me. The ship trumpeted its booming horn and we moored at the dock on the Rio Plata. In my pocket were hundred dollars given to me by Uri.

I grabbed my valise, one quite a bit bigger than the one I had taken on my last voyage, and headed for the gang plank. Even before I got there I heard a familiar voice.

"Freddy! Freddy!"

Nobody had called me Freddy in quite some time so I didn't respond at once. But that disconnected voice persisted, and it sounded hauntingly like my mother's or grandma's, so alike are the females of our clan. Then I realized that it was Aunt Rozsika and I turned toward her direction. She was standing in the crowd with Uncle David and a young man, and they were all waving like crazy. Waving back I ran down the gang plank, and in an instant I was being embraced and kissed. This was definitely a far cry from my reception, or lack thereof, in Haifa. They all hugged me and barraged me with questions about my trip, our kin back in Israel, and issues of health. I had left family, but here I was with family again. So far, Argentina felt good.

Aunt Rozsika introduced me to their son, Sonny who was as excited as his parents to have another member of the family join them. In the car on the way back to their house I must have spun my head around three hundred and sixty degrees. I imagined South America to be a collection of huts, but this was clearly the biggest city I had ever seen. And the architecture reminded me of Europe. Now, Argentine felt even better.

When we got back to their house I was treated to an amazing fete. Aunt Rozsika was a great cook and she had prepared a welcome feast of Hungarian delicacies. And they had made up the private room they had up on the roof especially for me. If love counts for anything in this world then I insist that nobody has ever been more royally received than me upon my arrival in Buenos Aires. Neither visiting diplomats nor conquering kings have ever been treated so graciously. Later Aunt Rozsika jokingly told me that David and Sonny were jealous of the attention lavished on me. Argentina was the best.

They all called me Freddy, because that's how they had been talking about me for years. Ivan was the name on my passport, and it's easy to pronounce in Spanish, but I would be Freddy to most of the people in Argentina, and Zev to a special few.

After a few more hugs and kisses I took rest in my private penthouse up on the roof. I looked out over the city and got my bearings. Silhouetted in the moonlight it reminded me of a cross between Jerusalem and Budapest. I compared my first night in Latin America with my first night in the Middle East, and felt relieved that my life was making more sense to me now. But, make no mistake; I was on a mission to educate myself better and ultimately improve my life. With just those hundred dollars from Uri there was no time to waste, and Uncle David's words about financial security reverberated in my head. With all that on my

Echoes Of My Footsteps

mind, as well as the excitement of being in a new continent, a sound night's sleep evaded me my first night in South America.

In the morning I had a hardy and more locally typical breakfast, lovingly cooked by Aunt Rozsika. We spoke Hungarian, but she peppered it with Yiddish which is what they mostly spoke at home. I ended up practicing that peculiar Jewish dialect with them until I became fluent. Of course, they were glad to help me learn some basic survival Spanish, especially Sonny. So I stumbled through a clumsy conversation of broken Castilian phrases, made tolerable by encouraging familial affection.

They gave me directions on how to get to the Ministry of Education, and I enjoyed the ride there, gawking again at the enormity of the city. I had been in the Middle East for a long time, and Buenos Aires felt as comfortable to me as my childhood. The broad boulevards and the way the people dressed were clearly like the old country. All of this made me feel at ease, and I proceeded to my appointment filled with confidence.

The Ministry of Education had arranged for an interpreter, though it turned out to be French, so I had to manage with whatever I remembered from my days at the Kolscey Gimnazium. After the tour I felt I had found something stable and worthwhile. Over the course of the next few days we had several more meetings, and every day when I got home Uncle David would ask me how things were going. But when I got home after the third day he was more than merely curious. When I responded to his inquiries with my usual reports about learning about their advanced education program, and how I would apply them in Israel, he stopped me in mid-sentence.

"Freddela. Teachers the world over are noble, and Argentina's no exception. They're noble, but underpaid. So, forget about it! I didn't have you schlep halfway around the world to suffer. You could have stayed in Israel and been noble and poor too."

I remembered how he talked to me at my wedding, and now I was starting to see that this was his master plan, why he had brought me here. And I was also starting to admit to myself that making money was not contrary to my total outlook on life either. My father had been good at making money, as were my grandfathers. I remembered their fine houses, as well as our elegant street side apartment in Budapest, and I had to confess that I was not averse to following in their footsteps. And now here was a caring relative trying to steer me in that direction. It was true what he said. I had respect and admiration in Israel, but couldn't deposit any of it in the bank. I was grateful to Israel for turning my life around, but I had to consider that I was now married, and that the responsibilities of raising children could soon ensue. So, after hearing Uncle David out thoroughly, I asked him what he thought was the best plan for me.

"*Gesheft!* Business! What else? You're not a doctor or a lawyer. So, it's business!"

"But what kind of business?"

"Well, most business boils down to one thing, selling."

"But I've never sold anything in my life! Anyway, what would I sell?"

"Well, you don't know if you can do something until you try. As far as what to sell I'd like to suggest that you start out by selling one of my products, cashmere sweaters."

What's cashmere?"

"Only one of the most luxurious fabrics in the world, *boychic*. People go crazy over it. Tomorrow you take that suitcase of yours, fill it with my cashmere sweaters, and I'll show you how and where to sell it."

"But I don't speak a word of Spanish."

"It's not a big *tzimis*, Freddy! We'll teach you a few phrases and the numbers. With *los numeros* you can go anywhere in the world and do *gesheft*. What?! You think I'm a big linguist? In three months you'll probably speak better than me! Anyway, I'm gonna send you to some neighborhoods where there are also some Jews. When they hear about your military experience they'll treat you like a hero and buy from you! But everyone loves this stuff. So get a good night's rest, *boychic*. Tomorrow you're a businessman!"

Alone in my quaint penthouse that night I considered what tomorrow would bring. Not figuratively what tomorrow would bring, but literally. When the sun rose I was going to schlep yet another suitcase through yet another strange city. I needed that? Back in Bat Yam I had an office, a secretary, popularity and family. Why would I risk leaving all that? The answer was simple. Money. Gelt. Dinero. Uncle David was certainly right about one thing, what I had in Bat Yam was not going to give me a substantial living. So, I shrugged my shoulders and said to myself, "Why not? Let's give it a try!"

Next morning I headed out with Uncle David for my baptism in business. He took me to one of the main streets in town, Calle Rivadavia, a long, broad boulevard, lined with shops. The idea was to visit the stores where I'd probably find my potential clientele. Besides the numbers he taught me to say, "*Yo fabricante*. I manufacturer. *Yo vender*. I sell." With this Tarzanish vocabulary he left me with best wishes and was off. With old images of schlepping a valise and the phony commie uncle abandoning me on the street, it all felt eerily familiar. But I was game to try my hand at selling.

With a suitcase full of cashmere pull-overs I at least had the motivation of lightening my load, so that meant selling some. At that time there weren't too many Jews on Rivadavia, but they were all charmed to meet me and practice a word or two of Hebrew. Uncle

David was right about that. As soon as they heard I was a soldier and fought in the Suez War they treated me like a hero. Of course, selling to them was easier than to anyone else, but making any sale at all gave me confidence, and I continued.

Somehow or other I managed to charm everyone on my first day and sell every single one of my dozen cashmere pull-overs. I was amazed! My profit was just two dollars each, but I had never made twenty four dollars in one day in my entire life. I felt great! The main reason I was elated was not the money, but the discovery that I was capable of making real money on my own. Maybe I was a born salesman? It's funny the talents we're born with, but never recognize until the need pops up. Who knew I was an actor? Who knew I was a sharpshooter? Who knew I could manage camps and educational programs? And who knew I could sell? Now, for the first time in my life I thought that I might actually rise above poverty. Still, my only safety net was Uri's hundred dollars. But my first's day gesheft found me in the black and I was eager to try it again.

Next day I told my uncle to give me twenty pull-overs instead of twelve. Unbelievably I sold those too. And the next day I crammed three dozen pull-overs into the suitcase and sold them out too. Everyday I left with a suitcase full and everyday I came back with an empty one. I thought I had found a career, but I didn't want to burn any Israeli bridges in case it was just dumb luck. After all, there is such a thing called beginner's luck, and I didn't want to make a rash decision based on some temporary streak of good fortune. So, I wrote Chaim Toam and asked for an extension of my vacation. He assented and I continued selling.

Everyday my sales, confidence and Spanish vocabulary grew. Then Uncle David came to me and said, "I have a friend who manufactures a line of children's clothing and he wants you to sell for him. The line is called Creaciones Mariel."

Now I schlepped two suitcases down the street, the cashmere pull-overs and the kiddies' clothing. My luck, or perhaps expertise, persisted. I got the children's wear on credit too, and I paid it all off daily, pocketing my profit afterwards. Things were going great until Mariel asked me to take on a partner.

"Freddy, I can't keep giving you so much credit any more. But if you will take on my Uncle Felix, who is struggling to maintain his wife and four kids, as your partner, I'll give you all the credit you can handle." I had no choice, so I agreed. Business continued to improve, and I was already speaking Spanish better than Uncle David. He was right about both things.

Argentina's population is generally descended from Europeans, but they're decidedly Latinos, as passionate and hot-blooded as any in South America. They speak their own brand of Castilian, characterized by an Italian sounding accent spoken at a very fast clip. Back in Israel it had been a real struggle to get used to Hebrew, but Spanish seemed to come much easier. Maybe it was my studies in another romance language, French, that gave me a more basic understanding. Anyway, everyday my vocabulary grew, and every day I was a better salesman. I even started selling to people right out of the valise on the street. While I concentrated on stores I was not averse to making a sale or two to tourists. Most of them were visitors from neighboring Bolivia, Paraguay and Brazil, and they were eager to buy my wares.

Things had progressed to the point that it was time to share plans with Hassida. I had been writing her regularly since my arrival, and she knew the score, business wise and marriage wise. The fact is, early in our days of wedded bliss, things were not always completely perfect. Sabras can be tough cookies and friction raised its ugly head early. She was gregarious and outspoken, to the point of finishing my sentences before I could, and that can try one's patience. But at the same time we shared a rather passionate relationship, which can blur more basic problems, especially when you're young. We always theorized that getting off on our own might create an atmosphere of interdependence that would nurture a sounder bond. Also, being a Sabra, Hassida didn't give up on anything. As she was emotionally and physically attached to me she wanted to make a go of it, so I sent her one way passage on the Israeli cargo ship Dorego. It was not the tourist experience I had on my crossing, but it had decent passenger accommodations. And the lack of a return ticket symbolized our commitment to make it work. Furthermore, I bought it with my own earrings. Uri's money was still untouched.

While Hassida was en route I made the startling discovery that Felix was a dyed in the wool communist. First Natan and now Felix. It seems as if I couldn't avoid Karl Marx' disciples. Of course, back in Israel I could roll my eyes, shrug my shoulders and laugh it off. But over here they took such things seriously, so I thought it best to break off all relations with him. I tried to tell the owner of Mariel that I couldn't work with his uncle.

"I'm sorry, but I don't want to get into trouble."

"My new line is coming out soon! You've got to stay!"

He begged me to stay, and I did, though it made me extremely nervous. Anyway Hassida was arriving and I wanted the merchandise to sell. Soon we were together again. Rozsika, David and Sonny took her in with an unconditional affection that elated me as much as her, and we rented an apartment of our own. Like millions of immigrants before us we started new lives in America. It must have been a sacrifice for her to leave the one country on Earth devoid of anti-Semitism and go thousands of miles away to sell *schmatahs* on the street, but she was

Echoes Of My Footsteps

game. And almost at soon as she got her land legs back she went out daily with me. We used to leave our apartment after an early breakfast and take the subway to downtown Buenos Aires. She schlepped along a suitcase just like me, and she stood shoulder to shoulder with me like a fierce Sabra, full of determination to build a solid life for us. I couldn't help but admire her for it.

Now that we were two I devised a tactic. Experienced salesmen know that nothing succeeds like success, so I decided to try and convince prospective clients that I was taking the world by storm. When we got to a client's store Hassida would wait outside on a bench with her suitcase. I'd go in and explain that I had my goods outside in my car, flashing the key, which was really just a useless copy of someone else's. To North Americans this sounds most unimpressive, because practically all of them own cars, but in 1960's Buenos Aires only the most affluent entrepreneurs possessed automobiles. We used this plan in all of the suburbs and it always worked. We'd also take the train to other outlying suburbs, all of which were set up like European villages, with shops around a central plaza with a church. Actually, Buenos Aires reminded me more and more of Budapest or Debrecen or Vienna. It was common to find apartment buildings or rows of two and three story town houses with facades that masked more opulent interior courtyards. This was identical to Hungary, only interior and exterior floor plans did not divide economic classes. Anyway, Hassida continued to wait on a park bench while I flashed phony car keys and came outside to retrieve the goods. The plan was working great, and we were both elated by our success.

Spanish didn't come as easily to Hassida as it did for me, but the income made that minor frustration tolerable. We were selling and we were filled with hope for our future. And we would need that confidence and a whole lot more, because Hassida soon became pregnant with our first child. I forbid her to continue schlepping, and she went out and found a good job with the Israeli tourist office. I carried on as before, alone. And to make my car story more believable I actually bought a car, *un carro*. It was an old BMW with the worst transmission in the western hemisphere, but it ran. I was reminded of what David had said in Israel. His was right again. I had a car. Next, a house.

Fate tested me by sending an expected curve ball. Though the Mariel company had pleaded with me to stay he now betrayed me. He said that there really wasn't enough in the new collection for both Felix and me, and he stopped supplying me. This was a blow and I was pissed. And doubly so when I realized he was going to sell to the very clients I had developed. So, I conferred with Uncle David.

"You're my business mentor. What do I do about this *momzer?*"

"What can you do? It's family! Naturally, he's going to give to his blood before you! Maybe you need to look for something else. I mean with a wife and kid to support you can't go out with just my pull-overs. You need something bigger."

Uncle David was giving me the *emis* -the truth- but I didn't like it. No Sabra or Israeli soldier gives up! But we did indeed need something bigger. So, we took all our savings and bought out a child's collection. We brought them home and took them apart to analyze how they were made.

Now, if I had been surprised to find out that I had an innate ability to sell, then I was absolutely stunned to find myself using what I had learned from working with those damn gunny sacks! But there I was, dissecting those seams like a pro. Wow! Sometimes life's just unfathomable! Oh, those burlap bags!

We dissected the top four or five best selling items from that children's collection and asked my uncle where to buy some fabric. We cut them exactly to match the ones we had taken apart and asked Uncle

David to direct us to where we could get them sewed. From the day I thought of it to the day we had our own collection was just two weeks. We visited all our old clients and they bought everything. What joy! We were ecstatic!

The joy that Hassida and I felt over our business success was now multiplied a hundred times over with the birth of our first son, Gabriel. Along with Rozsika, David, and Sonny we celebrated it like only real family can! And there was much to celebrate indeed. First off, we had a healthy son. But Gabriel's birth signified far more than the growth of one family and a proud papa and mama. Just a generation before a gang of hoodlums had tried their hardest to kill me and every other member of my tribe, and we had practically become an endangered species. So, Gabriel's appearance insured the preservation of a new generation, so that both our family and our people would endure. It was a *nachis* A-Bomb! Naturally, we named our company Creaciones Gabriel, and it brought us even more luck. Things were moving fast, and we negotiated with a small factory to manufacture for us on credit.

I was now committed to Argentina, so I did what a *mensch* does and let Chaim Toam know I wasn't coming back. He sent me a nice letter saying he never had anyone as competent as me, who did so much in such a short time, and assured me that the door was always open for me there.

The positive reply from Israel inspired me even more, and I appreciated the change of mood. After all, the last time I had left someone behind it turned out catastrophic. So, it was good to know that there were no hard feelings this time around. In every sense my Argentine experience was the exact opposite of its Haifa counterpart. There were no ill feelings left behind and my family here loved me without reservation. Rozsika was a loving carbon copy of my grandma, and she was out of her head over Gabriel. So far Argentina was incomparable.

We were living well, and the economy was strong. Our first year in the New World had brought nothing but happiness, and we were looking forward to the second one full of promise. It was the American Dream, even if it was the *la versión Latina*. Uncle David told me that his partner had an old two story house that I could move into for very little rent. It had a secondary house out back that was ideal for a small production plant, and we moved in without hesitation. Hassida was all Sabra and hands on, using her creativity to design and help me in any way possible. Then it happened.

I was analyzing the sizes that Creaciones Mariel sold and I noticed an extraordinary thing. This particular children's line only went up to size twelve. I found this odd, so I asked my uncle about this.

"What do the young ladies do after they're twelve years old? Where do they shop?"

"Vell, den dey just buy da small adult sizes. I tink dey even got petite."

I thought I misunderstood, so I persisted, just to be certain.

"You mean, they have no size thirteen?"

"Not dat I efer saw."

"Are you sure?"

"I tink so, boychic."

That sounded bizarre so we shopped around to confirm this, and it turned out that Uncle David was right. We were both stunned! Argentina had indoor plumbing, homogenized milk, and aspirins, but no apparel for females between the ages of twelve and eighteen. This country, eighth largest in the world, with a cosmopolitan, fashion conscious population of millions, didn't have junior sizes. They had subways, armed forces for their defense, and the electric light, but they didn't have juniors. The descendents of the Spanish conquistadores had planted vineyards, built ships, laid out broad boulevards and opened air-conditioned cinemas. They even developed the tango to its own art form. They resembled a developing twentieth century nation in most every way except that they didn't have clothes to fit a significant percentage of their citizenry. This nation, charter member of the United Nations and affiliate of the Organization of American States, had penicillin and rock and roll, but teens didn't have their own line of clothing! It was as if we were living in an alternate universe where everything was exactly the same, except girls had nothing to wear. But it was true! Argentina had no junior sizes! And better than that, nobody, especially clothes manufacturers, seemed to have thus far taken notice of this aberrant anomaly. The heavens opened up, complete with a fanfare of angelic trumpets.

And the Lord said, "I have heard the lamentation of the teenaged girls in Argentina, and lo I have sent unto them Freddy." And Freddy gave unto the afflicted girls the gift of junior sizes. And the Lord saw that it was good, and great was the jubilation thereof!

I had a realization, a bona fide epiphany. I had found my calling! We didn't even wait to start bright and early the next morning, but immediately went on a shopping spree to get samples of women's styles. For further inspiration we bought some international fashion magazines. Well, perhaps the word inspiration is a little disingenuous. We out and out copied them! At least, for starters. I sat and feverishly sewed piece after colorful piece. We didn't want to risk another cagey foreigner having the same insight, so I sewed on into the night. One thing I had learned by this stage in my life was that having a realization without acting on it was a realization wasted. If you're standing by the goal, with the ball coming your way, and you realize that the goalie's not paying attention, you have to act on that awareness, or it's all for naught. Well, I was standing by a goal that didn't have a goalie, and I wasn't going to pass this chance up. I was going to kick that ball into that net as hard and as fast as I could.

I sat at that sewing machine until my back ached, laughing all the while at the irony of using to such great advantage the skills that I had acquired working with gunny sacks. And I was still cutting, sewing and giggling like a man possessed when the South American sun rose on my last day of middle class aspiration. Hassida had stayed up with me all night, making me that strong coffee which had fueled the national economy for generations. I rose from the machine and laid out the dresses, tops and skirts on the table. We stared at them bleary eyed with admiration. Hassida broke the silence.

"Zev, you've done it! You got a whole line of juniors!"

"Not me, I corrected. We've got Creaciones Gabriel."

That same day we introduced Creaciones Gabriel to our clientele, and it took off! We took orders and deposits and because the little house out back was no longer adequate for such volume we had them mass produced. In no time they were on store shelves, and those shelves emptied as soon as they were filled. Girls simply swooned over Creaciones Gabriel. It was like giving food to starving people. Our success happened practically as fast as its telling. It swept the country. Every boutique on every street in Buenos Aires carried our line, and then, every other city after that. They all put signs in their windows announcing *Vendemos Creaciones Gabriel Aquí.* We sell Gabriel Creations here! And magazines were plastered with our ads featuring our model, Maria Angelos de Medrano. She was a cute, photogenic fourteen year old girl, and before long she became the fashion icon of her generation. Every girl wanted to look and dress like her. Within a year she parlayed her success as our model into a career as an actress, starring in a series of television soap operas, *novelas.* Everything we touched, or touched us, was golden! On top of that we had no competition. It was a phenomenon! Everyone wanted to know who the new designer in Argentina was, so we were interviewed by newspapers, magazines and radio. Even in my heavily accented Castellano I charmed the ladies and gentlemen of the press, garnering unlimited free advertising in the bargain. If anyone didn't know about us before those interviews the public media cemented our fame once and for all. They even splashed pictures of Hassida in her Israeli uniform. And her sexy persona didn't hurt our image at all. I was more low key about flaunting our heritage, but Sabras know no such timidity. That's how Sabras are. "Hey everybody, I'm Israeli! If you don't like it you can go screw yourself!"

After the first season we wondered if we could repeat our success, but we came up with a new line, and it sold even better than the first. Again, the press rushed to our doorstep to take pictures which they printed in their journals, giving us even greater gratis propaganda. Our product line became a household name, and we were celebrated from Patagonia to the Andes. Not since the Young Guard had I experienced such a heady rush of notoriety. But I had matured since then. Signing autographs in Budapest was a thrill for me once upon a time, but it didn't allow me to make any quantum leap in economic or social status. Uncle David had convinced me that a good life for my family was important, and I had come to the New World to find fortune before fame. So, while being celebrated as a designer was a thrill, seeing those designs sell by the carload was an even bigger one. We vacationed in Rio, spent weekends on our boat, and tooled around town in a beautiful Peugeot. As a matter of fact, we bought a new one every year. It was a golden epoch, and I remember, around that time, hearing that the American astronaut Neil Armstrong had walked on the moon. It was inexplicable, but I felt a synergy. Was his feat possible? Was our success possible?

It was an era of elation, but I feel I should qualify our success by putting into perspective. By Argentinean, or probably even South American standards, we were rich. But by the measure of developed nations we would have been classified as solidly upper middle class. But by any standard it still felt good, and our families on both sides of the ocean were thrilled. Rozsika and David couldn't have been prouder if I was their own son, and I took joy in repaying their kindness as much as they'd let me. Grandma wrote me that she wasn't even surprised, that she knew I had it in me all along, and Uri and Zsuzsika echoed those sentiments. Mother was congratulatory, if controlled. No matter what I did I could not put a chink into that wall. Had I offended her sensitive nature so much that I was truly locked out for good?

In light of her being related to and descended from such loving stock, her attitude was absolutely surreal. It was actually physically exhausting for me. It's not that I was doing all or any of this just to get her approval. I would've done it anyway. But at least she could've stepped back from this all-or-nothing position, and relaxed her position just a little. But it just wasn't in the cards for now. And to complicate this inexplicable female position it seemed to be hitting me at home. Getting the cold shoulder from my mother on the other side of the world was of course painful, but it was also perplexing to find my wife unsatisfied on this side. I thought Hassida would at last settle into her role as wife, but this Sabra just couldn't be an appendage to anyone. She was such an individualist she could only find fulfillment through her own endeavors. She respected and admired me for what I had accomplished, but our basic incompatibility persisted. You can gild a square peg with gold leaf, but it still won't fit into a round hole. Of course, part of the tenacious Sabra formula dictates that failure is not an option. So, as long as there wasn't out and out infidelity or violence, Hassida continued to tough out our marriage, what to mention making it tough on me. As far as I was concerned I had to consider the eventuality of falling short of our vow to let only death part us. I loved little Gabriel, and I didn't want to see him suffer the consequence of a divorce, a life as lonely as mine had been. So, I determined that he ought to have a sibling to keep him company, just in case his parents divorced. Without divulging my odd version of parental planning to Hassida we endeavored to produce his future playmate. It was a plan formulated in an atmosphere of matrimonial friction, tempered with a tenacious desire to see our marriage succeed. In any case, that part of my plan was apparently blessed, because Gabriel's kid brother soon made his appearance.

Baby Adrian hit like another nachis explosion, and family and friends joyously celebrated. Even the press was interested in the new addition to the family of Argentina's top designers. We brought these news clippings with us, along with the new generation of male Gabors, back to Israel for a short visit, and everyone was thrilled. The Schindlers, my old army buddies, Chaim Toam, my grandma, Zsuzsi and Uri all congratulated me while mother was her usual icicle. At least my conscience was clear that I had checked on her.

Being back in Israel, even for a short vacation, was exciting. I especially enjoyed observing my grandma. All her life she had been religious, but had never been completely free to express it. She had to endure anti-Semitism, the war, and the repressive commies, but now she was in her own element, and ecstatic to live in the Jewish Homeland. Zsuzsi had also become a well adjusted Israeli woman, and she found herself a nice husband. So, most of my ghosts were subdued, if not dead. I had family, money and self respect. It was almost too good to be true. And now, with very little nagging at my soul, I had the freedom to seek out a totally new kind of fulfillment. I woke up one day with the urge to paint.

Maybe my propensity to think up new fashion designs was just the tip of an artistic iceberg which I needed to explore. So, I went out and got myself some canvases, an easel, oils and some brushes. I started painting and found it to be quite relaxing. I was no Rembrandt, but it was great therapy. Even with money and love I was still the same emotional animal as ever, and I needed this outlet. I sat for hours applying paint to canvas, and found that whatever artistic expression I had as a child actor was now coming back to me. This time though I didn't need applause. I just did it because I liked it.

Around 1972 Argentina started to experience seriously bad inflation, so we decided to protect our money. I met an Israeli, who recommended the International Credit Bank in Geneva. Its owner, Tibor Rosenbaum, was also the treasurer of the World Jewish Congress, so what better recommendation could you need? Besides, what safer place for your money than a Swiss bank? So we wired about three hundred thousand dollars there and opened an account. That amount of money back then was the equivalent of between four and five million dollars at the writing of this book. From any perspective it was a lot of sheckles, and we were relieved to sock it away safely in a Swiss bank. It represented about half of our money, and we felt we could breathe easy. Argentina could face triple digit inflation, and our money would be safe. The idea that any bank could face problems in that alpine financial refuge was absolutely surreal. We had nothing to worry about. And while I luxuriated in that serene mental state of false security some mystic power looked down upon my scene of fame, fulfillment and riches, and determined that surrealism had been absent too long from my life. The International Credit Bank of Geneva went bankrupt and we lost the entire account. I flew to Switzerland with Jose Ryban, another friend who had also deposited in that bank, to see if there was anything we could do to salvage the situation, but we only ended up wasting more money on the flights. What a shock! Did I still deserve to be punished for abandoning my mother? Or was this for abandoning Yona or Pnina? Or was I confusing bad luck with destiny? Perhaps they are one and the same. Or maybe I was naïve and should have investigated the bank more thoroughly? But who does a background check on a Swiss bank? That's like making Sinatra audition. Whatever it was I experienced more than a little mental anguish over losing over a small fortune. Fortunately Creaciones Gabriel was as popular as ever, so the money kept flowing. Hassida wasn't about to give up on anything either, and she inspired me to not look back. Our factory continued to hum, and before long we had another comfortable nest egg. This time though we chose to keep it closer to home to keep an eye on it. But our own personal success couldn't keep Argentina from sliding into her own economic decline.

History teaches us that whenever national economies take a dive the incompetent and unfortunate politicians who cause it tend to assign the blame for it elsewhere. The world had already lived through an entire war caused by such lunacy, sacrificing fifty million lives to it. Now the seeds of such madness were being sown deep in Argentina's psyche, and one of the darkest chapters in her history was about to unfold.

Chapter XXI

Miami 11

Being recently divorced from Hassida she wasn't particularly well disposed toward me, so she only came to the hospital with the kids to see me twice. Although separation had been a persistent topic with us, I don't think she ever really thought I'd go through with it. I guess it's impossible not to take such a thing personally, and she certainly did little to hide her resentment. Our arrangement was the typical American settlement, with her getting the boys during the week, and me on weekends. As for property and possessions we split it all up to our mutual satisfaction, and there was no want on anyone's part. With my portion of the cash I bought some properties in Miami Beach and reopened Creaciones Gabriel in Miami. We both felt secure in our futures, separate though they now were, and most importantly, we were positive that Jews were as safe in Miami as they were in Israel. Hassida was raised in an environment devoid of such concern, and though Argentina's reign of terror was brief it deeply affected her, so it was vital to us as Jews to be assured we'd live in peace and security in the Untied States. Fortunately that is indeed the fact, and like generations of our people before us we kiss the ground of this wonderful country. Actually, with rocket armed Arab states all around Israel, the United States is probably the safest place in the world to hold a Bar Mitzvah.

The doctors wouldn't let Hassida, the kids or anyone else stay too long. They said I needed absolute rest, and even administered a sedative to make sure my blood pressure wouldn't go up. Regardless, I couldn't keep myself from thinking about Rebequita. The drugs imposed a relaxed state on my consciousness, but they couldn't stop my mind from working. Even in a foggy state I thought about her. Why was I holding on to this age equation? Hassida's father had been twice as old as his bride, and they were happy. And in South America I had plenty of occasion to observe the phenomenon of successful May/December marriages. Most importantly, if I didn't marry Rebequita I'd lose her. As she professed, she was not a common girl having a fling with an older lover. Apparently, she knew I was the one, and that was that. The angel on my right shoulder reminded me that I loved her too, while the devil on my left insisted I deny our union and make us both miserable.

Through the fog of medication I thought I saw Rebequita standing before me reproaching me for standing in the way of our happiness. Then I was gripped by horror when I realized it was Yona, rebuking me for refusing to marry her when I actually loved her. And here I was, about to make the same mistake twice.

The phone startled me awake. Although the doctors and nurses wanted me to rest they had neglected to turn off the ringer on my bedside telephone or tell the hospital switchboard operator to stop my calls. Did they ever? In any case, I picked up.

"Ivan, mi amor? Como estás?"

It was inconceivable to me. She was thousands of miles away in Italy, surrounded by horny young Casanovas, and she was calling this old Hungarian. She insisted she loved me, wanted to marry me, and would be coming back to me at once. But the imp on my shoulder forced me to deny her.

"You must stay in Italy and study. It wouldn't be fair to your mother to leave early."

I sounded logical and fair, but she didn't hear a word of it. Furthermore, she was as upset about my illness as my own grandmother would have been. A Loretta would have been disappointed not to have her love toy for the weekend and just gone out and found another. Not Rebequita. Not if I was her own child could she have been more distraught, and she called daily. Person to person long distance calls back then were quite costly, and she probably spent the equivalent of a round trip ticket to Italy on them. Then one day I got a call I could never have predicted. It was Rebequita's mother.

"Look Mr. Gabor, Rebeca loves you, and will have no other. I've done all a mother can do to prevent it, but she insists that she cannot live without you. So, I cannot stand in her way any longer. I just pray that you love her even half as much as she does you. But you must promise me one thing. I want you to swear that you will marry her!"

I do not know how long my jaw hung open in disbelief before I spoke. I was surrounded. Rebequita, Yona, Mr. Bar Cohen, and even Rebequita's mother, all made their case. The prosecution rested, and I knew I was guilty of loving her. So, I came to my senses.

"I swear it!"

"And she must finish her studies."

"I wouldn't have it any other way."

"Then Señor, you and Rebequita have my blessings. In two months she will complete her studies in Italy. Then, I want you to fly to New York and receive her. Good luck!"

1. My beloved Rebequita when I met her. I used this photo as the label for our clothes line in Miami.
2. Ecstatic newlyweds.
3. Celebrating. A small wedding, but a great love.
4. With new born baby Jessica.
5. My clothing company in Miami. Not a success, but at least I met Rebequita when I had it.'

1. Still my best friend after all these years. Natan and me in California.

2. 20 year reunion of our Israeli Defense Force company.

3. 40 reunio. Time has done more to thin our ranks than the enemy ever did.

4. I went to Hong Kong to find a cheaper manufacturer for our clothes line in Miami.

1. Back in Budapest after so many years.

2. I found my father's grave in Budapest and had a headstone made for him.

3. In the old synagogue of Baia-Mare.

4. One of the handful of Jews remaining in Baia-Mare shows me an important book. He is ninety years old in this picture, and he gave me that book as a gift.

5. In a park in Baia-Mare I had this fateful meeting with this gentleman who led me to the house where I received the photo of Nora and me.

1. Bearded orthodox Nandor,, forger extraordinaire of Swedish visas, lived to a ripe old age with Margit, the master forger on the right. They paid us a visit in the 90's. L-R Adi, Rebequita, Gaby.
2. Zsuzsi with me and our mother on her 90th birthday in Miami. 3. Ady and Jessica. 4. L-R Lili (Gaby's wife), Gaby and me at Jessica's Bat Mitzvah. 5. Jessica's Bat Mitzvah with her adoring parents.
6. Joshua is the next generation of Gabors. Gaby's son, my grandson, Armin's great grandson, clearly shows that we not only survived but flourished. The future is full of endless possibilities.

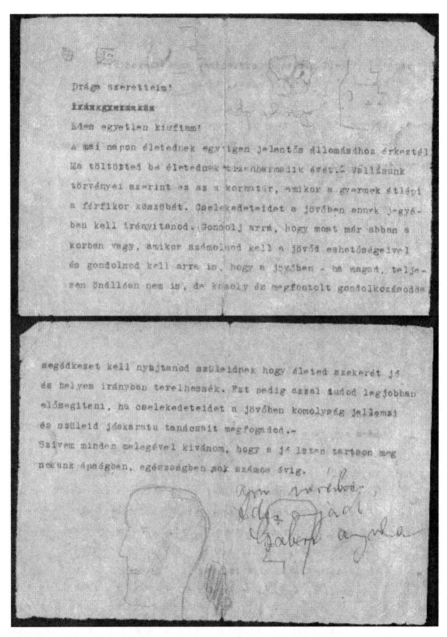

This is the letter that my father wrote to me as I approached Bar Mitzvah age. He knew he was dying and wanted to leave me with last words of advice. My mother didn't show it to me until she moved to Israel years later. The doodling is Zsuzsi's.

Chapter XXII

The Dirty War

By the time this is read the topics of this paragraph may be ancient and arcane history, requiring much research to comprehend it. Therefore, dear audience, I refer you to the popular theatrical work Evita in order to give you some perspective.

In 1973, when we had been living in Argentina for ten years, the populist leader Juan Peron assumed control of Argentina, determined to establish policies of a decidedly nationalistic fervor. This country had been so conservative for so long it was even sympathetic to fascism, and had recently offered refuge to escaped Nazis. He died only a year after his ascent to power, leaving his widow, Isabel Peron, in charge. A charismatic blond figurehead, constantly evoking the persona of his former wife, the legendary Eva Peron, she ceded power to the military, setting the stage for years of right wing repression against subversives, real and imagined. It was an old game in Latin America. A government regime plants the fear of communist subversion into the minds of the citizenry, and then carries out its own agenda under the banner of purging the country of the scourge of radical parasites intent on betraying the home land. Give the dog a bad name and hang it, all the while distracting the people from their own incompetence. By the time this particular game was played out over thirty thousand victims were claimed. Most of them were students and other young people. If anyone belonged to any suspect organization, and they suspected practically everyone, they were arrested and tortured. And once they were arrested they usually just vanished. And it didn't take much to end up on their list of undesirables. For example, if they found a victim's address book every single person in it got the treatment. The police and the military behaved just like Gestapo, smashing down doors and dragged them away. The only difference was secrecy. The Nazis or the Nyilasok carried out their despicable actions in broad daylight. It was war, and they had openly declared their hostile intentions. The Argentine government, on the other hand, did not declare civil war or martial law. They carried out actions against their own citizens without even a legal façade. This was a clandestine war, and its methods gave it a name that would forever characterize it. It came to be known as the Dirty War. The Argentine military had learned a lesson from the Third Reich on how to get rid of evidence. The Nazis incinerated the corpses of their victims, but the Argentine government was not so mechanized. They couldn't build concentration camps or ovens, because it would have attracted more attention than they could handle. So, they simply made their victims disappear. The poor unfortunates came to be known as *Los Desaparecidos*, The Disappeared. After enduring torture they were flown out over the Atlantic Ocean and tossed out of the plane. Thousands of victims were also drugged and their feet stuck in cement. Then they tossed them into the Rio Plata in front of Buenos Aires. With their feet weighted down by concrete thousands of cadavers stand upright on the floor of the great river, forming a grotesque forest of skeletons. At that time of course, nobody knew where the army was dumping the bodies, and without habeas corpus there is no crime. Among the victims were thirteen hundred Jews, killed for the same old scapegoat excuses as ever. We were communists or subversives, or somehow mystically responsible for the woes of the day. So yet another river was claiming our innocent. But we didn't have to see the evidence. We already knew what it meant when someone unpopular with a government disappears. Recognizing the familiar handwriting on the wall thoughts of fleeing crept into my head. I had seen it before, and knew what procrastination meant. The great irony was that we'd have to escape from a land that had once offered us shelter from the storm. The words of Judah Winter came back with a vengeance. One day we're welcome, the next we're not. South America, an almost entirely Catholic continent, harbored the age old paranoia for the foreign Hebrew. Just a year earlier there had been a violent anti-Semitic attack in Asuncion, Paraguay, six hundred miles to the north. A dictator named Alfredo Stroessner ruled the country for decades, and openly displayed his sympathy for fascism, allowing escaped Nazis to freely immigrate there. Though not officially sponsored or sanctioned by Stroessner, a group of gunmen blasted their way into the Israeli Consul there and shot several people. One of them, the wife of its Consul General, Moshe Paer, died in the attack. And now Moshe was serving in Buenos Aires as the Israeli Consul General.

Besides kidnapping, murder and torture, ransoms were common, and with everyone imagining that we were twenty times richer than we really were, our lives were in peril. One night a friend of mine who was very involved with Jewish life in Buenos Aires, called to tell me that his daughter had been kidnapped for a million dollar ransom. If she was alive maybe the money would free her, but the odds were that she was already dead. Regardless, we all pooled our resources. My friend had a lot of property, easily worth the amount demanded by the kidnappers, but it was a cash emergency. We were happy to help him and he repaid all of it. Miraculously, his daughter was released, but not before being sadistically raped by her tormentors. She was free, but mentally never recovered. This barbarity was our wake up call. We would have to make some concrete plan to get out of the country. Meanwhile, for protection, I bought some guns on the black market. I recalled an historian who theorized that, if the Jews would have met the storm troopers at the door with guns in their hands, then Hitler might have opted for alternate scapegoats.

I got a call from an official down at the Jewish school that Gabriel attended. He said we needed to organize security for the school, and position ourselves in front of it for protection. Armed, we spent a few nights on guard duty, but things seemed to settle down, so we went back to normal. However, we knew the situation was bad and getting worse. This was dramatically demonstrated when Moshe Paer personally came to visit me at my apartment. We were sitting in my kitchen, discussing various scenarios. A knock came to my front door and he just bolted out the back. Having already lost his wife to this insanity he feared he was next, and he didn't want to get me into any trouble either. His hasty retreat spoke volumes about the gravity of our situation. Shortly after that Dado arrived in Buenos Aires incognito. I never asked him if his arrival had anything to do with the political situation, but it might have, considering the circumstances of his entry into the country. Things were happening that certainly warranted it, but it wasn't my business to ask. My military training told me not to question my superiors. I was on a need to know basis, and if Dado wanted to involve me he would. Whatever the reason for his trip we became great friends while he was there. He enjoyed having another person with military experience to relate to, and we formed a bond that endured until the day he died. At that time another Israeli war veteran, Sergeant Gibli, famed for his rescue of thousands of Ethiopian Jews, had already been serving for two years as head of security of the Israeli Embassy. He and I went out on several occasions to aid threatened landtsmen. It seemed inconceivable that I was going to have to face this a second time. And worse, it was frustrating to have so much training in military tactics and strategy and still have to endure it. Finally, it all came to a head.

A close friend became prey for the paramilitaries, and his apartment on the fourteenth floor of one of the most exclusive condominiums in Buenos Aires was bombed. It was one of the most overt violent acts committed in that entire period. Usually, their activities were clandestine, away from prying eyes. But in this case they wanted to scare a lot of people, and they probably felt the publicity they would garner with this terrorist act would serve their needs. A huge section of the building was gouged out and twisted iron bars stuck out into the air. It was not what the military would call a surgical strike, and people were seriously hurt on adjacent floors. It was a miracle that my friend's relatives survived the explosion, and that their neighbors weren't all killed. My friend asked me to go over and pick up his wife and kids and take them to safety. It was dangerous to show my face there, but I couldn't refuse a friend in such dire need. So, I took them back to one of my apartments. The next day a letter arrived threatening us all. The fact that the letter arrived so soon, and that they knew where to send it, let us know that they were serious. Of course the situation was not so subtle as to require any speculation. They spelled out in black and white that they were going to kill them and all their relatives. And to confirm their ability the envelope included photos of all of us entering my apartment building. Now I knew that we would all have to take fast action to safeguard ourselves. My friends fled the country under heavy protection, slipping across the border into Uruguay after which they flew to Israel. While I was contemplating our own exodus another disappearance made me redouble my efforts. My accountant stopped coming to work, and when I went to his house to see what happened I discovered that his wife was gone as well. Things were happening almost daily now, but the last straw was a call I got at five in the morning from my friend, Jose Ryban.

"We gotta talk in one hour," he insists. "Meet me for an early breakfast!"

By now it had become routine for my friends to call me for help. I was an army veteran, as well as being personally acquainted with the Consul General to Argentina, so Jose thought I could do something. However the Israeli diplomatic mission had no influence in another country's internal affairs, and one ex-soldier, alone and unarmed, was hardly a competent foe to resist an entire army on their home turf. Unable to act caused me no end of anxiety. Back in Budapest I was just a kid, with no option but to hide. But now I was an adult, trained by the most competent military on Earth. With a single Israeli company I knew I could mop up the floor with these cowards. With just a platoon I could take the Presidential Palace. We would have rolled up our sleeves, clicked magazines into our Uzis, and gotten the job done. If only. But I was thousands of miles away from Israel with nothing more lethal in my possession than a couple of nine millimeter hand guns for last resort personal protection. The whole situation made me quake in frustrated anger. I prepared for the worst from Jose and got it. His nephew's house was bombed, and he barely escaped alive with his wife. But outside the ruins of their home a paramilitary squad arrested them. Tragically, Jose's nephew disappeared along with his wife. It was deeply disturbing to me. It had been over thirty years since Jews had faced such victimization and terror.

Though not publicly and officially sanctioned by the government, an atmosphere of terror pervaded our lives. I remembered Judah Winter's words from so long ago, how nations invited Jews in then changed their minds later. Now Argentina was behaving like some Slavic nation. It was not as widespread as the infamous holocaust, but it was far worse than any mere pogrom. Besides, if this situation was going to kill even a handful of Jews, just for being Jews, then it was infamy enough.

Our lives there were permanently through. My children were born here, and we had made our fortune here. I was well established and a pillar of the community. But that age old fear of the stranger now compelled me to do what my ancestors had done so many uncounted times before. We had to reincarnate ourselves elsewhere. From Romania east to Hungary. From Hungary south to Israel. From Israel west to Argentina. Now, it was time to go north.

What the Argentine military was doing to its citizens was shrouded in secrecy, but the conflict between Hassida and I was out in the open. Although she supported Creaciones Gabriel and was a devoted mother, she had a nature that was just naturally irritating to me. Her obsessively competitive nature made us constant rivals, and the only way that we could stay together forever would be for me to give in to her every whim. To do that though I'd have to be henpecked, which was impossible for me. I was a normal person with my own individuality, and a duel of wills would have been inevitable. She was honest, ambitious, and caring, but her strident need to dominate everyone and everything just wore me out. So, in spite of our successful business and wonderful children, and admittedly a basic mutual physical attraction for each other, we got a legal separation, with a divorce pending. By that time though the political reality obliged us to put marital problems on a far back burner and focus on our family's survival. I had already told Hassida not to send the kids to school any more, and now we decided not to invest in any more materials for Creaciones Gabriel either. We had to shut down the businesses and homes and slip out of Dodge as quickly and quietly as possible. We barely had time to sell our cars and boat and lock the doors of our properties. We left the keys in the care of Jose Ryban and took only what would fit into a few suitcases. Our financial status and notoriety made us attractive candidates for immigration to the United States, and we even received an invitation from the New York State Department of Commerce to reestablish Creaciones Gabriel there. As we were departing for America I had a chilling realization. Most Dirty War victims were young people and they might have been dressed in Creaciones Gabriel.

I flew ahead to Miami and rented an apartment. Shortly thereafter Gabriel came. Then Hassida and Adrian. I urged Rozsika and David to come too, but older people seemed to be out of harm's way in the Dirty War, so they preferred to stay put, assured that it would all blow over soon. And of course, Sonny wouldn't abandon his folks. Besides he was lulled into apathy by years of Argentine tolerance just as my father's generation had been in Hungary. "It can't happen here!" Later he was arrested for just being near some protest, but by then things had calmed down significantly and he was released. So we embraced them all and boarded a plane to our new home, the United States. In my pocket were Uri's one hundred dollars still in tact.

Chapter XXIII

Miami 12

With the last barrier of guilt banished from my soul I flew to New York to receive Rebequita at Kennedy Airport. I stood at the gate waiting to see her face, and when she appeared my heart leapt out of my body. We embraced and kissed, oblivious to our surroundings. Finally, we were free to publicly express our love. We went back to the St. Moritz Hotel and enjoyed a long and passionate Big Apple honeymoon. Our life together had started, and the joy has not abated to this day. As soon as we returned to Miami we got married. It was no gala affair, but simply performed in a lawyer's office with dignity, and only the most immediate family was present, including Rebequita's pleased if skeptical mother. We settled down and dove into married life which is all we ever wanted in the first place. We worked together at our business, and she helped me in my transition from clothing to beauty products.

When I first came to the United States I naturally came with the spirit to conquer the youth clothing market here, and expected nothing less than a repeat of my success with Creaciones Gabriel. Confidence is a good thing, a necessary thing, and in Argentina they say, *querer es* *pode*r which means that to want something is to empower yourself to get it. And while I certainly desired success I also had to contend with the wisdom of another Spanish expression, *el hombre propone, pero Dios dispone.* This saying has a more sobering tone, and reminds mortal man that he may propose anything he wants, but God ultimately holds sway over whether or not it becomes manifest. Whether you subscribe to such beliefs or not, a North American repeat of our South American success in the apparel trade was not in the cards. There was a vast sea of North American competition, heretofore nonexistent in South America, including manufacturing in foreign markets where labor and materials were less than half my cost. I even traveled to China and Korea to see if I could also avail myself of those methods, but it was too late for me to get in. Basically, I was way undercapitalized. So, being unable to compete in kids' clothing, I tried a series of other businesses, eventually settling on beauty products.

When we opened our first store of beauty supplies another ghost from the past surfaced, though it was a rather weak apparition. Henry Berger, my old salesman, and Rebequita's long ago ex-suitor, began badgering her at our store. He had never gotten over her, and despite the fact she was now married, he persisted in wooing her. He'd appear, beg her to run away with him, disappear for a year or more, reappear out of the blue with the same plan, and then vanish again. This went on for nearly a decade, but we never took his pathetic advances seriously. Finally, he vanished for good. I'm pleased and proud to report that I have always been her sole focus of romantic interest. She's a pristine figure of fidelity, and throughout our marriage we've always been able to count on each other one hundred percent. Only a selfish person would cheat on a spouse, and Rebequita hasn't a selfish molecule in her being. She'd no sooner break a heart than harm herself.

Although Rebequita loved and accepted me for who I was, it seemed a good idea to show her my background and what shaped me. Of course, I also needed to come to terms with my traumatic past, so we made a world wide heritage tour.

First we flew to Europe to face my old demons. We rented a car in Budapest, but drove to Romania in order to relive things chronologically, and went to Transylvania to explore the birth place of my first incarnation, Alfred Grossman. We headed for the town of Nagybanya, but of course it had been Romania since 1945, and would forever be known as Baia-Mare. It was still under the repressive communist boot of Nicolae Ceausescu, a man second only to Stalin in the realm of suspicion. He feared everything, and our border crossing reflected that. The guards saw in my American passport that I was born in Romania, but whatever favor that might have won me immediately faded when I demonstrated no ability to speak their language. Things went from bad to worse when I opened up my mouth and spoke Hungarian, the dialect of their traditional enemy. Thinking me to be a spy, no less, they searched for some contraband that they assumed I must be smuggling, and ended up keeping us there all day. Finally convinced that I posed no great threat to national security they let us in, but by then it was dark. There was no moon out that night and the impoverished communist government couldn't afford to install street lights, so it was pitch black. Only what was illuminated by our car's high beams was visible. But even by that dim artificial light it looked no different from when I was a kid, and especially compared to Miami it looked absolutely medieval. Everything, from the houses to the very trees, looked to me like the middle ages.

As soon as I saw the sign on the outskirts of Baia-Mare my entire childhood came back to me. I was only seven when I left but my memory of it was clear. However the nurturing warmth of my pre-war childhood was a long time ago. Now the whole town, like the whole area, was poor and uninviting. The political system that had pervaded since the end of World War Two was a grim totalitarian regime, and everything was dreary and bleak. Although the Soviets sport red flags no such gay colors were evidence in Baia-Mare. Wherever your eye came to rest it was gray or black.

At the entrance to the town lay its sole hotel. There was barely enough electrical power to run two small lights in our room, and there was no hot water. I thought to drop off Rebequita and continue on into the old part of town, such was my impatience, but the mood of the place made her tremble in fright. The thought of her staying there alone was unthinkable, so we pressed on together.

With nothing but the car lights I was somehow able to find my old kindergarten. The archaic stone structure still functioned, though it looked like it hadn't had any repairs since I was a pupil there. As we drove on it was amazing to find everything from that era still standing, but in the same condition. Our rental car seemed to function as much more than a mere land conveyance. It was like a time machine, transporting us back to a place unchanged by the passing of the years. Baia-Mare was like a Transylvanian Brigadoon. No wonder Dracula was ageless! The whole place was! I found the site where my grandpa had operated the town's first gas station, and so little progress in infrastructure had been made in all that time that I could actually see the rusted bolts in the cracked cement slab that had anchored his original pump. There was the bank where my father worked, our home, and even my grandparents' house. It was very nostalgic for me, but all poor Rebequita felt was discomforting fear. She had grown up in the sunny, verdant tropics, and these oppressive glimpses of dilapidated Slavic ruins were disturbing. I had to admit it was a little creepy, so I turned the car around to go back to the hotel, but at once I realized that, despite my familiarity with the location, I had to admit that I was lost. The sole man on the street offered us directions, but he turned out to be drunk. Rebequita begged me to drive on, but we needed this guy to guide us back to our hotel. He filled the car with his alcoholic stench, but he got us there in one piece. I tried to invite him into the hotel to thank him, but the authorities, big drinkers themselves, made a great hypocritical display of their disdain for public intoxication and chased him off.

The morning's sunshine was far more inviting. At least we could see. We drove by a famous art school near my grandmother's home and then decided to abandon the uncomfortably tiny time machine for a stroll in the very park where I used to play. We nodded at the people, unable to greet them in their language, but stopped when we passed a bench where an old man was chatting with a little boy. I heard them conversing in the same Hungarian dialect as mine, and I could tell they were grandpa and grandson. The man was more than happy to speak to me, and when I told him I was born there and what my name was he guessed that I was Jewish. Then he shared with us that he had always liked the Jews, and was horrified by what had happened to them in the war. He especially liked Jews because of the success they had made of the Phenix chemical company, his old employer. He had played soccer for them, as it was the common practice of that epoch for big business to sponsor teams. After some time he said he wanted to take us to visit an elderly Jewish woman in town. Apparently the fellow did have some synergy with Jews, because he knew where the few remaining ones lived. He especially wanted to take us to see a certain old, blind, Jewish lady, a visit that turned out to hold a secret from my past.

He pointed out the house where she lived, and then departed, vigorously shaking my hand. We knocked at the door and a voice, craggy from age, answered.

"Who are you?"

I was inexplicably nervous and hesitated, so the same challenge came from within.

"Who are you?"

"I am Freddy Grossman."

There was not even a moment's hesitation from the other side of the door.

"I don't believe you! You are the son of Ilushka Grossman. She was my dearest friend! And your father and my husband were the very best of friends too!"

This entire conversation was conducted through a closed door. Being blind I suppose she saw no urgent need to share a physical presence. But when she realized who I was she bade someone who was with her open the door. A woman, approximately my own age, let us in. She introduced herself as the old woman's daughter, and warmly invited us to sit on the sofa by her mother. The old woman felt my face with her hand to see if she could recognize me. Of course, the face of a man in his late forties is hardly reminiscent of a seven year old child, but she tried and became very emotional.

"Please tell me everything about your dear mother, and don't leave out a thing."

I did my best to bring her up to date on Israel and America. Finally, she spoke.

"I have a surprise for you."

She had her daughter fetch down an old shoe box that was high on a shelf. It was covered in dust, and had been reposing there for God knows how long, waiting for some unknown visitor to honor it. She opened the box, placing the lid down on the table, taking her time with the mystery of its contents. A smile played across her face as she plucked out an ancient photograph. Though she could not see it she took delight in holding it between her wrinkled fingers. A grin of ultimate satisfaction spread across her weathered cheeks as she reminisced.

"When I could still see I remembered I had a photo of you when you were seven. It's you and a group of children. I knew you were alive so I kept it."

She handed it to me, and as soon as I beheld it I was stunned. I had not been so overwhelmed by such an image in my entire life and was momentarily embarrassed by my tears. It's not that I was ashamed for the sentimental display, but the long hand of time can affect things as little else can. The woman's memory was accurate. I stood there among other children, all girls except for me and another little boy. We were all about the same size, so we must have been nearly the same age. From across the decades this moment came back to me as if it were yesterday. The picture was taken in 1941 on a small street in front of a friend's house. We were all together because it was the birthday of one of those little girls. The children were little darlings, smiling for a relative's camera. What had caused my shock was the face of one of those girls. It was Nora, my first sweetheart, my puppy love. We were very fond of each other and always sought each other out at play time. I hadn't thought of her for fifty years. Although afraid of what the answer was almost certainly going to be, I had to ask.

"What happened to Nora? What happened to all of them?"

The joy of the reunion dissolved, and the old woman's face dropped. I already had my worst fears confirmed. It was the usual answer to all riddles of lost persons of that era. The room became deadly still, and though she could not see her head turned away. It is unnerving that a sightless person can shed a tear. The daughter revealed the mystery.

"This picture is a birthday party photo. Two of those little girls were my sisters. One of them was celebrating her seventh birthday that day.

On the back are the signatures of each one, including yours and mine. I'm the tall girl in that photo."

By now Rebequita and I were comatose with trepidation. We knew what was coming.

"We were all taken to Auschwitz. Only my mother and I returned."

Rebequita was quietly sobbing. I knew the truth, but I had to be certain. I didn't have to dig any deeper. The woman knew what I needed to know.

"Yes, Nora too."

I looked down at the floor fighting back more tears. Of course, scenes like this have been common for over half a century. Whenever survivors meet it inevitably leads to the list of the dead and the mourning. The cruelty that the Nazis committed lives on, and the holocaust casts a long shadow. But the war killed so many why mourn just a few? Why? Because it is the nobility of humanity. The inhuman Nazis slaughtered millions without batting an eye. A normal human observes a single victim and the eyes fill with tears.

The old woman recovered and told me to keep the picture. She was a little ashamed for her lack of hospitality, but Romania was not a land of plenty, nor was she one of its richer citizens. There was no coffee or sugar in the house and our visit was a surprise. I didn't want to embarrass her by offering her money, but very quietly I passed some notes to her daughter who graciously accepted. Knowing the poverty of the country Rebequita and I also divested ourselves of everything that was nonessential to us and gave it all to her. Rebequita and I were shaken by the visit, yet inexplicably glad for having come.

Thousand of Jews had lived there a century before but now there were only about fifteen individuals left. We could actually hold a meeting and meet them all. So we did. Sitting in the old synagogue we spoke about the world before the war. It was amazing, but some of them actually remembered my parents.

"Oh, she played the piano! Such a beauty!"

While I was legal heir to our Romanian property the system of government made it impossible to claim. So, this part of the world would belong to me only in memory.

We crossed the border back into Hungary as my family did back in 1941, and drove the two hours to Budapest which, even under the Soviets and badly in need of a paint job, was still one of the grand capitals of Europe. It also has one of its largest Jewish populations. Technically, I was the landlord of our old outside apartment at Csengery Utca, but communism made reclamation here just as unlikely as in Romania.

We started our visit on a light hearted tone by visiting the National Theater. Rebequita already knew about my great acting triumph there and was delighted to see it. The theater, in all its granite grandeur was very nearly identical as I had remembered it. Years later, when communism made its final curtain call it would get a face lift and total renovation with a gorgeous garden around its entrance. Its entrance would also get a beautiful statue of my old costar, Hilda Gobi. It was a thrill to revisit the old theater, but I had not come thousands of miles just to reminisce. It was time to revisit the scenes of my greatest terror. I went by that building next to the Hotel Royale, whose splendid salons and patios stood in proximity and contrast to the neighboring Nyilas center of torture and murder. My mother and I had been two of its few war time guests to have ever checked out. I also walked by the hospital where we sought refuge that night, but I did not stop to reflect. Nor did I stop on the spot where I had been so savagely beaten. I passed these places, scenes of suffering, as if in a trance on my way to the river. The day was as gray as the last time I stood there, clutching my mother's hand, and listening to my grandma pray. We had stood by the edge of the river where violent death brushed up against us so close we felt its fetid breath. A monument of brass shoes now memorializes the exact spot on the cement banks where we trembled. I approached it uneasily, feeling the shadow of that distant afternoon's terror. The echoes of the guns and the screams invaded my mind and my whole body became tense. Many decades had passed, but I still could not fathom why it happened at all. What was the point of murdering any of us? Nothing fundamental about their lives changed at all, except that they became murderers, wasting the opportunity of their precious human life to do something of value. The war was the same savage mystery it always had been. The blue of the Danube was turning red before my eyes, and the same confusion that gripped me then did so now. Violent, brutal death was all around me once again. The events of forty years before now overwhelmed my senses. Then Rebequita squeezed my hand and brought me back.

"Mi amor, I feel as if I am walking in your footsteps."

My pulse relaxed. My vision cleared. The raging storm within me subsided. The sun was shining down on us and its warmth made me feel grateful for life. And throughout it all my darling bride shared its emotion and meaning. She wasn't even born when any of this happened, but she understood it all. She was young, but with a very old soul.

Next, I tried to see if I could locate our old maid Sonia who had tried to help us in the war. It was she who had contacted that woman who might've hid us had we the right amount of precious jewelry. After the war Sonia found my mother back at Csengery Utca, and the two women continued to communicate for years. Perhaps she had passed away, because my inquiries led nowhere.

I had revisited all the scenes of my trauma of Europe and felt closure. I confronted the scenes of my greatest suffering and came away stronger. With my greatest trauma behind me we were off to Israel. Of course, I went through great emotional upheavals there as well, but I managed to overcome them while I still lived there.

Israel had been the great metamorphosis of my life. But I had witnessed so much of its progress I was curious about every aspect of life there now. One fascinating thing I discovered was that my Aliyah group had achieved a degree of fame for their myriad accomplishments, of which I was part, and a book was even published about it. I went to the Kibbutz Dalia and discovered that it had been converted from agricultural to industrial. One of the kids that was with me on the original Shomer Hatzair Aliyah still lived there. Of course, there were no more tents, and he lived in a nice apartment with his wife. He even knew how I could get in touch with Judah Winter, and I couldn't resist calling him. With a few reminders he remembered me and even seemed excited to talk to me. Then, after all those years, I finally had the opportunity to reproach him for what he had done.

"Judah, how could you do that to a troubled holocaust survivor? How could you trick me into leaving my family without any consideration for me as an individual? Do you have any idea how much pain that has caused me over the years?"

I had been waiting a lifetime to hurl that gauntlet at him, but he seemed to have a ready reply. Obviously, I was not the first to say, "Je accuse!" His answer was surprisingly simple.

"I was only a little older than you. I was naïve and innocent. Just a kid like you!"

I heard his explanation, and was tempted to press on. After all, it was his deception that caused the rift between my mother and me. It was he who set the stage for a lifetime of emotional hell. I could've gone deeper, but hearing his blithe response I decided that there was no solution to be found there. What's done is done and best to leave it alone.

We visited my grandmother and mother, and it was exactly as I expected. My grandmother approved and was open and loving, while mother was civil and guarded. We visited the art school I helped to establish, and I'm proud that it's still one of the most important in Israel. And the Rebach Museum in Bat Yam continues to host important exhibitions. You can even see the works of that kid whose creative décor of the summer camps did me so proud. Yankel Ginzburg became an internationally celebrated artist. The legendary Marc Chagall recognized the young man's talent even back then.

"It took me forty years to capture Paris. This young man will capture the world before his hair turns gray."

Yankel generously gave me an early canvas, and it graces my home even now.

Another artist from my past was Janos Nyiri. It was his suggestion that led to my brief career on the stage, and my mother was always eager to hear from him again. They had communicated before she went to Israel, but had somehow lost contact with each other. He fled the repressive Soviet regime and was given asylum in England where he became a huge theatrical and literary success. There he wrote the best seller Playgrounds and Battlefields which was translated into various languages worldwide. Unaware of this at the time I searched in vain in the wrong places, and I finally learned of his whereabouts just months before he passed away.

When I took Rebequita to visit my old office I had an experience I'll never forget. Years earlier, when we were running the summer camps, there was a blind person we became aware of who needed a job. We naturally felt sorry for the gentleman, because we imagined that jobs for the sightless were few and far between. At that time we were looking to install a new telephone system which included a switchboard. With this fellow in mind we investigated and found that there was indeed one that a sightless person could easily use. We convinced the administration to buy it and to hire that gentleman. So now, as I walked in the building, I was surprised though delighted to see him sitting there. I greeted him, and as soon as he heard my voice he called out, "Gabor. I don't believe it. How are you?" I was moved to be remembered like this, and I gave him a big hug. Later, this fellow made great progress, eventually becoming an attorney.

By now Israel held nothing but warm memories for me, so I satisfied my curiosity without risk of trauma. I showed Rebequita the building where I slept between stinking mattresses which was now boarded up, pending demolition. And the place where I worked on burlap bags had been converted into a state-of-the-art mechanized factory. Israel no longer needed make-shift businesses. It was a sign of the times.

Though the barrier built by my mother was still sturdy it was a great pleasure to visit Israel. It was a true joy to introduce Rebequita to Natan Schindler and the rest of my old friends and comrades. And now, with Europe and the Middle East crossed off the heritage tour list, we had only Argentina to relive.

With the Dirty War a memory which nobody even dared talk about, we had no trepidation about going back there. Besides, compared to the horror of the war in Europe, what went on in South America was mild. So, if we could brave a return to Budapest we could certainly risk Buenos Aires.

It was a joy to see Rozsika and David and Sonny again. I had told Rebequita so much about the love of my grandma and Rozsika, and it was a special thrill to present her to both of them. In our tour around the city I couldn't help but notice that Budapest and Buenos Aires shared something dark in common. In the Hungarian capital I had shown Rebequita the venue of torture next door to the Hotel Royale. And in the Argentine capital I showed her the infamous Marine Mechanics School where Dirty War victims were conveniently tortured before they were dumped in the water. Apart from that Buenos Aires shared more synergy with Transylvania. Neither had undergone any transformation. They were both by and large unchanged. If it weren't for Israel the whole trip would have been like that dust covered shoe box off the shelf in the blind woman's home. It was like giving Rebequita a tour of a museum. Only the people were different, and then only by age. Israel, on the other hand, was totally transformed. Progress was so rampant there that even the desert was abloom. But the capital of Argentina, from Rivadavia to the government buildings, was identical. And with nothing new or different to confuse me I easily maneuvered to all my old properties. My friend Jose Ryban had rented out the factory and store, but they still looked the same. The factory, the store, and my old apartment were time capsules. The apartment was unchanged and the key still fit the lock. The door creaked open and everything was as I left it when we fled. It was still decorated with my old paintings, and my old hand gun was still down in the hidden floor safe. I remembered how we used to keep cash there, and Gaby bragged at school that it was a deep hole stuffed with money.

Though Argentina and Europe looked the same to me there was one big difference. All of our property in Buenos Aires still legally belonged to me. Jose Ryban had sold one of the apartments for me, and the rest was still under my name. And now that the political turmoil had subsided I was free to sell it. Eventually we negotiated every property, but for *bubkis*, peanuts.

When we left Argentina it was the conclusion of my world heritage tour, and I had hoped that it would have been the close of every emotional wound, the real motive behind the whole trip. But the irreparable rift with my mother made a hundred percent healing impossible. My salvation was my darling angel Rebequita and our life together. Even before Rebequita reached voting age she had the maturity to commit totally to a relationship. And that mood of adult responsibility also let her settle comfortably into her life as an instant parent. She got along wonderfully with Gabriel and also enjoyed Adrian's weekend visits. She was, and has always been, sister, friend and second mother to my boys. Pure love, acceptance and confidence have always characterized their relationship. But women are women, and eventually they seek the ultimate fulfillment of having a child of their own. Rebequita was no different, and it was only natural that our love bring forth a child. We were encouraged by Adrian and Gabriel as well. They assured us that any child of ours would not be a mere half or step brother, but be accepted as a full sibling. And this is something else for which I am grateful, that my two boys are so open and caring. They were never resentful of Rebequita, and they were as thrilled as we were to have our family grow. So Jessica, a beautiful baby girl, was the next addition to the Gabor clan, and she completed our bliss. We have no need to search any further for elusive happiness, because we live it every day.

How can one man be so lucky? I look back at generations of my forefathers, and forward to my descendents, and see a river of love. It's a strong current, reaching all the way back to Baia-Mare, and flowing on through America. I easily maneuver my craft through its tranquil waters, and my heart swells from the journey. My joy is such that words fail me, so I'm lucky to be able to express it through my painting. I'm no Yankel, but my art is a most rewarding part of my life.

In 1982 my dear saintly grandmother passed away in Israel. In spite of the ravages of the Second World War she managed to live robustly into her ninety-second year, happily living almost half of those years in what she considered her homeland. She was a beacon of love to me throughout my entire life, and I rejoice that she survived her tormentors, ending up in the best place in creation for her. I visited her several times in Israel, and I always came away knowing that she was truly content to be there. Her photo is right on my desk, and I talk to her daily. God bless her and rest her soul.

With her own mother gone, and herself twice widowed, my mother moved to Miami to be near her family. Zsuzsi came too, along with her own husband and baby daughter, Orli. There were expectations on my part that time would have healed the rift between my mother and me, but I was sadly mistaken. In some ways it was even worse. With no other man to occupy her time she became obsessed with me and my abandonment of her, blaming it for all her woes. "You left me! I didn't leave you!" All conversations ended like that. And she would not hear my argument that I was just a dumb kid. "But mother, I was just fourteen years old, and traumatized by the war. Can't you forgive me?" But she wouldn't, and I couldn't comprehend why not. A fourteen year old is little more than child. And in my case I really was just a child. My folks had brought me up in an illusory cocoon of their own making, and only the harshest period of the war finally ripped through it to educate me enough to survive. But there was no reasoning with her. She never forgave me, and I never again was permitted to feel the same warmth from her as I did in my childhood. She was tough, which is probably how she survived the war. Doubtless, I inherited some of that characteristic from her, enabling me to endure those tough years on the streets of Haifa. Sadly her antipathy toward me extended to my issue, and she denied her grandsons the warmth she denied me. She was civil and formal even with my sons and Rebequita. She passed away in Miami in 2003, ninety three tenacious years young. Our large extended family had many friends, and her funeral was well attended. When I stepped up to deliver her eulogy I opened my mouth to speak and found that I was like a child again. Speaking in both Hungarian and English, through the first tears I had shed in decades I tried my best to make peace.

"You've gone to heaven, so perhaps you can't hear me. But if you can I know I will understand if you don't answer. I know I hurt you, and cannot overcome the pain I caused you. I ask for forgiveness. Moreover, we have to forgive each other. All of our actions came as a consequence of the war, and we're both victims of that terrible tragedy of the holocaust."

It's a fact. The twisted destiny which is the legacy of the Nazis, led to that moment when I closed the door behind me at Csengery Utca., number fifty-one. And it shaped the future from which there was no escape. But I certainly do forgive her for feeling that way. I thought I had buried the ghost of regret long ago, but my emotions betrayed me, and I left her graveside quite shaken. The woman lived for nearly a century, and she was so tough she carried to her grave a mother's heart opened only a crack to her only son. It is a melancholy that has tempered my life, and still knows no relief.

I started out hating Israel and suffering like a dog, and ended up one of its proudest citizens and contributors. After some years I served a stint as chairman of the Friends of Israel Defense Forces, Florida Chapter, and one day my secretary there told me that she had received a call from Israel. Sara Yacabovitch, my old secretary from Base Number four, had spent a year combing the world for veterans from my era in the army to make a gala forty year reunion. She finally tracked me down through a chain of acquaintances who informed her of my chairman post. If I hadn't held that temporary position I never would've gotten that message. I called Sara back and the next thing I knew I was sitting on an El Al flight for Israel. When I landed they received me with a banner proclaiming: Welcome Zev Gabor, F Company. What a thrill to see my old comrades in arms. They had come from all over the world, from as far away as California, Australia and even Uganda. I saw people who had trained me, and people whom I had trained. Some were in wheelchairs, but for a few hours we were hardy kids, traipsing the hills of the borders, flanking the enemy. Our company commander, Colonel Massa, was there, and I saw Dado with whom I remained friends until the day he died. Of course, while I was there I didn't miss the opportunity to visit Natan Schindler. He stayed a welder all his life, but the constant exposure to the intense heat and gas of that occupation did some permanent damage to his health. Another thing happened over time. His political extremism mellowed to mere socialism. We're friends to this day and speak constantly.

Sadly, some of Israel's legacies are more tragic than they are nostalgic. Hassida's brother, Ariel, was shot to death at night while sitting in a car with a girlfriend. The same bullet killed them both. The girl died at once, but Ariel managed to drive his car halfway to a hospital before he lost consciousness and crashed into a lamp post. Nobody was ever caught or even arrested for the crime. Ghosts from Argentina haunt us too. The murderers of Jose Ryban's nephew are still at large. But my accountant surfaced, and I actually heard from him. He just hid until it all blew over. I knew from experience exactly what he was talking about.

I was successful enough in business to do more traveling, and while in Montreal one time I was able to visit one of the original Shomer Hatzair kids there, Janos Schwitzer who had become a dentist. He had an amazing memory, and the first thing he said when he recognized me was that I was the kid who was the famous actor. He even remembered my role in the play. And he held another bit of information for me. By the greatest of coincidences he had taken a cab and was surprised to see that his driver was Tomy Blau. We all got together. He too had lived in Montreal his whole life with Cathy, the same girl with whom he had fallen in love in Israel. Not long after he passed away, content to have lived all his life with his true love. He was survived by Cathy and their kids.

Running into Janos Schwitzer in Montreal cast its own peculiar shadow. When I asked him where he had studied dentistry he told me Budapest. It turns out that he was able to return there thanks to his parents paying his way back. That's all it took. They forgave him for his clandestine Aliyah, received him like the prodigal son, and put him through school. At first this only served to remind me of my own mother's refusal to do the same, and once again that heavyhearted mood engulfed me. But, in so doing, I was forced to compare myself with Janos, and acquire some objective analysis of my trouble.

His parents must have also sacrificed themselves to protect him during the war. There's no other scenario that is conceivable. Then, he got swept up in the Zionist fervor of Shomer Hatzair and made the same naïve decision as me and hundreds of other kids. Yet his parents excused him. Others had similar stories. But, as far as I've been able to learn, nobody else experienced total rejection as a result of their idiocy. There's no denying that we were stupid, but I can't dilute my culpability simply by assigning some portion of it to the misguided actions of others. Purely and simply, I've always admitted that I was dumb. We were all so young and vulnerable it really shouldn't shock anyone, including myself. What's left is for me to see my mother through the same objective lens. Children see their parents as nothing less than heroic and perfect. As adults though, we have to come to terms with the fact that they too had feet of clay. As nobly and courageously as they behaved under the pressure of war, and the pride it gives us, we must yet know that they too were human, heir to a thousand natural shocks. Any one of those shocks, visited upon us by that damned conflict, would have traumatized the best of us, and most easily a woman, a sex so vexed by frailty. The constant threat of violent death, the pregnancy under dire circumstances, the loss of her husband, the hunger and cold and deprivation, all took their merciless toll upon my mother's sensitive nature. The result was a consciousness equally capable of a wrong decision. I made a wrong decision, and so did she. In not forgiving me she all too humanly erred. Ultimately my mother and I are both guilty of exactly the same sin, brought about by exactly the same stimulus. Had we not been persecuted in Europe Zionism would not have had the same resonance, and Shomer Hatzair could not have so zealously steered me to Israel. And my mother's resentment never would have been so vehement had she not experienced the heightened maternal awareness necessary to protect her brood in such extraordinary and dire circumstances. I truly made a stupid decision that night while a cinematic Hamlet pondered his existence next door, but my mother also committed that same mistake. The reverberations of that epoch persecuted us for a long time, but now I release myself from its curse, and accept the fact we, beings conditioned by environment, behaved imperfectly. It happens.

My life has been greatly influenced by many women all of whom have shaped my comprehension of love. I do not refer to love as a pseudonym for pleasure, but to a deeper meaning that is both serene and selfless. Anyone can use the word love, but it takes generosity of spirit and deed to manifest it. It has to be given without self interest. And all my life I've been on the receiving end of that total sacrifice. From my birth to my Aliyah Ilushka Grossman lived and breathed for me. She confronted armed thugs and a world gone insane to shelter me. And, like all mothers, there was nothing in it for her. She did it all for her child. What came later could not tarnish fourteen years of dedicated sacrifice. My grandmother was all that and more. She was the essence of love, not just for me, but for her husband, my mother and sister too. If she ever had a thought just for herself I never saw it. Rozsika was every bit as giving, made from the same Old World mold as my grandma, and she helped turn the New World into a cozy home for me. Yona helped restore self worth to me. Hassida gave up everything, including the beloved land of her birth, to accompany me on a bold new adventure. Rebequita happily exchanged the liberty of youth for familial responsibility with tenderness and joy. She gave true love to me and my children, and continues to do so to this day. And her love is beyond evaluation. These generations of women have sacrificed for me more than I could ever repay. And I also observed this sacrifice in the people of Israel. Those pioneers and soldiers gave willingly so that a nation of unseen families could thrive and build a secure future. Yes, any sentimentalist can use the word love. But it only exists when it is freely given. Until then it is invisible. The act of giving brings it to life, and only the fortunate few are on the receiving end. And mercifully, mystical love surrounded the surrealism that mocked my life for too long, and forced it to surrender. I pray that I am worthy of that love, and have been able to absorb it and pass a little of it along to future generations.

Epilogue

So many ancient echoes land on my ears that I am no longer surprised to hear from old friends, and I have nothing but good will toward anyone who might take the time and trouble to contact me. We have a lovely apartment in Sunny Isles, Florida, and it's quite a bit more comfy than that room in Haifa that I traded for ration books so long ago.

Hassida lives nearby, as does Zsuzsi, and we're all close. Whenever I see my sister it reminds me of the war and how we barely survived. My mother had carried her when she was starving, and only through some miracle she was able to give birth. And then there was nothing to eat to allow her to make milk for her delicate baby daughter. Poor Zsuzsi was a victim of the holocaust after the fact, like my father and so many others.

Gabriel and Adrian both enjoy successful lives, and Gaby and his wife have guaranteed the next generation of Gabors by giving us a handsome grandson, Joshua. The Nazis could not do away with our family after all! My blessings are many and I'm grateful beyond description. First, I had Hassida and two beautiful sons, and then I got a new lease on life with Rebequita and Jessica. The most intriguing thing about our enduring union is that all of her relatives, who warned her that I would never marry her or stay with her, got divorced. To a one.

I still have a tendency to bounce back and forth between the past and the present, but its negative affect has diminished with time.

And, thanks to Rebequita, my head is a little less awhirl than in my younger days. Life continues to hurl itself at us, but together we meet its challenges with resiliency and tenacity. Besides, even at their worst, modern dilemma fade in the shadow of all that has gone before. The memories of ancient crises drown out the threat of new ones, and the promise of tomorrow always shines bright in the shadow of a yesterday when my footsteps echoed off the banks of the red Danube. Having now walked in my shoes I hope your own steps are sure.

Sunny Isles, Florida
July 1, 2009